CALIFORNIA DREAMERS

SALLY DAVIES

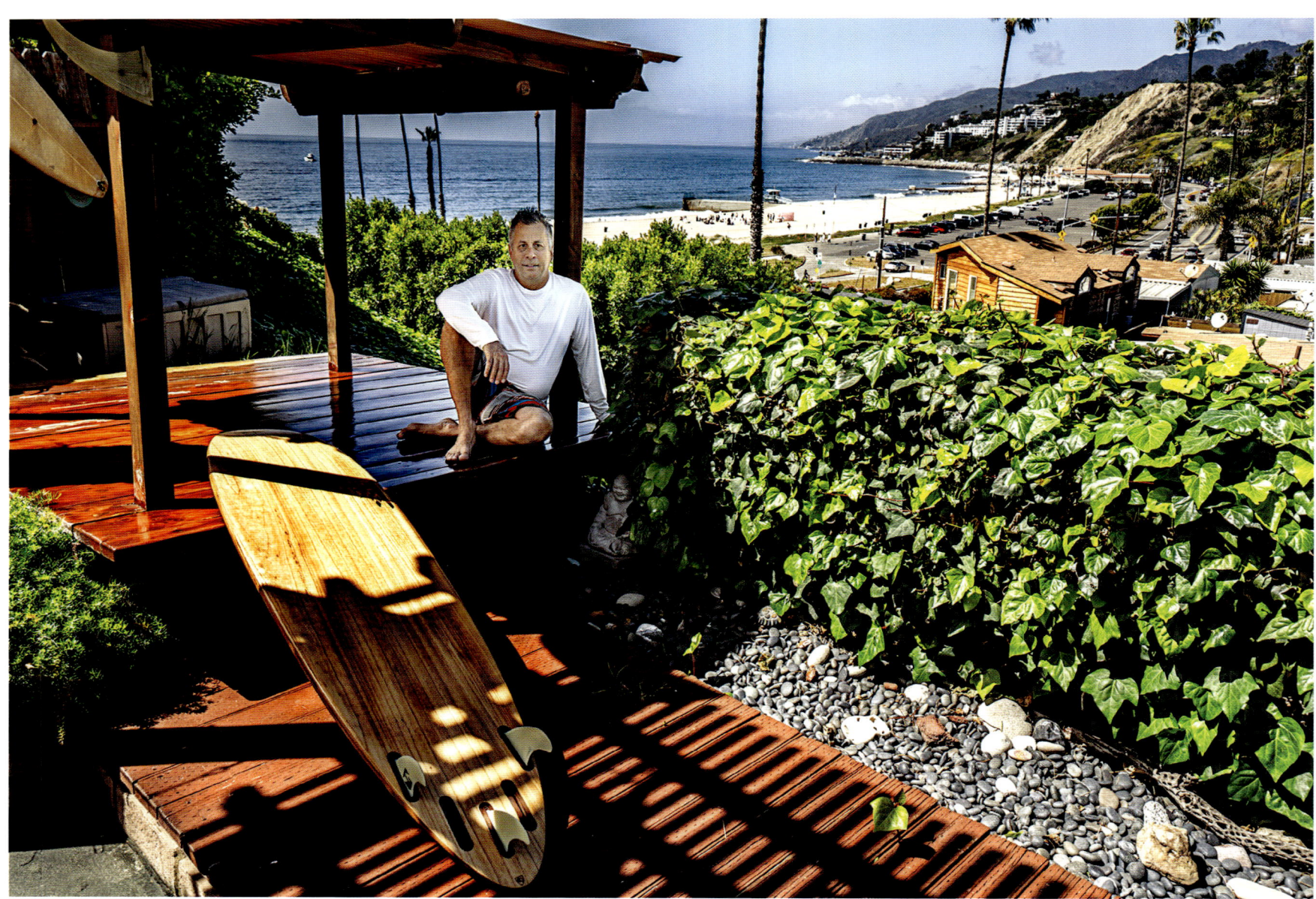

CALIFORNIA DREAMERS

SALLY DAVIES

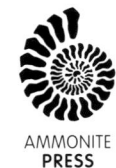

AMMONITE
PRESS

PREVIOUS PAGE

MARK STORHAUG

Photographed at home in the Pacific Palisades on March 18, 2022.

Mark was born in Santa Monica, California in 1965. He was the youngest of three for Duane and Azar. Dad was an accountant and Mom had a travel business and taught tennis. He spent his young years growing up in Malibu and New Jersey, but mostly Malibu. He was an average student, playing tennis, crosscountry skiing, and skateboarding. By the time he was 13 he was surfing, and working. He counted dump trucks, worked in restaurants, and parked cars. Mark spent a year living in Spain and went to college in San Francisco. After college ended, Mark moved to Santa Monica. He lived there for eight years, working first for the city then as an elementary school teacher, which he still is. He became a teacher so he would have lots of time off to travel and surf. He's been teaching grade school for 29 years. In 2001 Mark met his sweetie, Irma. They spend their time between her apartment in West Hollywood and Mark's vintage trailer in Malibu.

Mark moved into this Malibu mobile home park in 1999.

"I grew up driving by this place to go to high school and college. I love it! Ocean view, waves, sunsets, bike path. What's not to love? Los Angeles is a fantastic place to be in the world. The fact that you have a huge amount of humanity, then the vast, empty Pacific Ocean right there, makes for a nice contrast. It's also super easy to get out into nature from most places. It's also nice to take advantage of all the cultural happenings here. You don't really need to leave the city to get a taste of other cultures and cuisines. As a surfer, there's plenty of spots to go surf as well. I hate the soot from the cars on Pacific Coast Highway, but what you going to do about that? Not much."
—Mark

First published 2023 by
Ammonite Press
an imprint of Guild of Master Craftsman Publications Ltd
Castle Place, 166 High Street, Lewes, East Sussex, BN7 1XU,
United Kingdom
www.ammonitepress.com

Text and images © Sally Davies, 2023
Foreword © Stuart Horodner, 2023
Copyright in the Work © GMC Publications Ltd, 2023

ISBN 978-1-78145-465-7

A catalog record for this book is available from the British Library.

Publisher: Jonathan Bailey
Designer: Robin Shields
Senior Project Editor: Virginia Brehaut
Editor: Robin Pridy

Author photo on page 160 by Linda Heidinger
Back cover photo by Sally Davies, car courtesy of Deke Dickerson

Color reproduction by GMC Reprographics
Printed and bound in China

Set in Futura

The
California Dreamers

FOREWORD

by Stuart Horodner

In 2021, after producing an acclaimed photographic testament to New Yorkers and the domestic spaces they inhabit, it made sense that Sally Davies went west ... to the other coast, full of "good vibrations and excitations," according to The Beach Boys' song. Despite being warned that she'd hate it out there, the opportunity to challenge the official brand of California was just too alluring. In truth, she'd been visiting there for several years and knew all about the palm trees, shiny vintage cars, and ubiquitous screenwriters.

Davies recently told me she'd analyzed Annie Leibowitz's images in the 1980s to learn about lighting and composition, and Arbus's photo of the albino sword swallower at a carnival is a touchstone for her. But it is painter Alice Neel's probing portraits that inspire her when she meets people in their homes. "Her canvases are not judgmental," Davies said. "She's telling you something about the subject, and the person is also talking about themselves through Alice."

By photographing a few friends and many strangers with their stuff, this transplanted Canadian captures a sense of intimate otherness. She did not have a car during her time in California, relying on Uber drivers and Vin, her weekend assistant. If her first book was the result of getting numerous people to trust her, these residents were willing protagonists. They knew what they were getting into from the start, and welcomed Davies into their bedrooms, garages, and patios. Like their Manhattan counterparts, these folks pose with confidence. They lay on couches, sit at pianos, dress up or stay casual, and show off cherished items (movie posters, music gear, and at least one Emmy Award).

According to Davies: "Everyone has a dog because they all have a yard. LA is a house culture, NY is not." And it's true, these photographs are airy and horizontal, with windows and sliding doors revealing beckoning exteriors. At least ten of her "dreamers" pose barefoot. The sun is ever present, because so many of the photos include shutters, shades, curtains, and blinds contending with it.

Tina Barney, Carl Corey, Alec Soth, and Larry Sultan are image makers who examine the lives of specific individuals in the contexts of their surroundings. Like them, Davies revels in the details of everyday life and what people's choices (partners, pets, clothes, homes, furnishings) say about their position in the American context. But with her *California Dreamers*, I could not stop thinking of David Hockney, another artist who came from elsewhere to see a place with fresh eyes and an open heart. In 1964, he moved to Los Angeles and started painting poolside boys with suntanned bodies and one, *Beverly Hills Housewife*, his elegant portrait of art collector Betty Freeman. Almost 50 years later, Sally Davies has abundantly answered the question: "What does it mean to be seen?" in the environment that Hockney called, "the promised land."

DONNA LEE

Photographed with her dog Roddy at home in Larchmont Village on February 21, 2022.

Donna was born in Lowell, Massachusetts in 1966. She loved to roller skate and she wanted to be an Egyptologist, a cowgirl, or a movie star when she grew up. At 16, she discovered Boston's punk scene. Donna worked at a record store, a video store, and at the first CD store in the country. Somewhere around 1985 she started spending time in NYC, and in 1991 she moved there. She worked as a waitress and at a film archive. In 2003 Donna moved to Los Angeles, and continued working in TV. She works for the Film Noir Foundation doing research, and meditates every day. Donna moved into this cottage in 2021 and lives there with her pit bull Roddy.

"Like everywhere, LA has changed drastically in the last few years. It's gotten much more dangerous and grim, but my friends in other cities tell me the same thing."
—*Donna*

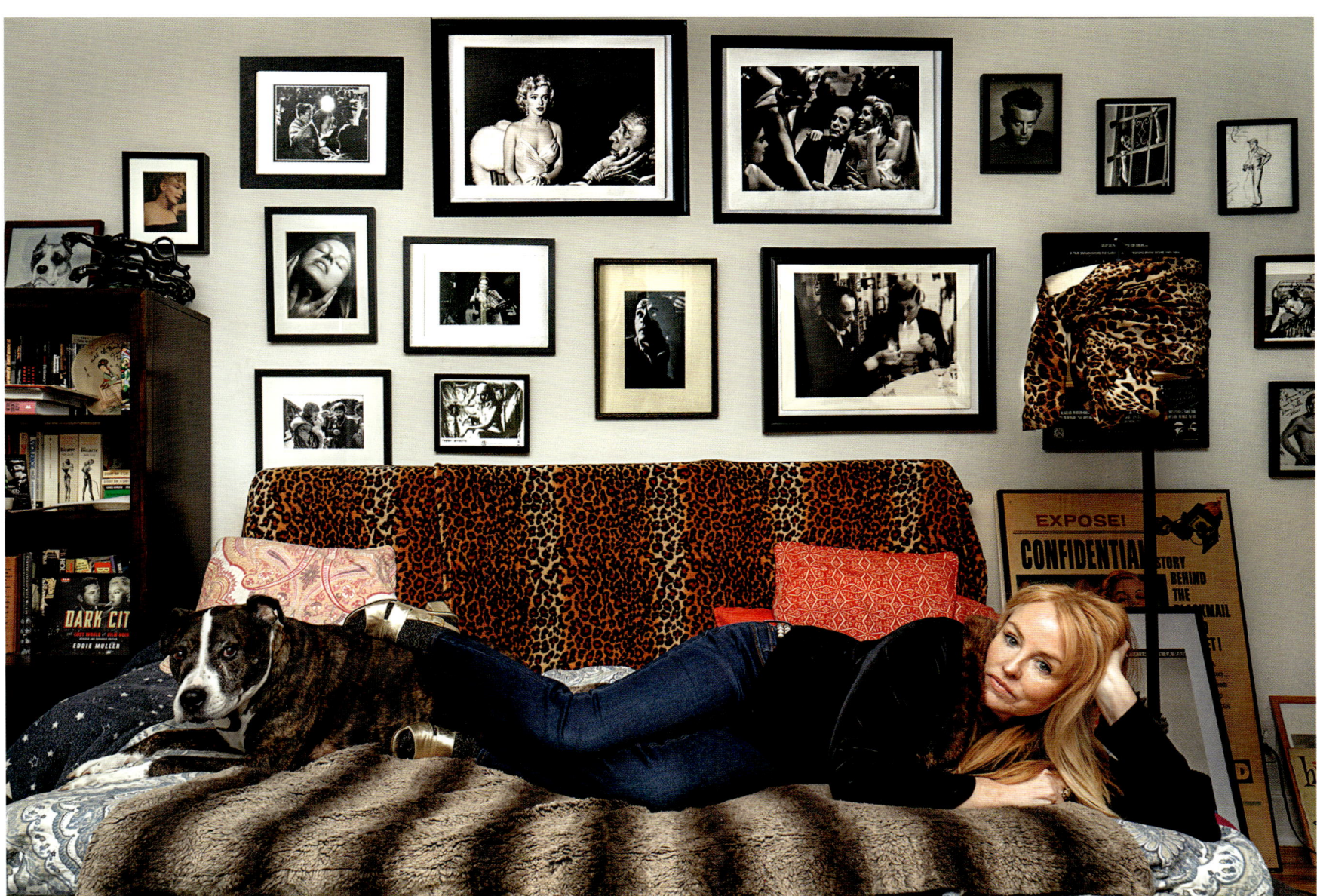

INTRODUCTION

Buried deep beneath the pile of old Hollywood glamour and Schwab drugstore stories lies a chuck wagon and a map for gold. Whether you are a snowbird from Canada escaping the winter's cold, a traveler from a faraway land looking for a better life, or a kid from Cleveland in hot pursuit of a Netflix deal, California beckons. Like some angel with wings, we believe in her. Generations of immigrants have headed west to plant their flag in the years following the great Gold Rush: moviemakers, farmers, artists, oil drillers, starlets, writers, and so many more. California became the destination for new beginnings, and it remains a place where one might strike it rich with a little luck, and a lot of hard work. So for all the waitresses, the software developers, and the kids pumping gas who still come here to make good on a dream, hope remains the glue that binds them all together.

As was true with the making of my *New Yorkers* book, a particular story unfolded while I continued to photograph these Californians at home. The cliché of palm trees and sunny interiors was there for sure, but that was only the first layer of the onion. And while I did have the good fortune of photographing some well knowns, I also found others who had redefined their goals as time went by. If their dreams fell short they just looked for new ones, because the same shared spirit that brought them all here in the first place, shines on.

The magic and the promises that wave us in: Joni Mitchell, Mama Cass, the Beach Boys, tail-finned cars, and sunny skies, are immediately at odds with the earthquakes, drought, and end-of-times wildfires. The choice then becomes ours, and as the myth of Icarus gives rise to the warning: don't fly too close to the sun, I found myself wondering instead, if I might just be a distant relative of Peter Pan.

Sally Davies
www.sallydaviesphoto.com

TARRAN MERRILL

Photographed at home in La Quinta on April 28, 2021.

Tarran was born in 1971 in La Quinta, California. He was the youngest of two boys for Doug and Peggy. When Tarran was 17 his brother died in a car accident. Dad was a Mormon from Los Angeles and Mom was a Mormon from Utah. Dad worked until the day he died for the Thunderbird Country Club as a purchasing agent. Mom was the boss of all the paper boys at the *Desert Sun* newspaper in Indio. Tarran wanted to be a lawyer when he grew up. When he was a 12-year-old Boy Scout he had a bad accident and fell 30 feet off a mountain ledge. He had four brain surgeries after that. He finished Palm Desert High School and spent the next several years addicted to drugs. On June 19, 2004 Tarran got clean and remains clean to this day. When he left home, he moved into an apartment, then he bought a house three blocks away. In 2003 a house came up for sale directly across the street from the house he grew up in. He bought it and moved in. In 2004 Tarran went to a neon school near San Francisco. He worked as a paper boy, a busboy at a restaurant, thought about being in the construction business, worked with neon, and started a successful carpet-cleaning business in 2012.

"I love the desert. I love La Quinta most of all the cities in the desert, because there is no light pollution, no street lights so you have beautiful stars. It is the gem of the desert. I plan to run for Mayor of La Quinta."
—*Tarran*

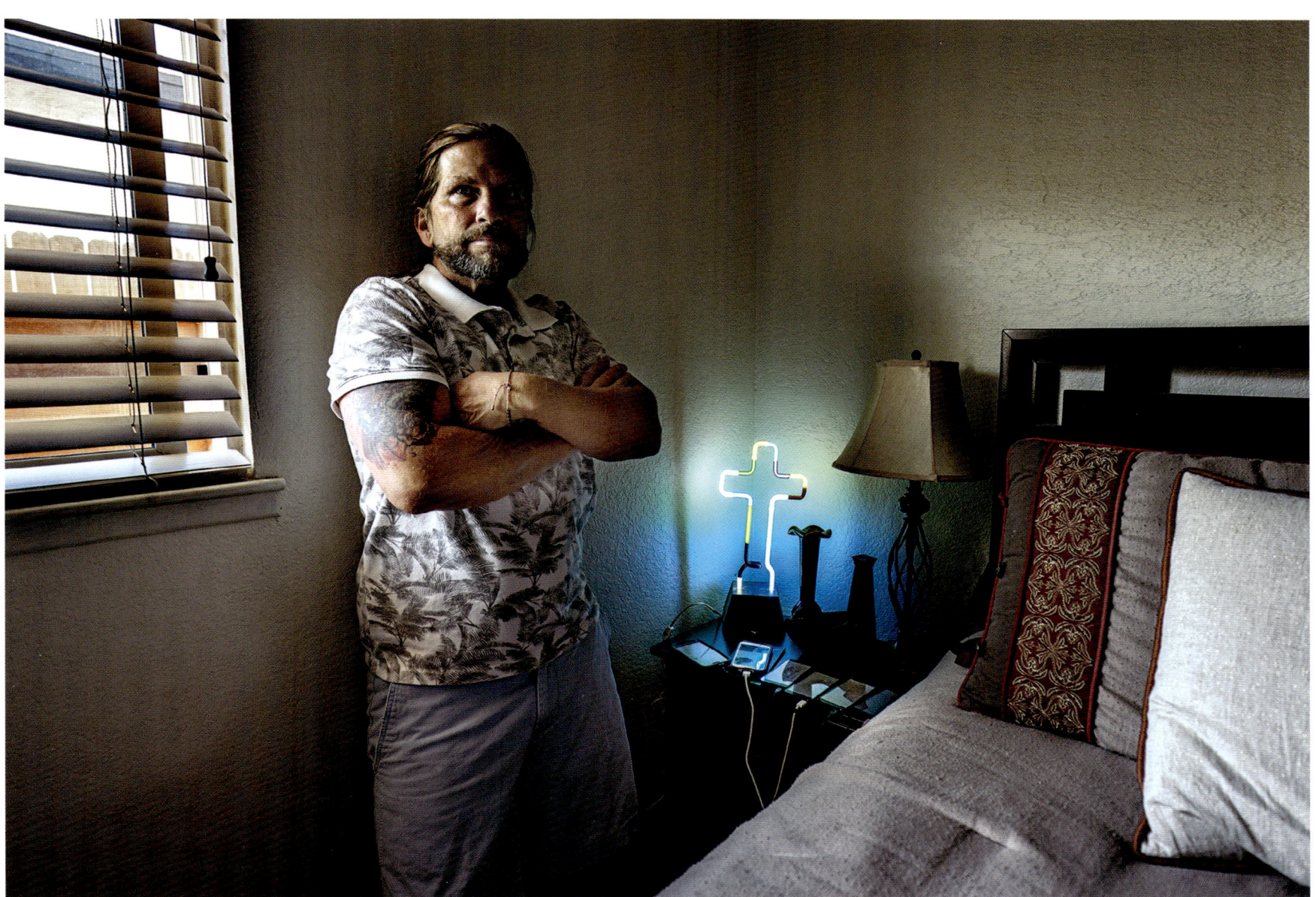

OSBALDO AND ROSA CASTRO

Photographed at home with their two kids Harmony and Michael in Cathedral City on May 1, 2021.

Osbaldo Castro was born in 1974 in Acambaro, Mexico. He was the last of five kids for 19-year-old Sara and Antonio. Sara was a homemaker who also read people's cards, and Dad delivered groceries. When he was a little baby his mom took him and two of the other kids and moved to Texas, leaving the other kids at home in Mexico with Antonio. His mom fell in love and married a Texan man there named Geraldo, who Osbaldo really loved. Osbaldo spent his youth growing up in Alamo, Texas. He was a very lovable little boy. He wanted to be a truck driver when he grew up. He got good marks, and graduated high school. He was a devoted football player with number 34 on his team jersey, and he was also a very, very good *quebradita* dancer. Years later his mom moved from Texas to Cathedral City in California with the family. Geraldo went to see, but he didn't like it and returned to Alamo, where he was murdered years later. Osbaldo stayed in Cathedral City with his mom. He always loved music, especially country and Mexican banda. Not long after graduating high school in Cathedral City, he met Rosa at Fandango's night club. He left home when he was 22 and they married soon after. Osbaldo sold newspapers at the border and worked in the Texan fields picking cotton and fruit. He worked as a bagger and restocker at a grocery store, worked in retail at Ross's department store, worked for a mobile car wash company, sold plumbing parts to plumbers, and worked at a hardware store. Now he sells Bluetooth speakers complete with custom music.

Rosa Maria Castro was born in Guadalajara, Jalisco, Mexico in 1963. She was the fifth of seven kids for Cresencio and Rosalia. Dad was a construction worker and Mom was a homemaker who also took in laundry and babysat to make extra money. Mom and Dad were never married but they lived together their whole lives. She was a quiet little girl and was a good student, never causing problems. She wanted to be a teacher or a secretary when she grew up. When Rosa was nine and ten years old she worked with her uncle at a diner. She did dishes and cleared the tables while still going to school, but the next year, she quit in sixth grade. Rosa left home when she was 20. Her mom didn't like her boyfriend, so she sent her to the USA with relatives. In 1983 Rosa, her brother and a cousin were smuggled across the border by "coyotes," landing in Palm Desert. Not loving the desert, she stayed for one year only then returned to Mexico, but it was short lived and she returned to the USA for good. She realized working here she could make enough money to send some home to help her parents in Mexico. She lived in Palm Desert with her brother for 13 years. She was a dishwasher and then a cook. In 1995 she met Osbaldo at a nightclub. A year later they moved to Cathedral City. They lived for one year with Osbaldo's mom then got their own place, where they lived for 15 years.

Osbaldo and Rosa got married in 1997 on Valentine's Day. In 2006 he and Rosa adopted Harmony and Michael. They all moved into this house six years ago and live there still.

"Things have changed here and yes, that's for the better, except for the homeless problem. But I don't love it here, it's boring. I would rather be back in Alamo."
—Osbaldo

"Back in those early days I liked that the city was quiet, with no traffic. But, these days the desert is more beautiful and more modern than it used to be, and I like that. I like to wake up early in the morning and get ready for the day. I like to be ready."
—Rosa

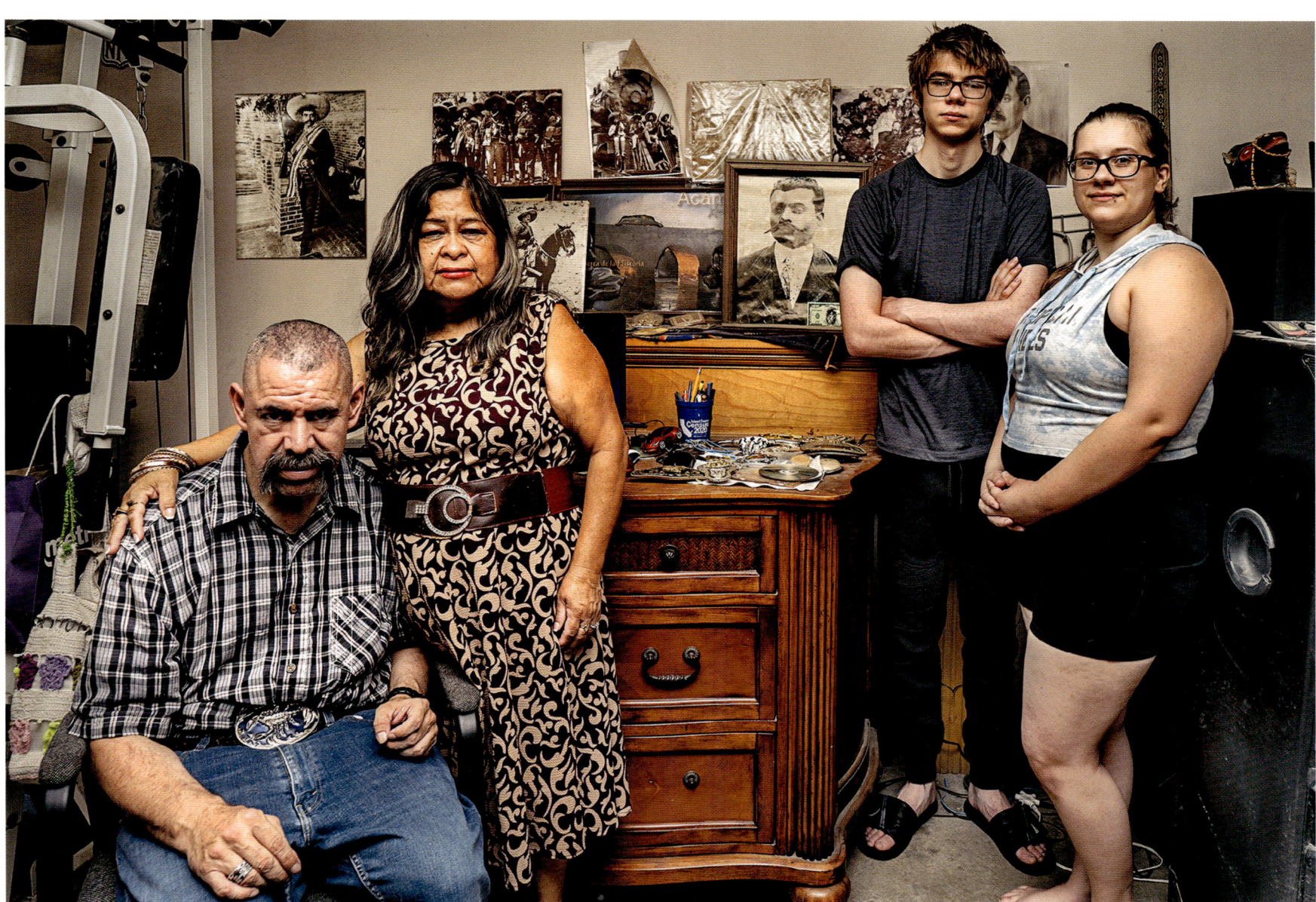

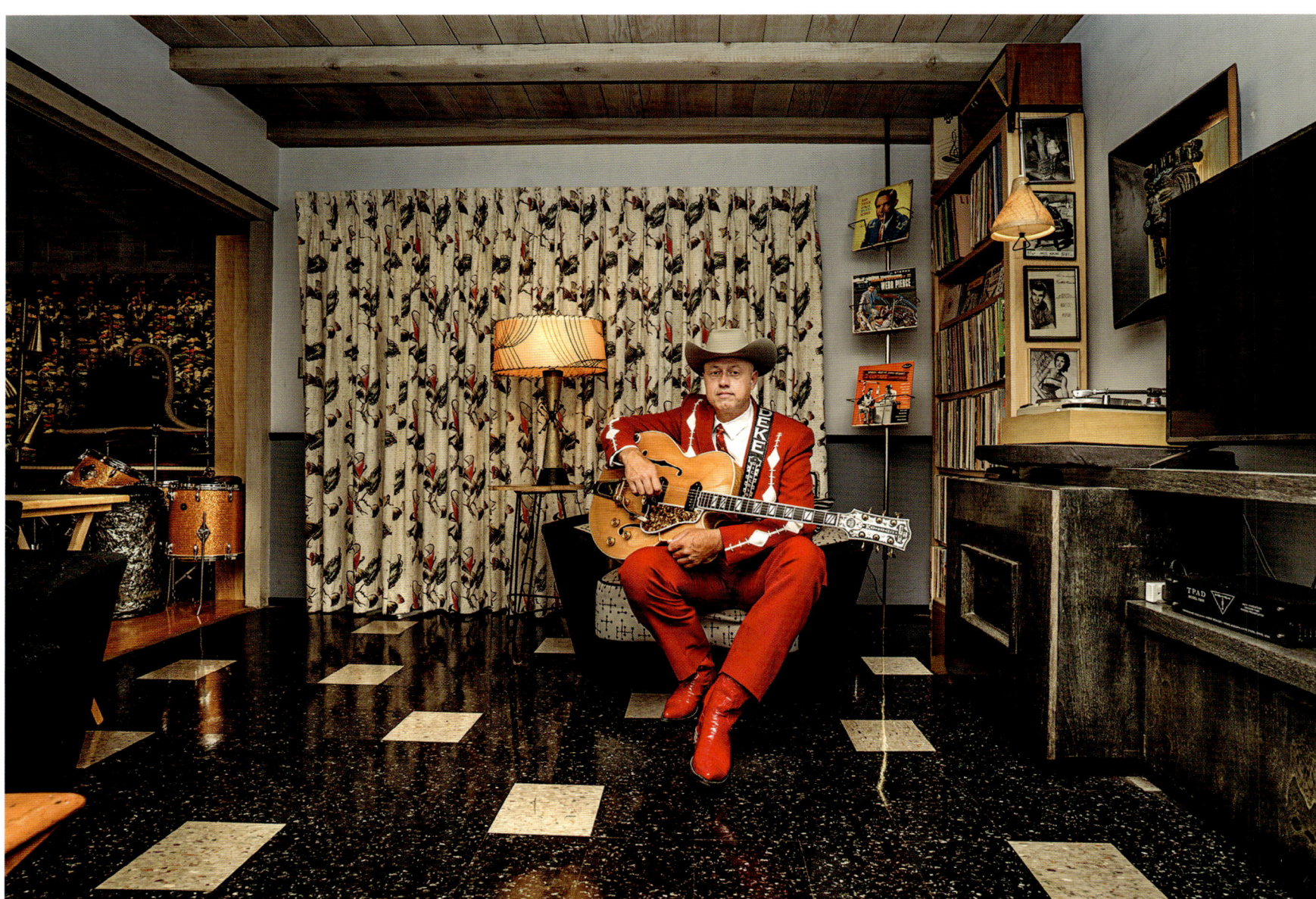

DEKE DICKERSON

Photographed at home in the Valley on May 19, 2021.

Deke was born in 1968 in St. Louis, Missouri. He was the oldest of two for Harman and Kitty Lee. Dad quit a desk job with the Army to restore vintage airplanes in a barn behind the house. Mom was a college professor and she also wrote textbooks. Both were from Floyd, Virginia. Deke spent his childhood years moving around a bit because of his mom's jobs. He wanted to be a singer and play guitar when he grew up. When he was 13 he started playing in bars. He was six-feet-two-inches tall, so no one suspected he wasn't old enough. He went to college for two years to study journalism, but rock 'n' roll won out and he moved to Los Angeles with a band. He was 23. That band broke up but Deke started other bands along the way, finally starting his own solo band in 1998. He's been playing ever since and has not had a real job to this day. Deke was also married a couple of times, and 12 years ago had a daughter named Evelyn. He worked at low-paying hard labor jobs in Missouri but when he moved to California, he got a job at a self-help organization that paid four times more. When he had to lift anything that weighed a couple of pounds, the bosses told him to take a regenerative nap. That attitude agreed with Deke—he loved California. He's made 12 albums, 40 singles, and has songs in movies and TV shows. He has his own signature guitar through Hallmark Guitars, and has produced the Guitar Geek Festival since 2004. He tours non-stop throughout the USA and the world, and has written two books on vintage guitars. He wrote a biography on songwriter Merle Travis, and in 2019 was voted Best Musician in the Ameripolitan Awards. Deke moved into this house in 2006. He lives there with his girlfriend Sally-Jo and his daughter.

"There are pros and cons to every place in the world. All I can say is that the first time I came to Los Angeles, when my band was on tour back in the 1980s, I said to myself: 'How long until I can live here? Because I'M GOING TO LIVE HERE.' I've been here 30 years and I wouldn't live anywhere else. I think it's funny Los Angeles is so universally hated across the USA, because I've always loved it so much."
—Deke

DENISE COOK

Photographed at home in Inglewood on March 20, 2022.

Denise was born Denise Lynnette Youlanda Lyles in 1958 in Los Angeles, California. She was the seventh of eight kids for Leon and Erma. Dad was a pharmacist and Mom was a registered nurse. Denise spent her young years growing up in Los Angeles. Later when the Watts Riots broke out, the family moved to Pasadena. She was a bright, spirited kid who had attention deficit hyperactivity disorder and she asked "Why?" a lot. She was a popular kid who was liked by adults. She began producing talent showcases when she was seven. She grew up with dogs, exotic fish, and homing pigeons. She wanted to be a dancer and a teacher when she grew up, and became both of those things. She had her own dance company that toured Europe and she taught at the same time. She was an overachiever who did well at everything she put her hand to. She became a member of the Honors Society, and excelled at all types of sports, even training for the 1972 Olympics. When Denise was 17 she moved in with her sister until she graduated school. From there she was Hollywood bound with her godmother. She attended college in Los Angeles studying dance, education, and the performing arts. She worked at Burger King and as an assistant to an accountant. After college Denise mostly taught dance. She got married to Gregory Cook in 1987 and they had two kids. She was on a TV show, and continued dancing in various companies. Denise teaches virtually now for the Los Angeles school system. She is a motivational speaker, a published author, an educator and artist, and is known as a healer of the heart. Denise and Gregory moved into this apartment in 2019 and live there still.

"I love Inglewood. I live near shopping, Space X, SoFi, Hollywood Park Casino . . . It is relatively quiet here and peaceful, but I do hate having to climb the stairs to my apartment; I have arthritis in the hips. I do love the close proximity to the freeway and retail and grocery stores."
—Denise

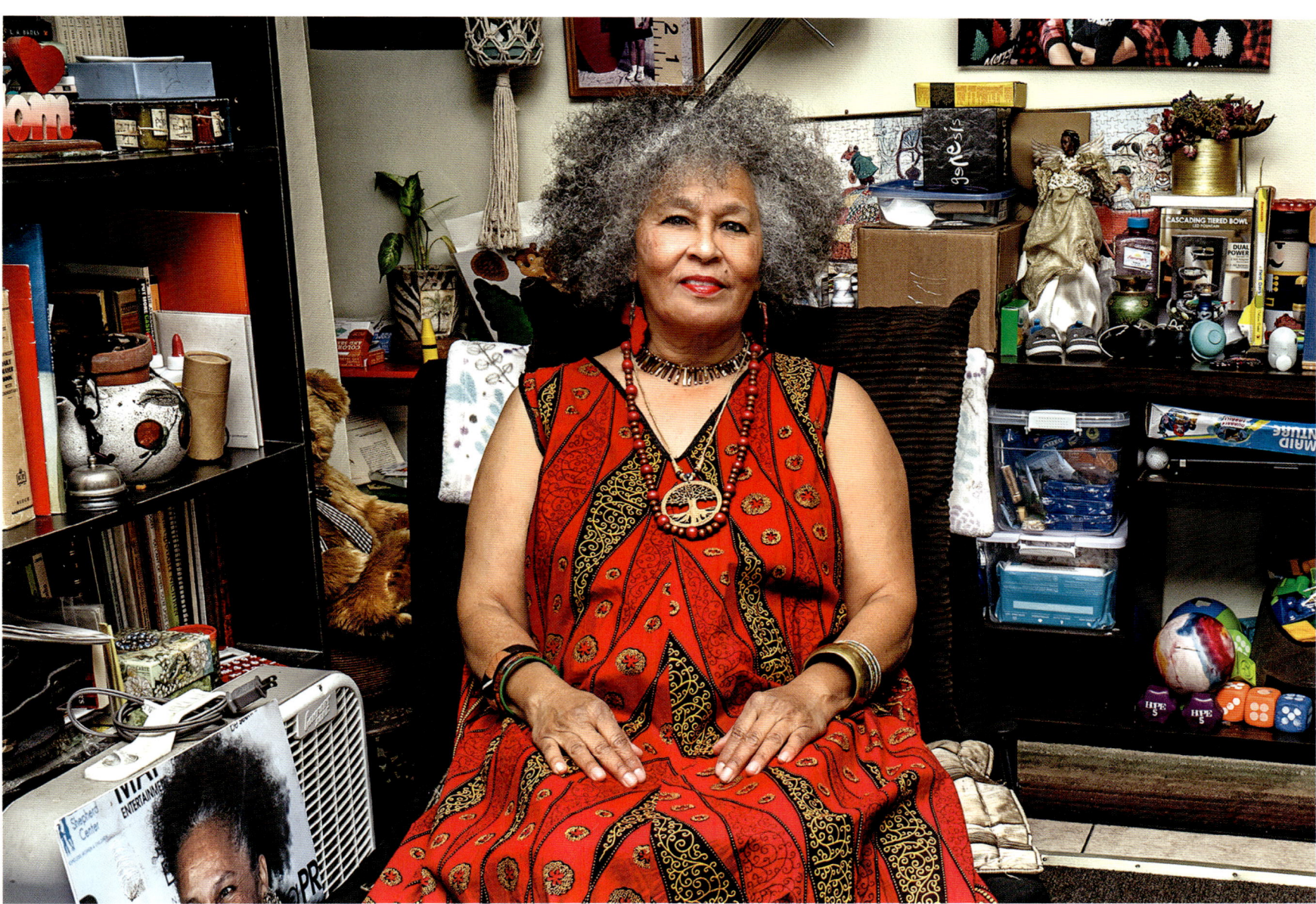

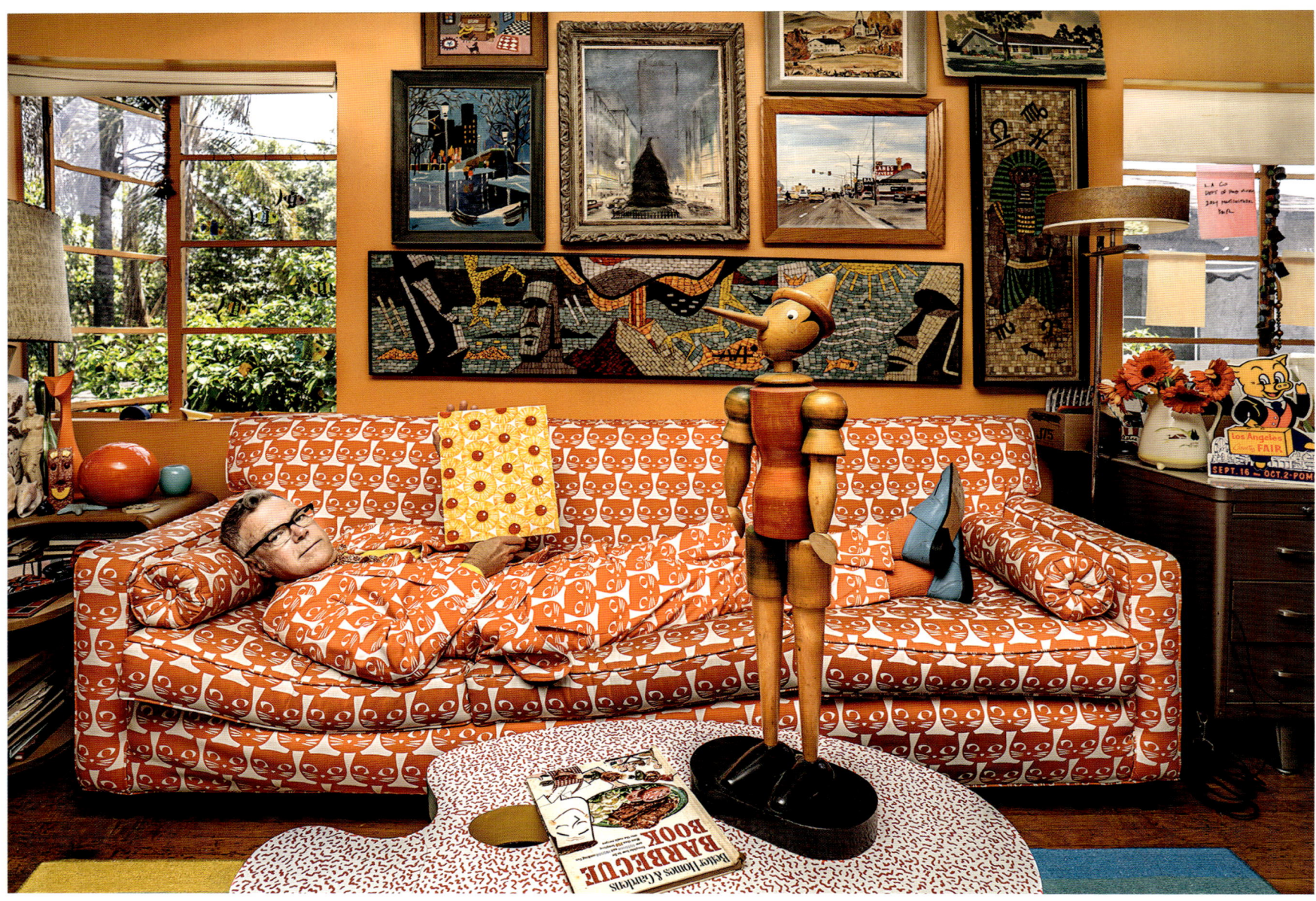

CHARLES PHOENIX

Photographed at home in Silver Lake on May 18, 2021.

Charles was born in 1962 in Ontario, California. He was the youngest of two boys for Gary and Donna. Dad was a used car salesman and Mom was a homemaker. Dad died when Charles was only 14 and Mom remarried. He spent his childhood in Ontario and wanted to be an artist when he grew up. When he was only four years old he knew he wanted to leave behind a legacy when he left this earth. He spent his teenage years with the local community theater, shopping at thrift stores and working at the movies. Charles left home when he was 19 and moved to Hollywood where he attended the Fashion Institute, becoming a fashion designer. He designed clothes for nine years. After that he bought and sold vintage cars. While he was selling cars, he found a box of photo slides from the 1950s and 1960s in a Pasadena thrift store, and that changed the course of his future. He continued to collect vintage slides and eventually started giving slide shows at the California Map and Travel Center in LA. His slide shows were a hit and were reviewed by the *LA Times*. He travels throughout the USA in search of vintage Americana. Charles collects vintage American cars, has been on TV, has been a commentator on NPR, has written seven books, and continues to give his critically acclaimed "Retro slide shows." Charles moved into this Silver Lake apartment in 1987 and lives there still.

"Los Angeles is loaded with people working in creative industries. You can have a wide circle of friends here that are working in a creative capacity somewhere, and that represents people who are forward thinking, who know how to think for themselves, and are visual people. The Internet changed the world and replaced so much. Environmental experiences in Los Angeles are getting really rare. Dining out, which used to be commonplace, is becoming a luxury. I only go to old vintage restaurants. I love Canter's Deli. I want history, a story, soul, integrity, staying power, I want genuine and authentic. We still have some of these places left, but they are folding quickly."
—Charles

BRANDON WARGO AND THUC DOAN NGUYEN-BROPHY

Photographed at home in East LA with their dogs Bea and Jasper on February 19, 2022.

Brandon was born in Colorado Springs, Colorado in 1981. He was the oldest of three for Paul and Rebecca. Dad was a landscaper and later a handyman. Brandon spent his youth growing up in Ambridge, Pennsylvania. He wanted to be a doctor when he grew up, or maybe a veterinarian. He played some little league, and spent his formative years absorbing pop culture: music, TV, movies, and such. Brandon wanted to move to New York when he was 17 and do music, but his parents made him go to college. So he left home when he was 18 for college and got a degree in computer science. He cooked at Pizza Hut, worked at landscaping with his dad, and stocked shelves at PetSmart. Brandon was 24 and college was done. He stayed living in Pennsylvania for four more years working at some office jobs and playing in bands. In 2009 Brandon moved to Los Angeles to do music. He worked at tech start-ups during the day while he moonlighted at night playing in bands. He has a band now named Tiger Beat. He sings and plays bass.

Thuc was born in Can Tho, Vietnam in 1976. She was the oldest of two girls for Danh and Ti. Dad taught history and Mom taught biology. When Thuc was just a toddler, they fled Vietnam, escaping the persecution of intellectuals under the communist regime. They became boat people drifting at sea, eventually spending time at refugee camps in Indonesia, before they were sponsored for immigrant status in the USA. Thuc was four years old. She spent her childhood years growing up in the rural North Carolina and Maryland area wanting to be a writer when she grew up. Thuc was a busy kid playing field hockey and basketball, doing art and taking African and modern dance. When she was 17, she left home for college. After college she spent a summer depressed and eating food from the local gas station. Hoping to delay her adulthood, she headed to London, England. She worked at Amnesty International and at Saatchi & Saatchi. After one year in London, Thuc hopped on a plane for NYC and spent three years living in the East Village there. Then in 2001 she went west to LA for a break, and ended up staying there. She worked as a receptionist, a waitress, a candle maker, a warehouse worker, a hostess, and as a go-go dancer. Now she is a studio screenwriter, an author, and she writes for magazines like *Vogue* and *Esquire*.

Thuc lived in Hollywood, Downtown LA, and Marina del Ray before she moved into this house in East LA in 2017.
Thuc and Brandon met in 2019, and he moved in with her in 2021.

"There's certainly a better quality of life and more access to things in LA than the rust belt. It was easier for me to meet like-minded people here to make music with. The pandemic and turning 40 kind of changed my priorities in life, made my social circles smaller. Life can be good or bad here like anywhere else. I used to love that there was always SOMETHING going on here before the pandemic. Nowadays, I enjoy nature and going places with very few people. I guess I hate the same things about LA as others do: too many people trying to "be seen" and the traffic."
—Brandon

"LA is roomy. People often stick to their neighborhoods instead of driving across town—too much traffic. It's impossible to be friends with people in certain neighborhoods if it takes an hour to find parking there—ha. I like basic aspects of life here like having nice parks nearby—if I don't have to go further than five miles from my house. I do hate that all the stereotypes are true, how people are truly plastic and delusional. Gentrification is happening where I am now. The audacity and entitlement of some people is simply incredible."
—Thuc

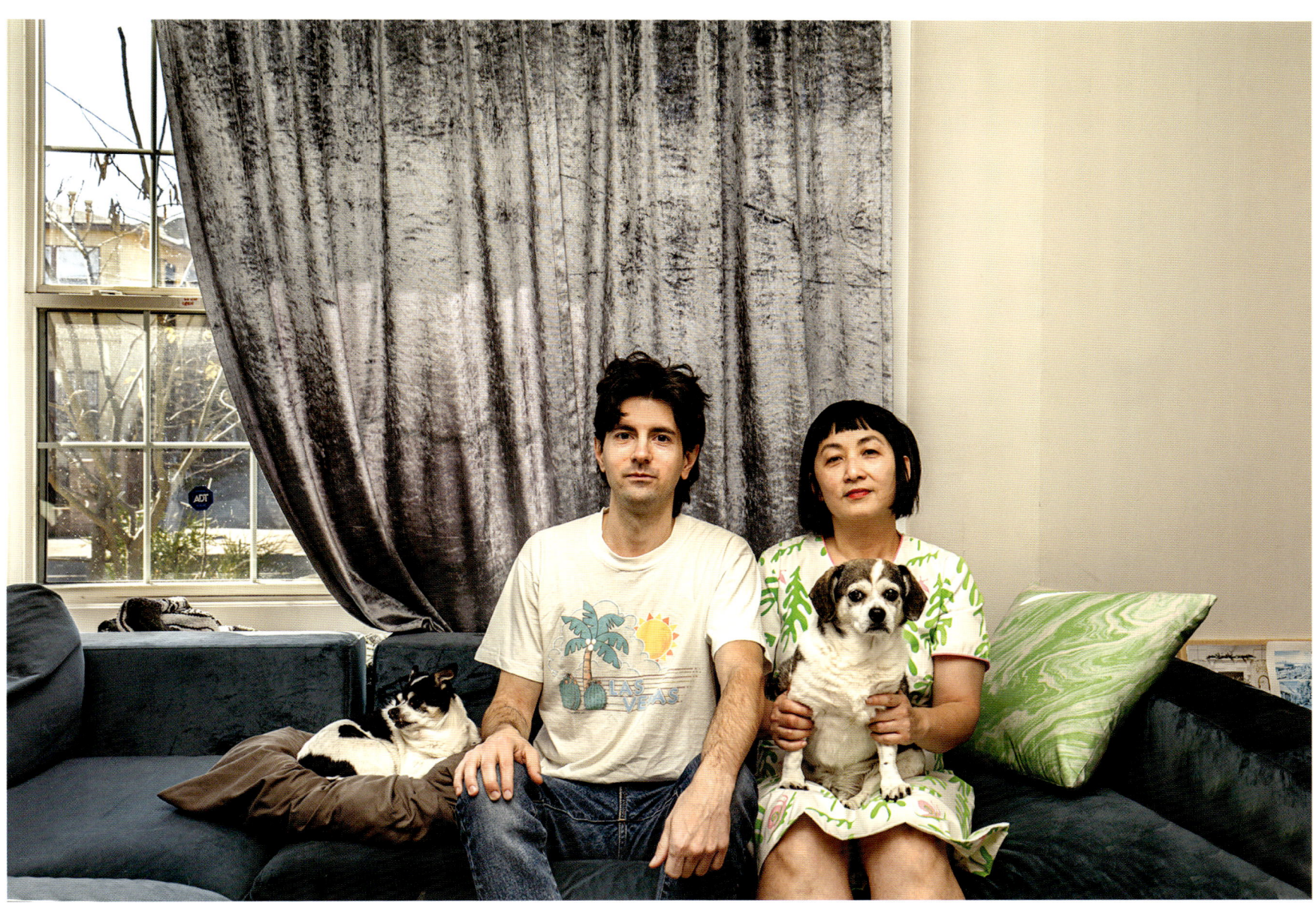

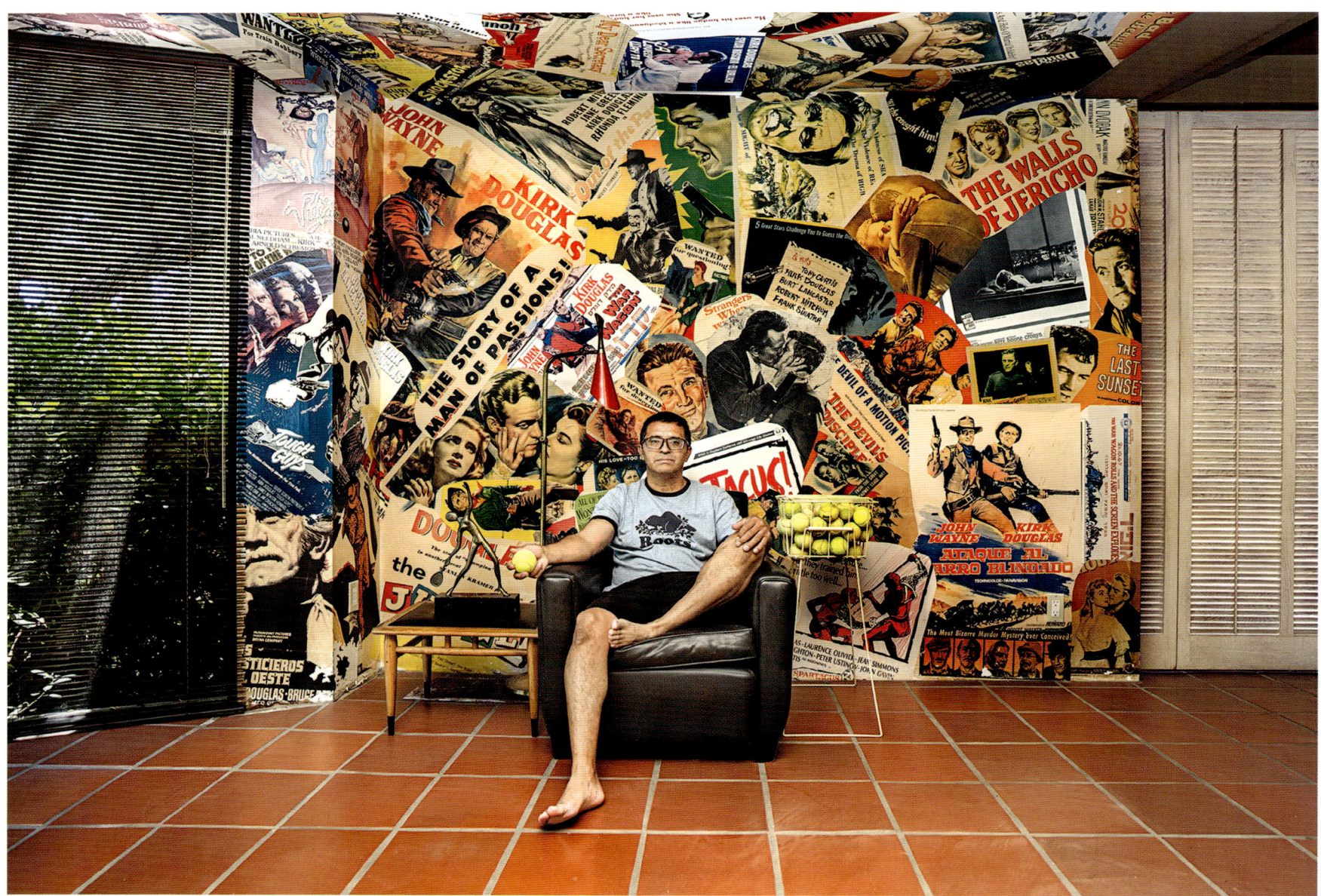

ARTURO MIRAFUENTES

Photographed in the tennis pavilion at the Kirk Douglas Estate in Palm Springs on May 2, 2021.

Arturo was born in 1967 in Mexico City. He was the second of six kids for Cristina Santamaria and Arturo. Mom was a neighborhood nurse and Dad was an electrician who later opened a shoe repair shop. When Arturo was ten his mom and dad split up. Arturo liked to play basketball and was pretty good at soccer. He was a very smart kid, and got really good grades, even though he was a rebel. He wanted to be a military pilot when he grew up. Before he left for the USA, Arturo worked sanding wood furniture, went door-to-door vaccinating dogs (his mom taught him how to do that) and helped a neighbor bake sweets to sell door-to-door. He sewed denim jeans, worked at a broom bristle factory as a machine operator, and worked at an office job at the health department. He worked in the accounting department at a small auto parts store and was a painter for his stepfather. Arturo was very enthusiastic about life as a young boy. When he was 18, Mexico City suffered a huge earthquake. He was still a Boy Scout and volunteered on the rescue mission. Arturo went to college in Mexico City. He studied architecture for three years, leaving for the USA shortly after that. He lived in LA, San Diego, Santa Barbara, and Carpinteria, but they all felt like Mexico City and Arturo wanted something different, something smaller and quieter. In 1992 he moved to Palm Springs. Once he was in California, he worked as a grape picker for six hours, at a car wash, as a dishwasher, as a pastry chef and baker, as a line cook, a bus boy, an assistant manager at a bagel place in Palm Springs, and as a newspaper delivery man. He delivered construction materials, drove a garbage truck, and was a limo driver. He was a swimming pool cleaner, then he and his brothers started their own family business in the pool industry. Finally, Arturo started a handyman service on his own, and that landed him a job working at the Kirk Douglas Estate in Palm Springs. He worked up from that and became the grounds' property manager. Twenty-one years and two owners later, Arturo still manages the estate and lives on site.

"I was sitting in the back seat of a car driving away from LA. First I noticed less big buildings, then less houses, until finally I saw a pure desert: no houses or anything on the side of the freeway. As we cleared Windy Point coming into Palm Springs I knew I liked this small, calm town. I can still enjoy 'old Palm Springs'—all I have to do is stay away from downtown."
—Arturo

ERIC GRAY

Photographed at home in Culver City on March 20, 2022.

Eric was born in Trenton, New Jersey in 1966. He was the oldest of three for Johnnie and Evelyn. Dad repaired city pipelines for the water department and Mom was a homemaker. Eric spent his childhood years growing up mostly in New Jersey. He was a laidback, streetwise kid who wanted to be a successful musician when he grew up. He was a good student who made the honor role in high school. When Dad got laid off and times were tough, Eric got a job at McDonald's so he could help out. He liked sports but really liked music and listening to the radio. When Eric was 18 he left home. He went to college for about a year studying music and he also started his own record label, releasing some successful underground recordings. He studied at a music conservatory when he was a teenager, but mostly he was a street hustler who survived the late 80s and 90s crack era. He went to Europe when he was 21 and spread hip hop music there. The Berlin Wall had just collapsed. He was the first on record to establish hip hop in West and East Germany while fighting against the fascist right wing. He got record deals with two big labels and was featured on MTV too. Eric met his wife in Hamburg, Germany. Five years later on a vacation to New York City they got married. They returned to Germany but in 2000 they moved back to Brooklyn and bought a brownstone. Their son was born two years later. Eric worked a security job in the Bronx and they rented out the upper level of their building for extra income while he continued working in his private recording studio. In 2014 they sold the brownstone and moved: first from Brooklyn to New Jersey, then from there to California. Eric plays guitar now, busking from Venice Beach to Culver City.

"California is a great place to live. The weather is really good out here and if you have a dream it's possible—but you have to work at it every day. You have to be out and about and meeting people. Just believe in yourself and build your empire from nothing if you have to. As for me, I did it before, I will do again. Don't Stop Believing."
—Eric

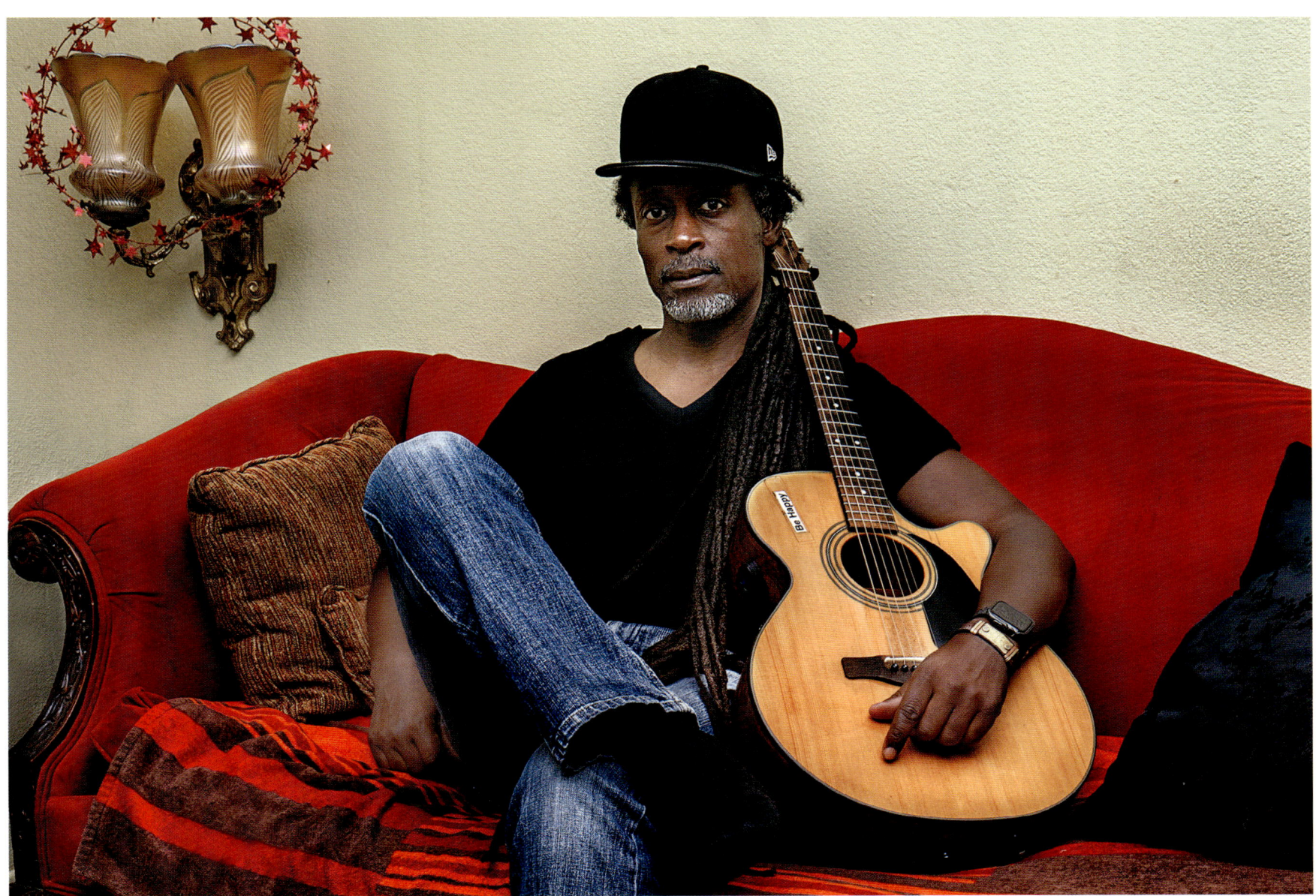

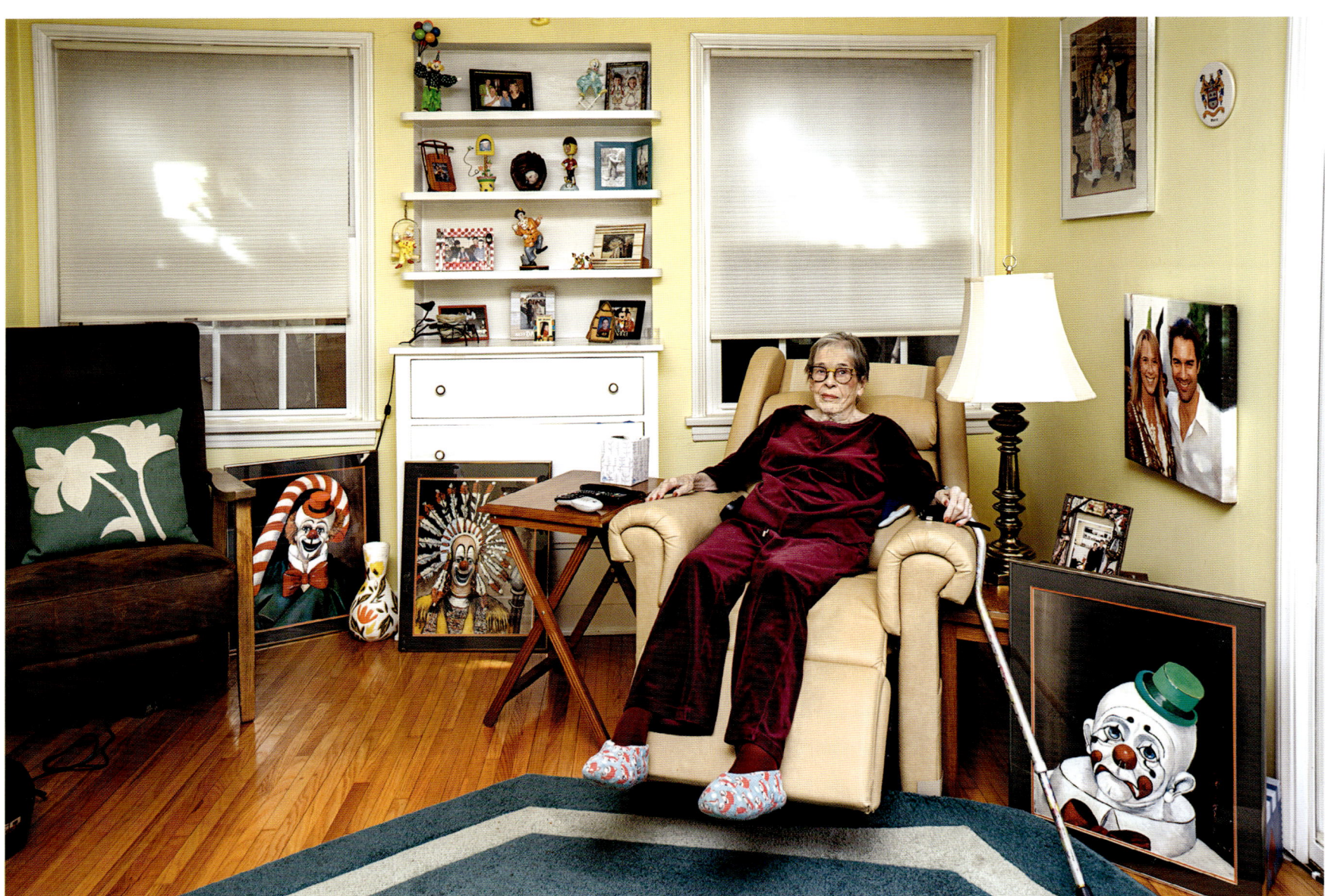

CAROL HOLDEN

Photographed at home in Toluca Lake on February 20, 2022.

Carol was born in Edmonton, Canada in 1938. She was the first born of three for Robert and Dorothy. She had a twin sister named Janet. Dad owned an insurance company. Carol spent her young years with her dog Smokey in Alberta, Canada. She wanted to be a nurse when she grew up, and excelled at English and history in school. Carol did what most Canadian kids do; she skated and played curling. When she was 18, she got married to Allan Holden, and left home. She worked at a hardware store and then later wrote commercials for a local radio station. Carol and Allan had two sons and one daughter. Much later, she left Canada and moved to Los Angeles to live closer to her daughter and family. She moved into this house in 2012 and lives there still.

"I love the weather here, the small town atmosphere, and the friendliness of my neighborhood."
—Carol

MARCO FRANCHINA

Photographed with his dog Luna at home in Palm Springs on April 8, 2022.

Marco was born Fabrizio Narducci in Pisa, Italy in 1961. Nick and Angela adopted Marco when he was three years old and brought him back to Encino, California. Dad was a lawyer and Mom was a fashion designer. Marco was a spirited little kid who was often in trouble. He loved fast cars and wanted to be a race car driver when he grew up. He suffered with attention deficit hyperactivity disorder and had a hard time with school. He barely graduated but he loved to play baseball and football. Marco worked at a vintage car lot and at his cousin's motorcycle shop. When he was 20 he left home and headed east to New York to learn photography. Two years later in 1983 he moved to Italy, where he worked as a fashion photographer for a couple of years. His photography had him traveling around: back to New York, then to Australia and back to New York again for eight more years, where he worked at Andy Warhol's *Interview* magazine. In the late nineties Marco returned to LA to continue his photography career and to take care of his mother who had fallen ill. Marco moved into this apartment in Palm Springs in 2020 and is still a photographer.

"I wanted to get out of Los Angeles—I'd been there way too long. The city was really getting bad. Palm Springs is 100 times more mellow: a small town that really hasn't changed since I was coming out to vacation when I was a teen. The bad is the summer. It hits triple digits for months. It can get as high as 115 degrees for weeks."
—Marco

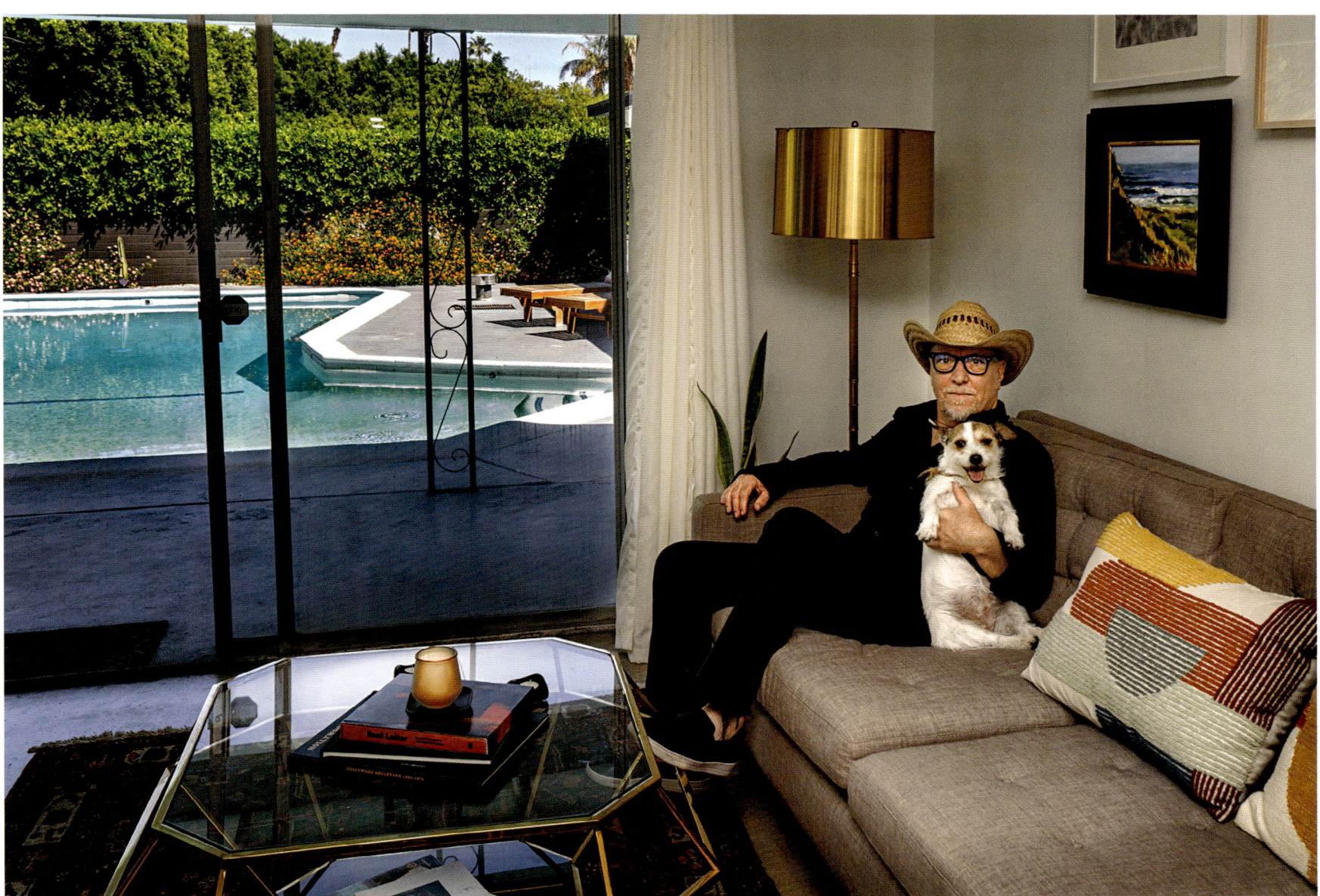

RYDER NOYES

Photographed at home in Los Angeles on February 26, 2022.

Ryder was born in 2000 in Los Angeles. He is the youngest of two for Phil and Lisa. Dad produced commercials and Mom was a model and an actress. Ryder spent his young years growing up in Los Angeles with his dog, two cats, and his pet white rat. He loves them all very much. Ryder makes puppets too, and hopes to some day work at the Jim Henson Muppet Company. He would also like to be a voice actor. He really hated school and is not sure to this day how he graduated. He worked at Petco and at Gamestop. He is currently learning to drive, looking for a job, making fantastic puppets, and watching horror movies.

"LA is not as glamorous as some would lead you to believe; it's hot with harsh wind and full of hobos. Even so, it's my home and I have good memories here. Something about listening to music while sitting in the back of a car and staring out the window as the sun sets is particularly magical. LA is a place where you can find all sorts of people, places, and things. I've lived here my whole life so far and there's still parts I haven't seen. It's like living in a David Lynch film."
—Ryder

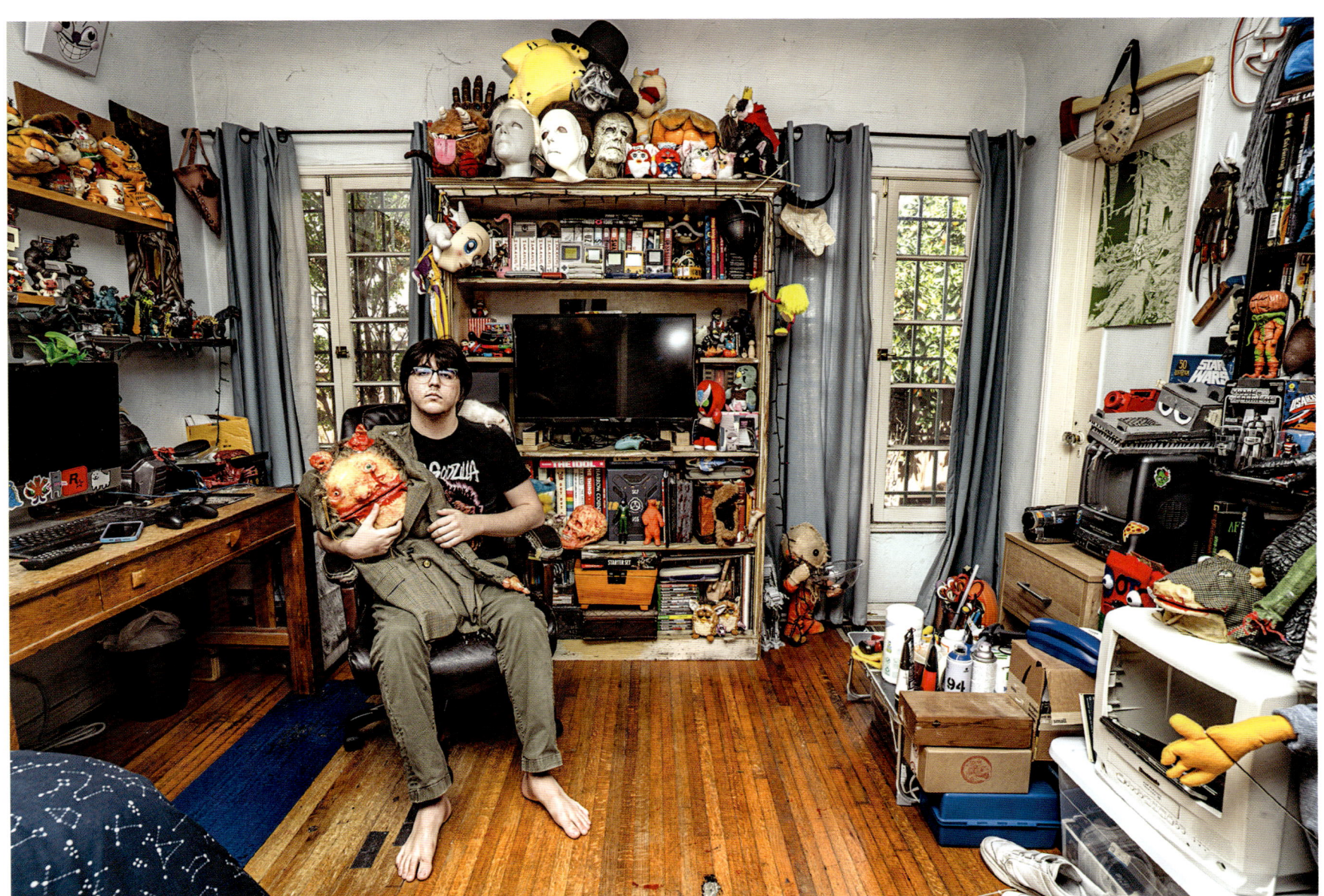

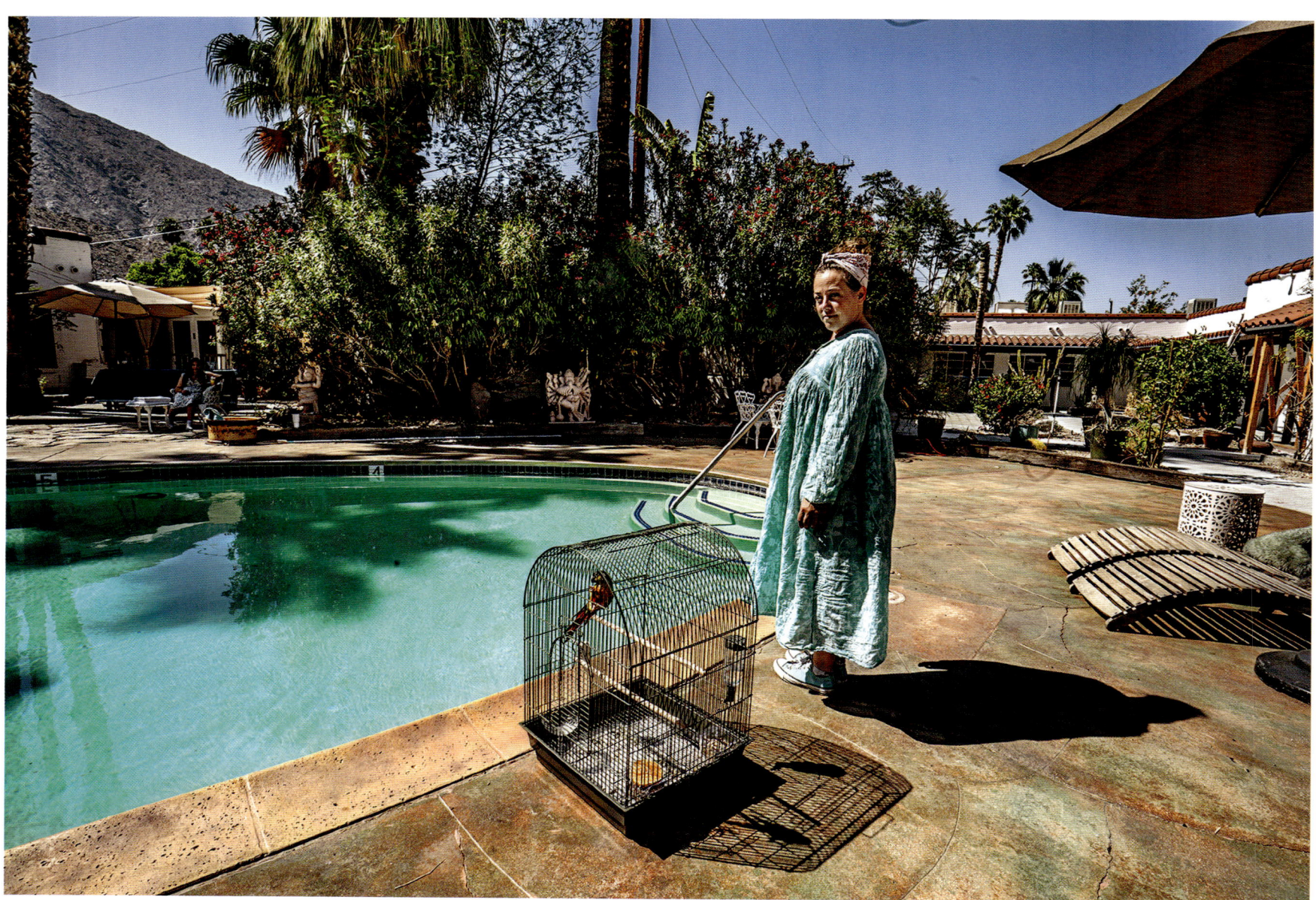

GABRIELLA REDDING

Photographed at the motel pool where she lives in Palm Springs, with her parrot Baxter, on May 8, 2021.

Gabbi was born in Long Beach, California in 1976, the year of the dragon. She was the oldest of three kids for Sharon and August. Mom and Dad were both teachers and both from California. Gabbi spent her childhood at Belmont Shore, Long Beach. She wasn't sure exactly what she wanted to be when she grew up, but she had a definite knack for selling things. She sold more Girl Scout cookies than anyone in her area and after school she sold her drawings on the sidewalk. Except for phys-ed, Gabbi did really well at school. She was a synchronized swimmer and in the evenings of her high school years, she sold kegs of beer to people who were having parties. She left home when she was 15 on a foreign exchange student program, and spent grade ten in Italy. She ditched school most days there, hopping the train to Milan or Rome or Florence. She learned how to speak Italian, how to smoke cigarettes, and was pretty sure being famous was in her future. Gabbi went to college for five years studying printmaking and puppetry. She fell in love with an artist she met at the Art Institute in Chicago. After only knowing each other for a few weeks, they got married and had two kids: Illiana Rose and Aliyah. She also founded a hula hoop company in between having the kids. In 2006 they all moved to LA. She delivered pizza, worked at The GAP, sold pot, sold her art, worked in head shops, and sold stuff on the Venice Beach Boardwalk. Some years later they got a divorce and Gabbi moved to Palm Springs. She bought this motel, and even though it was the last lesbian motel in the whole country, she decided to expand the clientele and started to fix it up. Before it was even open to the public a terrible storm blew through Palm Springs and the motel was destroyed. Gabbi works now as a full-time chef serving BBQ and pie, and is temporarily living at the motel.

"The desert can heal and the desert can destroy. Sometimes, the universe offers you no solution. It is relentlessly unforgiving and destroys until there is nothing, and from nothing, we can design newly, again."
—Gabbi

MANDON LOVETT

Photographed at home with his dog Ace in Pasadena on March 15, 2022.

Mandon was born in 1982 in Pasadena, California. He was the youngest for Leonard and Marie, with three half-brothers. Dad was a preacher and Mom was a schoolteacher. Mandon grew up in Pasadena and Virginia. He loved sports but didn't do so well at school otherwise. When Mandon was 18, he left home and headed east to Schenectady, New York to study political science at college. He worked as a busboy and as a lifeguard. When college was done, he stayed in New York. He worked as a paralegal there for three years before moving to Miami to go to law school. Somewhere around year two of law school, Mandon found film, and fell in love with that. He stayed the course and graduated with a law degree, but once he was out of school he hit the ground running and worked as a videographer, filming everything he could from weddings to rap videos. In 2014 when Mandon was 32, he moved west to work on his film career. He felt he had made the best of everything Miami had to offer and it was time get to California. Mandon works now as a documentary filmmaker. He moved into this apartment in 2019 and lives there still.

"Love it here in Pasadena. Feels like home. I was born here, left at the age of ten, and now am back again."
—Mandon

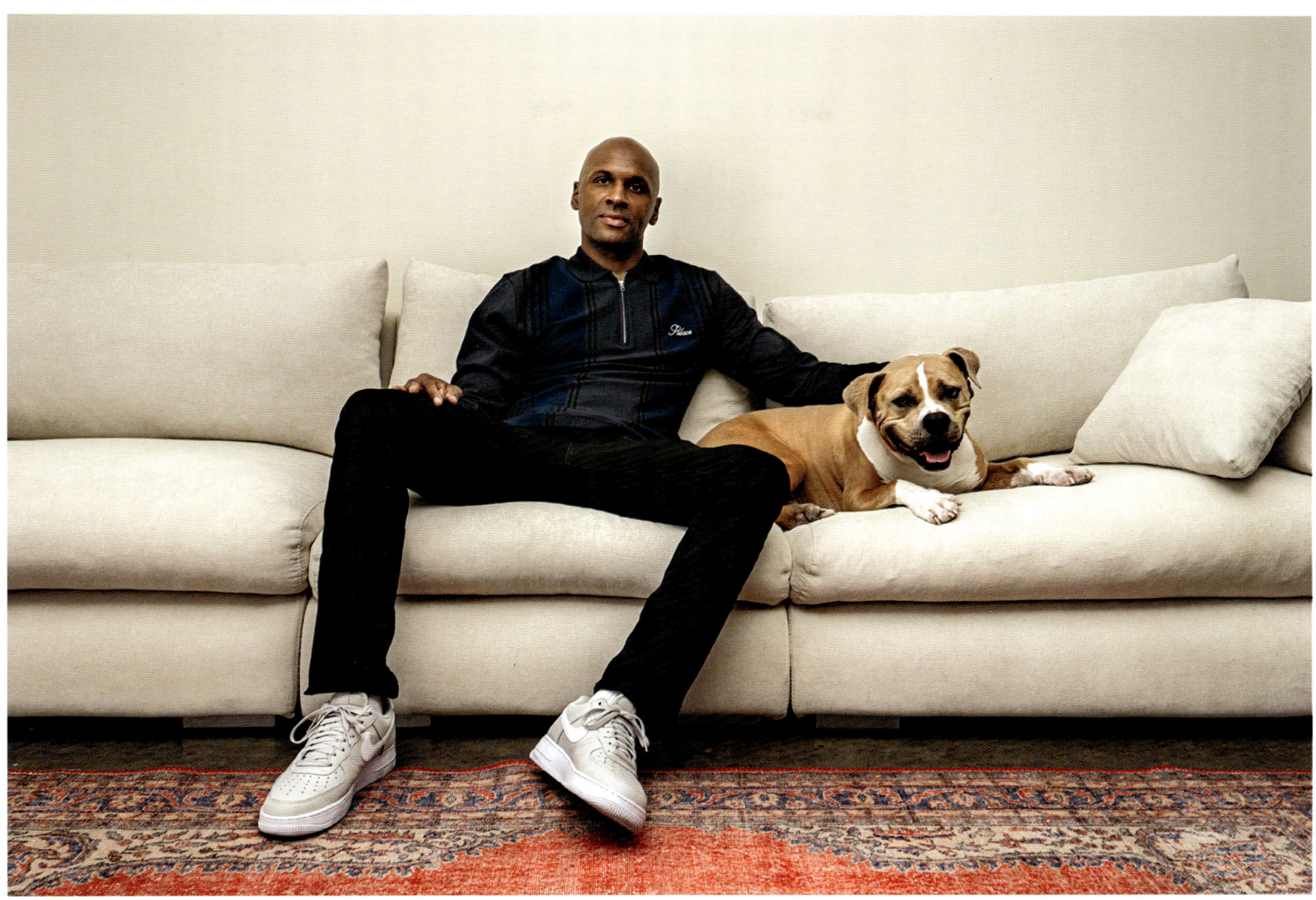

KIMBERLY BIEHL BOAZ AND GREG BOAZ

Photographed at their home in Los Angeles on March 12, 2022.

Kimberly was born in South Bend, Indiana in 1965. She was the first of two kids for Cheryl and Bob. Dad was an author and had a consulting firm, and Mom ran Dad's company. The family moved around and Kimberly went to 14 schools. She wanted to be like her mom when she grew up, and she wanted to marry Shaun Cassidy. Because she moved a lot, she was great at socializing, but just average with schoolwork. She studied interior design for two years then moved up to Los Angeles. She worked at a famous modeling agency and at a famous talent agency. She sold skin-care products and answered mail from prisoners. Her parents had a friend who was a preacher, and he had a prison pen-pal group. She also sold commodities, later finding out it was a scam when government officials told her she could never sell commodities in the state of California again. Kimberly worked for a jewelry designer and moved to New York City for a couple of years. When she returned to LA she did two more years of college and started her own design company. Kimberly got married when she was 32, had three kids, and got a divorce in 2004.

Greg was born in Fullerton, California in 1959. He was the second of two boys for Lorraine and Bob. Mom was a nurse and Dad was a teacher. Greg's parents split up when he was four and he spent his young years with his pet reptiles and his dog in San Diego. He was a quiet kid who wanted to be a musician when he grew up. He wasn't that great of a student. What he loved was music and mostly he excelled at getting stoned in high school, as he surfed and skateboarded through those years. He attended college briefly in San Diego, studying photography. He delivered flowers, delivered the *LA Weekly*, and drove a limo to support his music. It was 1982 and Greg moved to Los Angeles to immerse himself in the music scene. He worked in construction, drove a limo, played music and sold drugs. Somewhere around 1990 his music career really kicked in. Greg got married in 1993, had a son, and got a divorce in 2001.

In 2010 Kimberly and Greg met at a gig he was playing. Kim is a designer, Greg is the bass player for Mavis Staples, and the two of them run an art business, The Hollywood Collective. Kimberly moved into Mae West's old apartment in 2016 and Greg moved in two years later. They live there still.

"I am in LOVE with Los Angeles. I am constantly exploring this town and have loved every minute of my life here. I am always on the hunt for the hidden gems, places, or things I have never seen or experienced. I have loved Hollywood and specifically old Hollywood since I can remember and never will tire of the history we are surrounded by and live in. I love going to look at houses that belonged to old movie stars, which is how I ended up in Mae West's apartment. About four months after I moved in, I started hosting salons here. I miss 1980s Hollywood. I feel like some of the gritty, grimy soul that I loved was sucked out of it, but I still LOVE LA."
—Kimberly

"The Hollywood music scene in the 1980s was like a family. Maybe it was what was happening musically, or maybe it was our age, or a combination of both. So many of us came from dysfunctional families so found our new chosen family there. It was a special time. Maybe that is why Hollywood still feels like home to me. It's strange … places like Echo Park for example … you couldn't even walk around the lake at night back in the eighties. Now there are swans in the lake. Gentrification sucks, but life isn't fair. I guess you take the good with the bad. I love the weather, I still hate the traffic. LA is a nice place to live, but I wouldn't want to visit."
—Greg

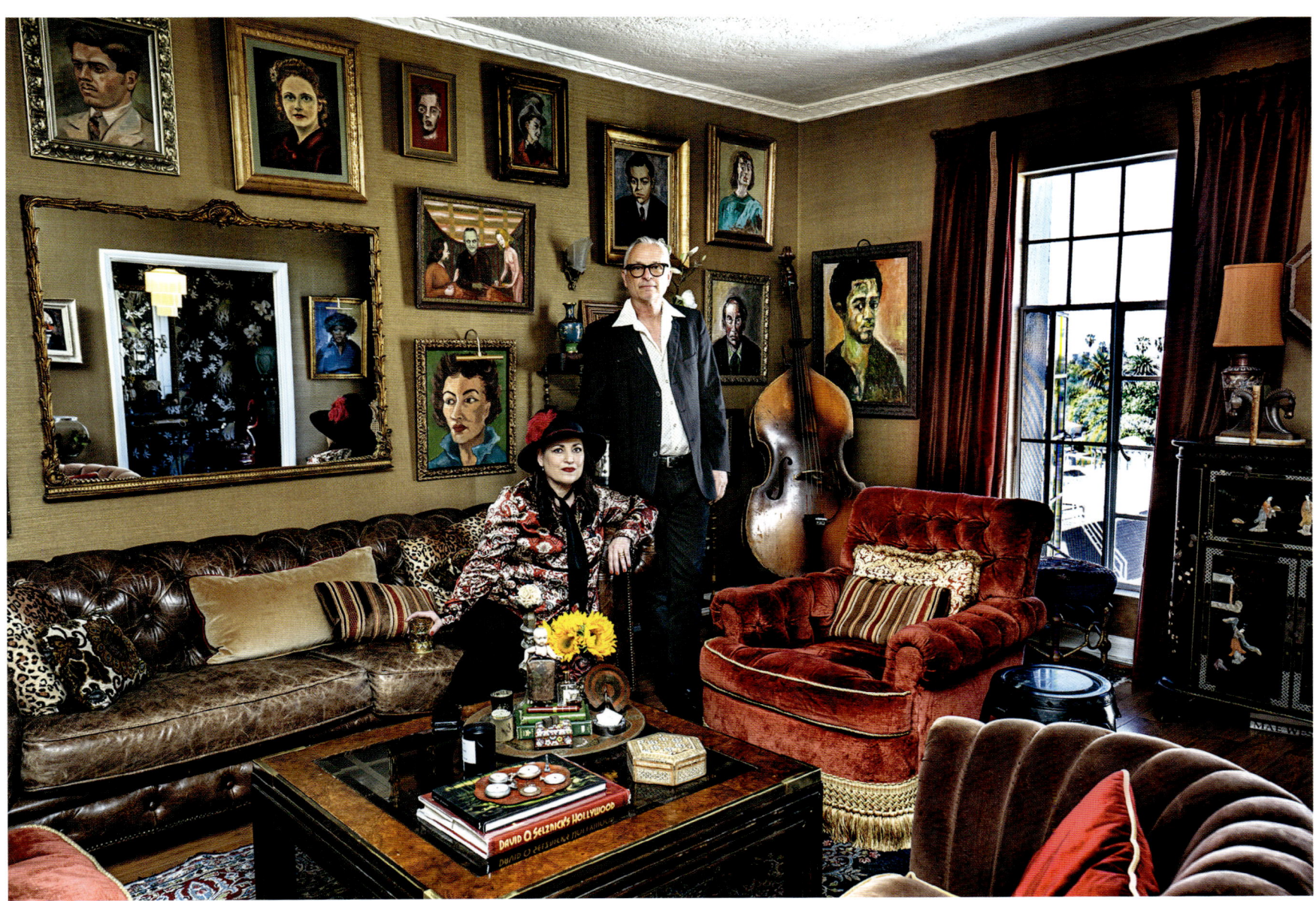

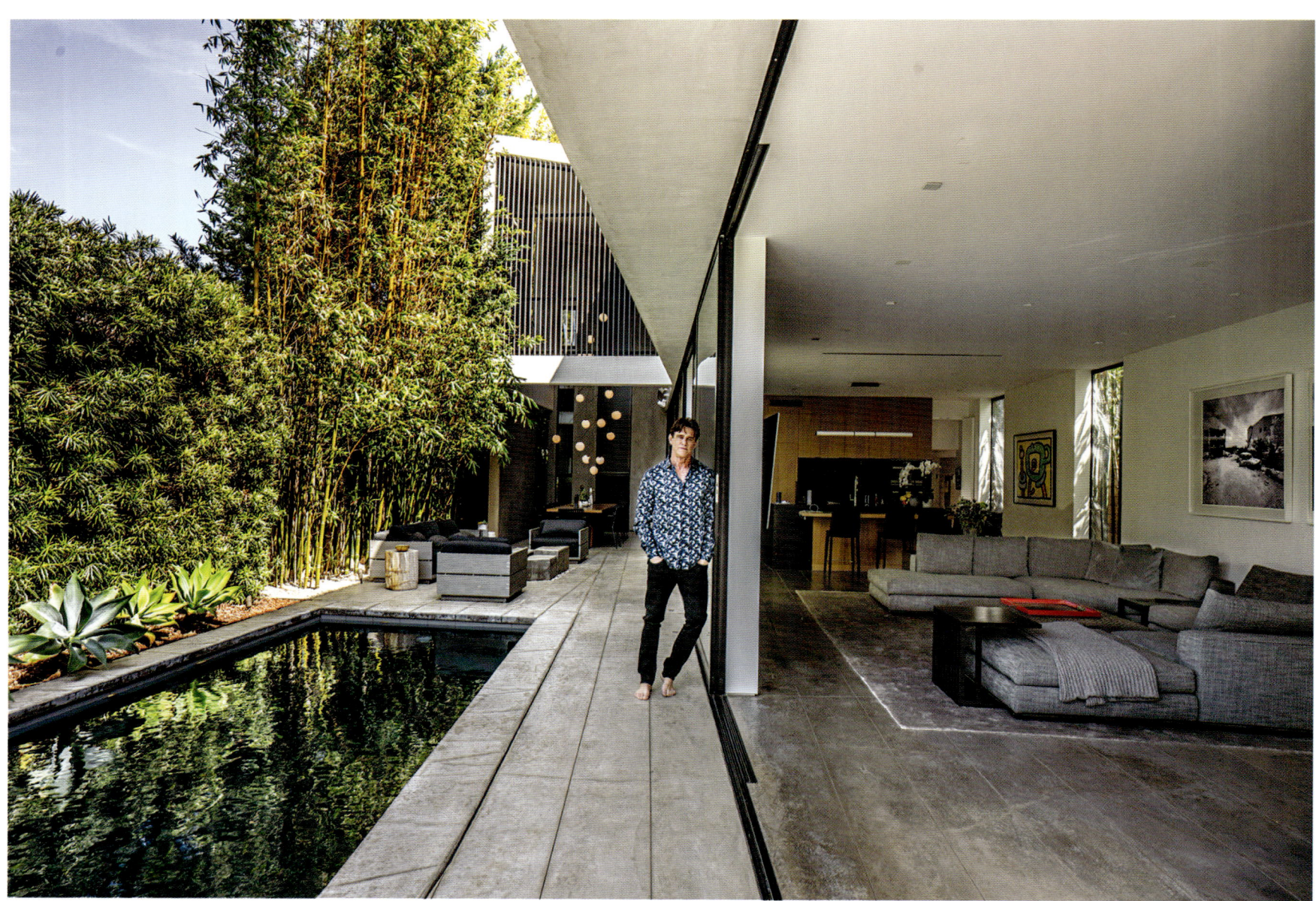

JEFF GUTHRIE

Photographed at home in Venice on May 25, 2021.

Jeff was born in rural Indiana on July 30, 1958. He was the fourth of five kids for Warren and Louise. Mom and Dad were both schoolteachers, and Dad was the athletic director at the school. Jeff spent his childhood years working on his neighbor's farm. He wanted to be a baker when he grew up and was a stellar student. Jeff was a swimmer and had a crush on his swim coach. He also wrestled. Jeff graduated from high school and moved to Purdue University straight away. He worked his way through school as a busboy, a van driver at a Holiday Inn, and as a concrete pourer. He also worked for the United Auto Workers union at a car factory. It was an assembly line job where they made tailgates for trucks. He also got married, had a son, and got a divorce during those college years. Jeff was super smart. He graduated with not one but two degrees, and hit the road for Los Angeles—this time with a boyfriend. With some money that his grandfather gifted him, he went back to school one more time in LA, with his sights set on law school. Not too long after he graduated with that law degree, he met and became lifelong friends with Clive Davis. It was 1986. Clive encouraged Jeff to move his law career into the entertainment business. Jeff found a job in the back-page want ads of the *Hollywood Reporter*, at Paramount Motion Pictures. Next job after that was HBO, where he has worked for 30 years. Jeff bought this property in 2013 and built a house. In 2017 he moved in, and lives there still.

"I drove from rural Indiana to California in the summer of 1982 to attend law school. I was determined to drive as far west as possible and I ended up on the beaches of Venice and Santa Monica. Venice has changed dramatically from the counterculture of the early eighties, but the local art scene still inspires me—as do the sunsets into the Pacific."
—Jeff

HELEN AND GENE GLEASON

Photographed at their home in Huntington Park on February 27, 2022.

Helen was born Helen Adams in Dayton, Ohio in 1931. She was the youngest of four for Harry and Flora. Dad worked in aviation and knew one of the Wright brothers. He was an executive at Douglas Aircraft but because had entered the US illegally from England during World War I he was demoted to sales. His job was to get drunk with the generals and sell them airplanes. He died of severe alcoholism in 1952. After he died, Douglas Aircraft hired Helen's mom to work in their offices. Helen spent her young years growing up in Cleveland and then in California. They moved to California when Helen was nine, because her dad got a job there. She wanted to be a nun when she grew up. She studied theology for one semester at a Catholic convent, then she moved back home and married Gene instead. Much later, when Gene's office manager quit, Helen would drive every morning to open up the factory. It was the first time she ever used her social security number.

Gene was born Eugene Gleason Jr. in Rochester, New York in 1929. He was the oldest of five for Eugene and Edith. His dad owned a machine shop making parts for cars and agricultural machines but lost the business in the Great Depression. Gene spent his childhood in Georgia, and moved to California when he was six because his dad got a job there, working in a boiler room at an aircraft company. His mom was a burlesque dancer in the 1920s. When dad proposed marriage, she quit the burlesque and later ran a hamburger stand on the Santa Monica Pier in the 1940s and 1950s. Gene went to college where he built a radio transmitter that became what is now the radio station KCRW. He was a radio engineer for live radio broadcasts. After college, Gene worked in machining and started his own machining business. He still goes into his factory a few days a week and is currently inventing new machines … at age 92.

Helen and Gene got married in 1952 and they had a family of four girls and three boys. They moved into a condo in Huntington Park in 1985. In 2009 they bought the condo next door and made their condo much larger by joining them together.

"The Starbucks is close by. I like that."
—Helen

"Every day that the weather is nice, I wonder how the poor fools who don't live in California are managing."
—Gene

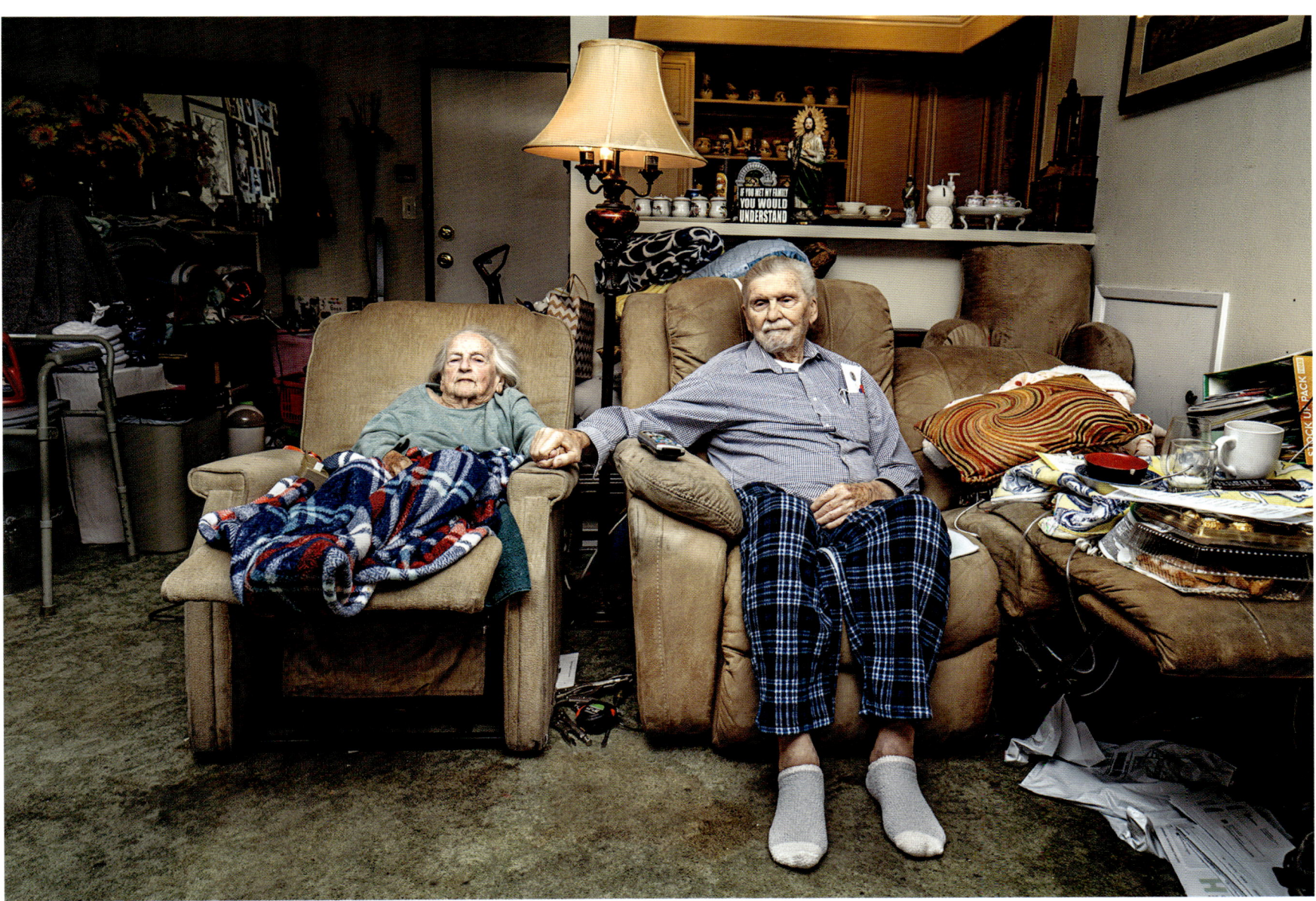

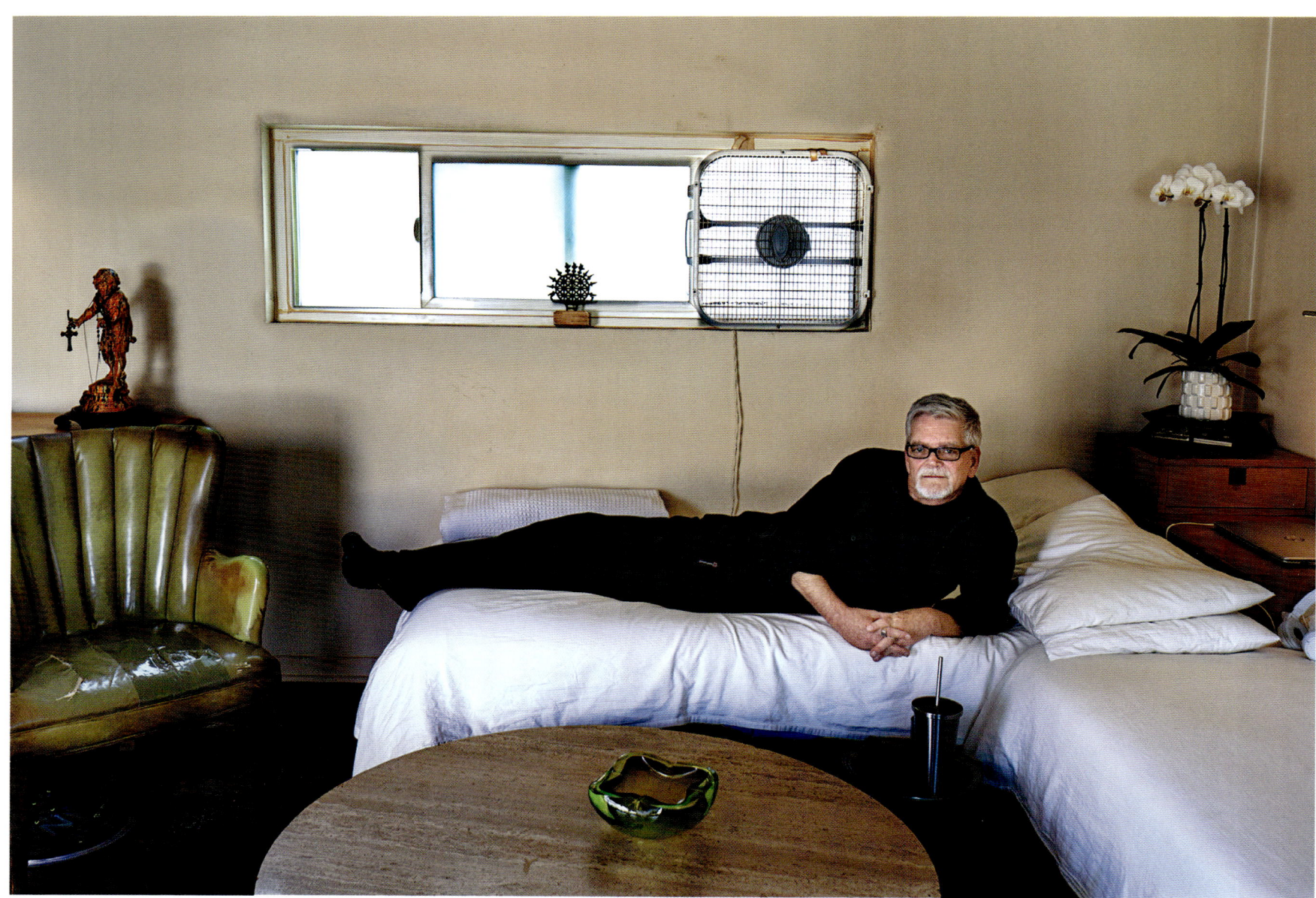

VICTOR SPENCER

Photographed at home in Venice on March 19, 2022.

Victor was born in Middleton, Ohio in 1963. He was the youngest of two kids for Bill and Barb. Dad was a barber and mom was an executive secretary for the school system. He spent his youth growing up in southern Ohio. Victor wanted to be an artist when he grew up, but had a leaning toward law and politics too. He was junior class president when Woody Harrelson was senior class president and he worked at a wine store during high school. It was 1980 and Victor was 17. He left home and headed east to New York City where he studied illustration at Parsons. He worked at a library, as a photo assistant, and at Studio 54. When school was over, Victor stayed in New York for a while, where he exhibited his paintings at the OK Harris Gallery, before heading west back to Ohio for four more years, where he continued to exhibit his art. Finally he moved west to Los Angeles in 1994, where he worked in the flower business for many years. In 2013 he started to photograph the high and low culture of the Boardwalk, and he continues to document the beach community. Victor moved into this Venice apartment in 1994 and lives there still.

"I will always consider myself a New Yorker but LA, and especially Venice, has been amazing. I love the artists, the musicians, the people, the Boardwalk, and the sunsets. Gentrification is a constant. Venice got caught in the tech boom and many of my friends were priced out. The homeless situation and the drug abuse in my neighborhood is out of control as well. I don't leave my place without pepper spray. I have found myself up against people who are out of their minds on Fentanyl at noon on a Tuesday. At the last sweep of the Boardwalk, 211 homeless people were offered housing and only 44 of the people were California residents."
—Victor

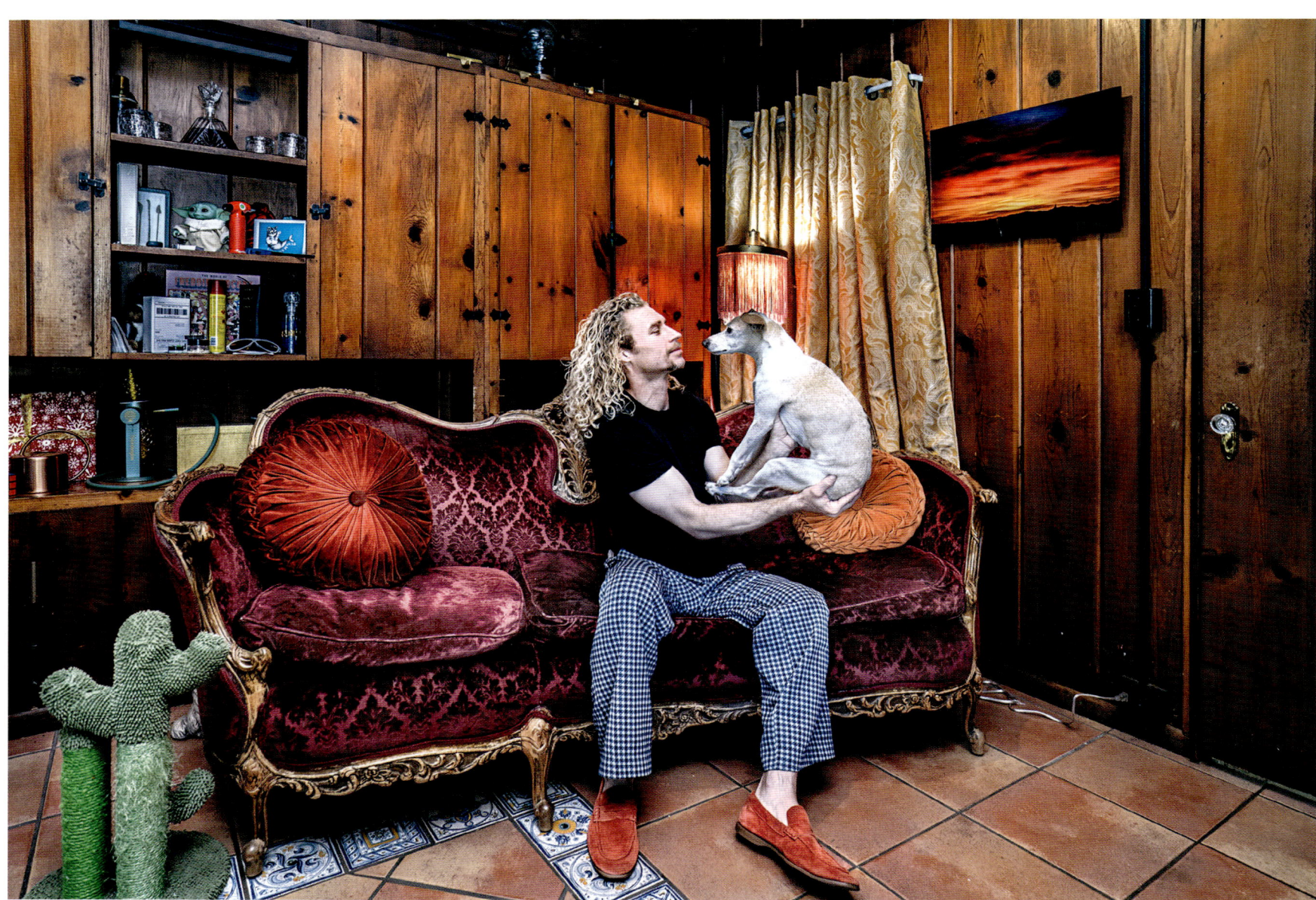

MICHAEL VEGAS

Photographed at home with his dog Kali in Arcadia on February 19, 2022.

Michael was born Micheal Boehler in Huntington Beach, California in 1984. He was the youngest of two boys for Connie and Ted. Both Mom and Dad worked as college administrators. Mom was also a stunt woman in the movie biz and Dad was a filmmaker. Michael spent his young years growing up in Garden Grove and then Fountain Valley. He wanted to be a stunt man and make movies when he grew up. He learned how to ride a unicycle when he was 12. He was a very busy kid: scuba diving, hockey, skateboarding, juggling, special effects makeup, and sewing, just to name a few. When he was 22 he left home, attending college for several things: the most recent was nursing school. Michael worked in a costume store, as an EMT, a firefighter, a nurse, in construction, and in a reptile zoo before he started working in the adult entertainment industry. When Michael was 25 he moved to LA, working odd jobs and performing in adult films. In 2011 he was nominated for an AVN Award for Best Male Newcomer and an XRCO Award for New Stud. Michael has been married three times, divorced twice, and now lives with his current wife, Siouxsie Q. He moved into this house in 2019 and lives there still.

"LA is beautiful like no other, ripe with opportunity for hard workers and determined folks. This is my home and I love it here."
—Michael

VERONICA HUNT AND DAN BIGELOW

Photographed at home with their dogs Rascal and Prisma in Silver Lake on February 26, 2022.

Veronica was born in Boyle Heights in 1963. She was the middle of three kids for Jimmy and Maria. Dad was an X-ray tech and Mom was a bank teller. Veronica spent her youth growing up in Monterey Park, California. She was an adventurous little tomboy who sold flowers, lemonade, and handmade things on the corner of where she lived. She produced plays and carnivals in the backyard and ran a snack bar too, where she sold burritos and orange juice. She wanted to be a beautician or a detective when she grew up. She did well with art and English and not so well with math. She produced and directed plays for the younger kids at school. She also took dance lessons, swimming lessons, and played the guitar. When Veronica was 20 she left home and moved to Hollywood. After a few years there she decided it was time to get it together, and went to college and studied merchandising and graphics. She worked as a file clerk and played in an all-girl band. When college was over she moved back home for a few years. Her first job was designing shoes. Now Veronica makes ceramics, jewelry, and clothing.

Dan was born in Ithaca, New York in 1970. He was the oldest of two for Christine and Bill. Mom was a singer/songwriter and Dad was a minister. When Daniel was seven, his parents got a divorce. Mom remarried and when Daniel was 15, she got another divorce. He was a creative kid who preferred tinker toys and Legos to action figures. He wanted to be a firefighter when he grew up. When he was in third grade he played the ukulele. He was an average student but did really well in geometry. Later he studied art and band after school and, in 1983, he won a breakdancing contest. He also worked at Six Flags drawing caricatures. Dan graduated from a high school for the performing and visual arts and at 17 he headed to Chicago for college to study film and video. Dan is an animator and an illustrator. He draws on paper, paints on wood, and designs with computer software.

Veronica got married and divorced and then met Dan at an art opening in 2006.
Dan moved into Veronica's house shortly after that. In 2016 they got married, and they live there still.

"LA has too much traffic and most people don't know how to drive. I love my neighbors, my hood, and all our local parks. I hate gentrification ... too many modern monstrosities!"
—Veronica

"LA is a different landscape than where I came from so I had some culture shock when I got here. I didn't have a car yet, and the hills were the primary obstacle for me on my bike. All the flora is amazing, and plants bloom in my neighborhood all year long! I sometimes miss snow, but I can occasionally see it on a faraway mountain when my family is freezing on the other side of the country. Freaks walk down the street in full costume all the livelong day and I love that brand of weirdness. Sure, it's got problems like everywhere else, but creative culture is everywhere!"
—Dan

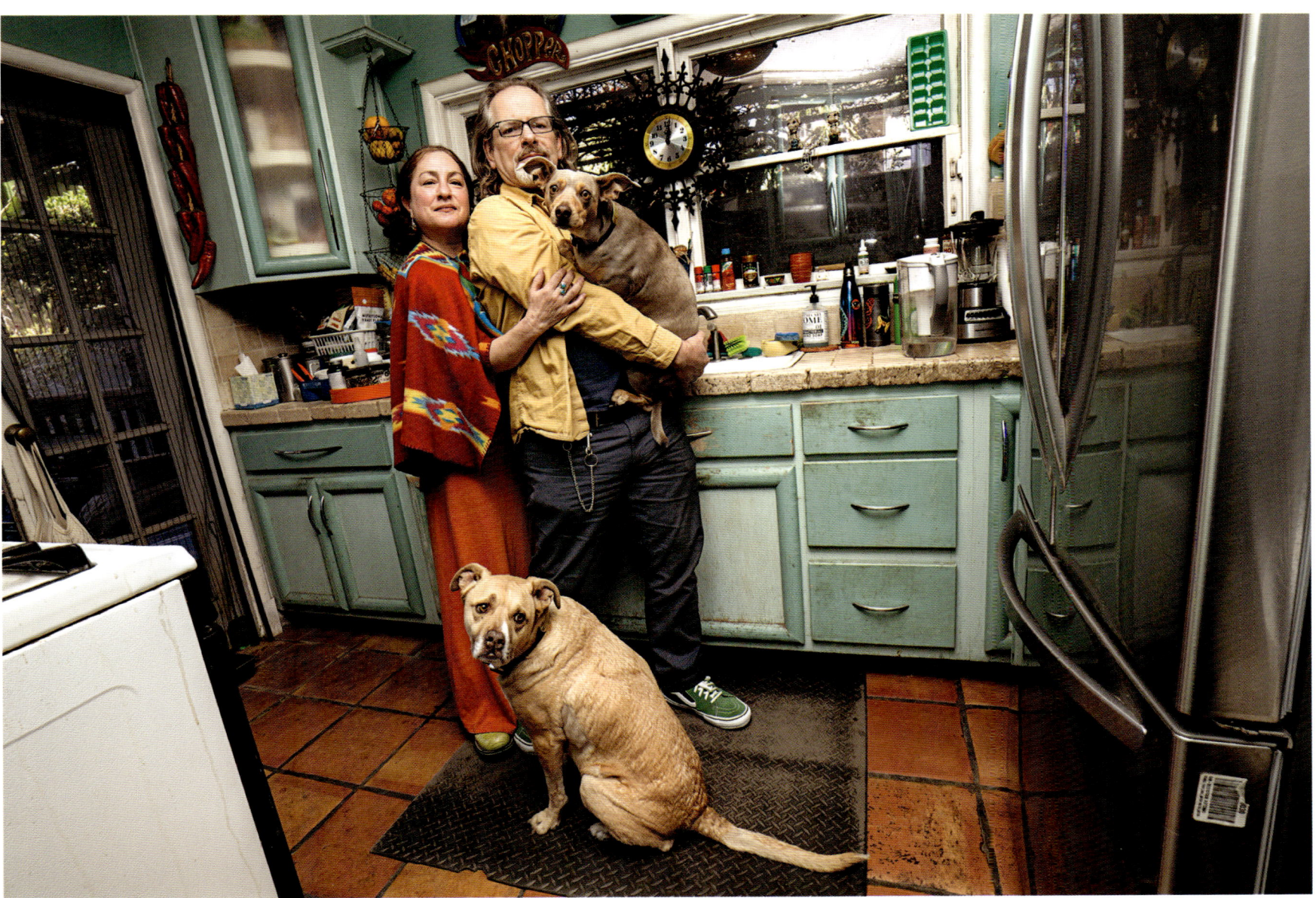

LINDA RAMONE

Photographed at home in Sherman Oaks on March 30, 2022.

Linda was born Linda Marie Daniele in Queens, New York in 1960. She was the youngest of two for Frank and Rose Mary. Dad worked for the sanitation department and Mom sold Avon beauty products. Linda spent her young years in Queens, hosting Tupperware parties. When she was 14, her brother Joseph turned her on to the New York Dolls and she started going to CBGBs and Max's Kansas City. When Linda was 16 her mom and dad split up, and a year later she moved out and headed west to Los Angeles. She worked part-time at Fiorucci. When she was 19 she started dating Joey Ramone. Linda traveled around with the band and eventually they all moved back to New York City. The Ramones wrote lots of songs about Linda. She and Joey broke up and then later in 1984, she married Johnny Ramone at the office of the city clerk in New York City. In 1996 she and Johnny moved to California and into this house. Linda worked as a hairdresser. The Ramones retired in 1996 and Johnny died of cancer later in 2004. Linda stayed living in the house. She starred as herself in a comedy television show called *Portlandia*, and Linda is also the president of Ramones Productions and the president of the Johnny Ramone Army. She is a philanthropist for cancer research. She collects fashion, music, and movie treasures and has theme rooms in her house: an Elvis room, a Barbie room, a Horror room, a Disney room, and a Rock 'n' Roll room. Linda lives in the house now with her sweetie, J.D. King.

"I love LA. I love my house—the "Johnny and Linda Ramone Ranch"—with all its theme rooms. Sitting by the pool and having lunch and cocktails is the best thing ever."
—Linda

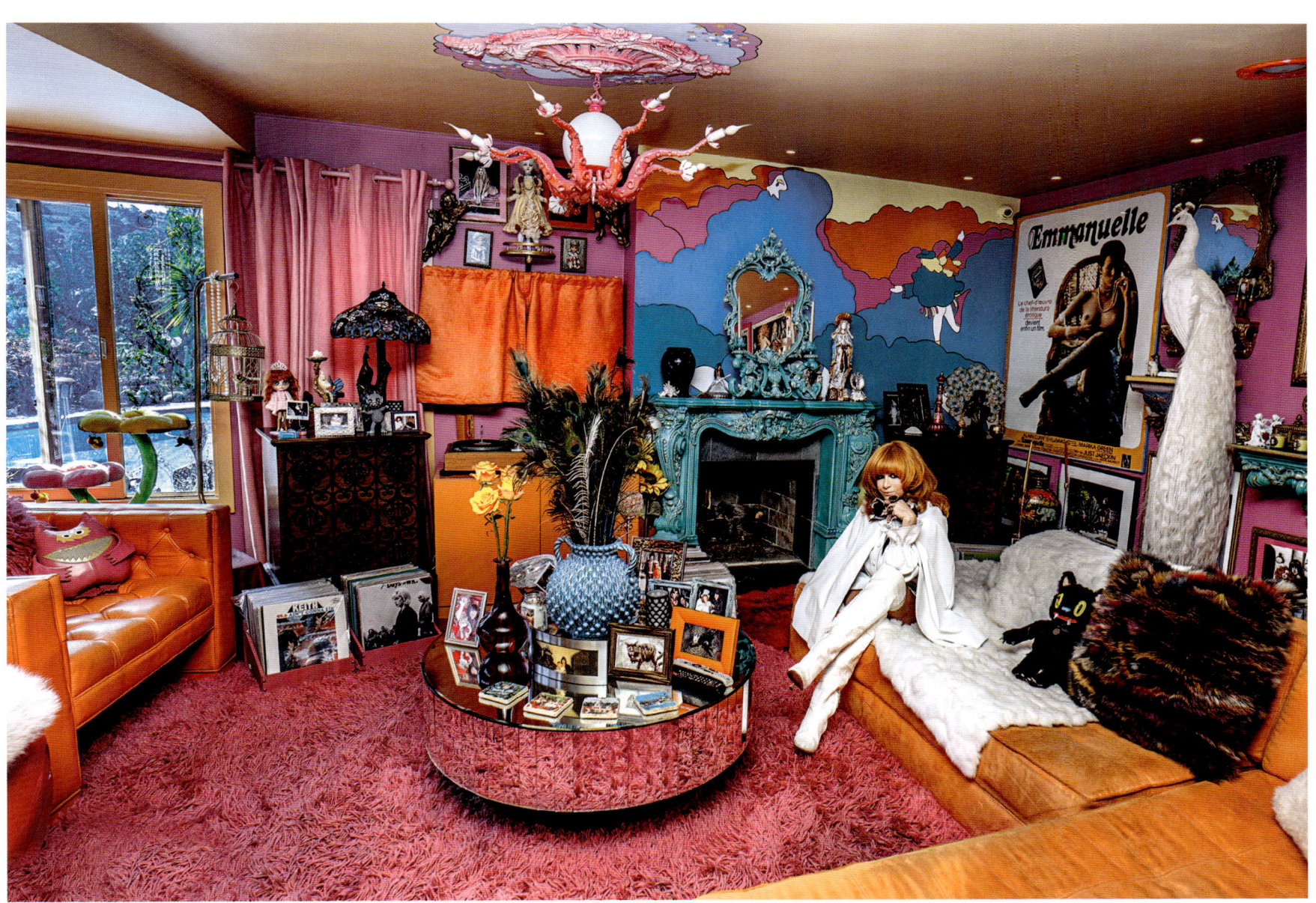

LYNDA KAHN

Photographed at home in Holmby Hills on March 12, 2022.

Lynda was born in New York City in 1952, arriving ten minutes after her twin sister Ellen. She was, therefore, the youngest of two for Marjorie and Melvin. Mom worked at a university library and Dad was an insurance broker. Once the girls arrived, they all left New York City and moved to Long Island. Lynda spent her young years growing up in Merrick, Long Island. She was a good student and was very passionate about art, hula hoops, and cartwheels. At 17 she left home for college: Philadelphia first, then Chicago for an advanced degree at the Art Institute. Lynda worked as a waitress, a bartender, a college professor, a window display person at Bloomingdale's, in an antique store, and as a computer artist. She stayed in Chicago after college was done, bartending, teaching at the college and working on a solo show of sculptures. After that she headed back to New York City where she lived for ten years. She started a company there called TwinArt with her twin sister. Lynda's sculpture designs turned into fashion items: jewelry, belts, and pillows that sold at fashionable shops and museum stores. The twins' evolution as digital artists propelled them to succeed later as Emmy award-winning creative directors in the entertainment business. In 1989 Lynda moved to Los Angeles and worked directing music videos and commercials. Lynda and her twin sister were storytellers, designing storyboards, animation, graphics, and logos for hundreds of award-winning television titles. In 2015 she began selling architectural and mid-century real estate. In 2016 Lynda moved into this apartment and lives there still.

"I love the unobstructed view! It makes me feel like I am on top of the world! I love the culture, LACMA, the Hammer, the Billy Wilder Theater, mid-century and modernist architecture, indoor-outdoor relaxed lifestyle, swimming pools, succulents, citrus trees, beach, mountains, deer climates, my car, and my friends … all being part of a horizontal city … what I don't like is traffic and the homeless situation taking over the LA I love."
—Lynda

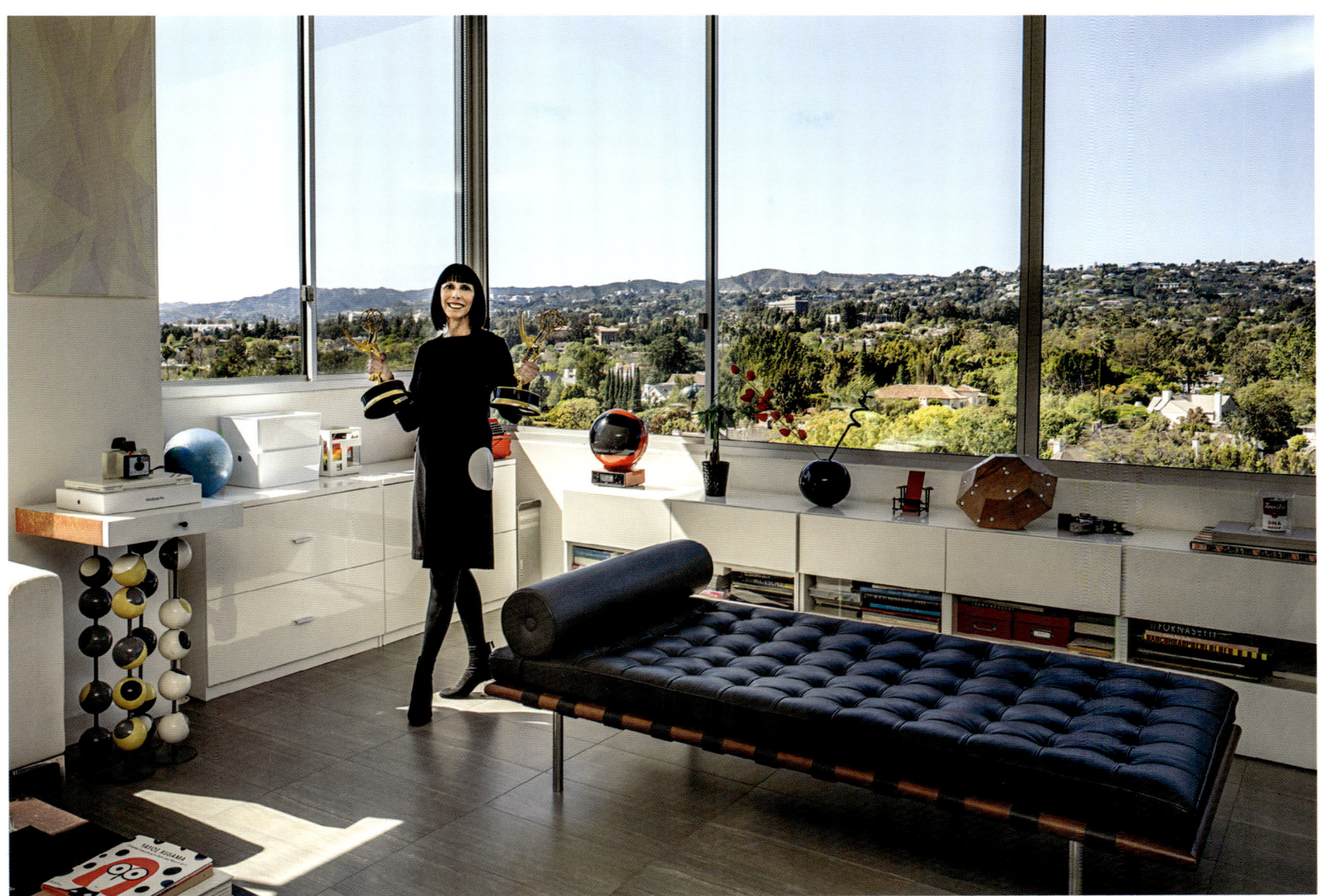

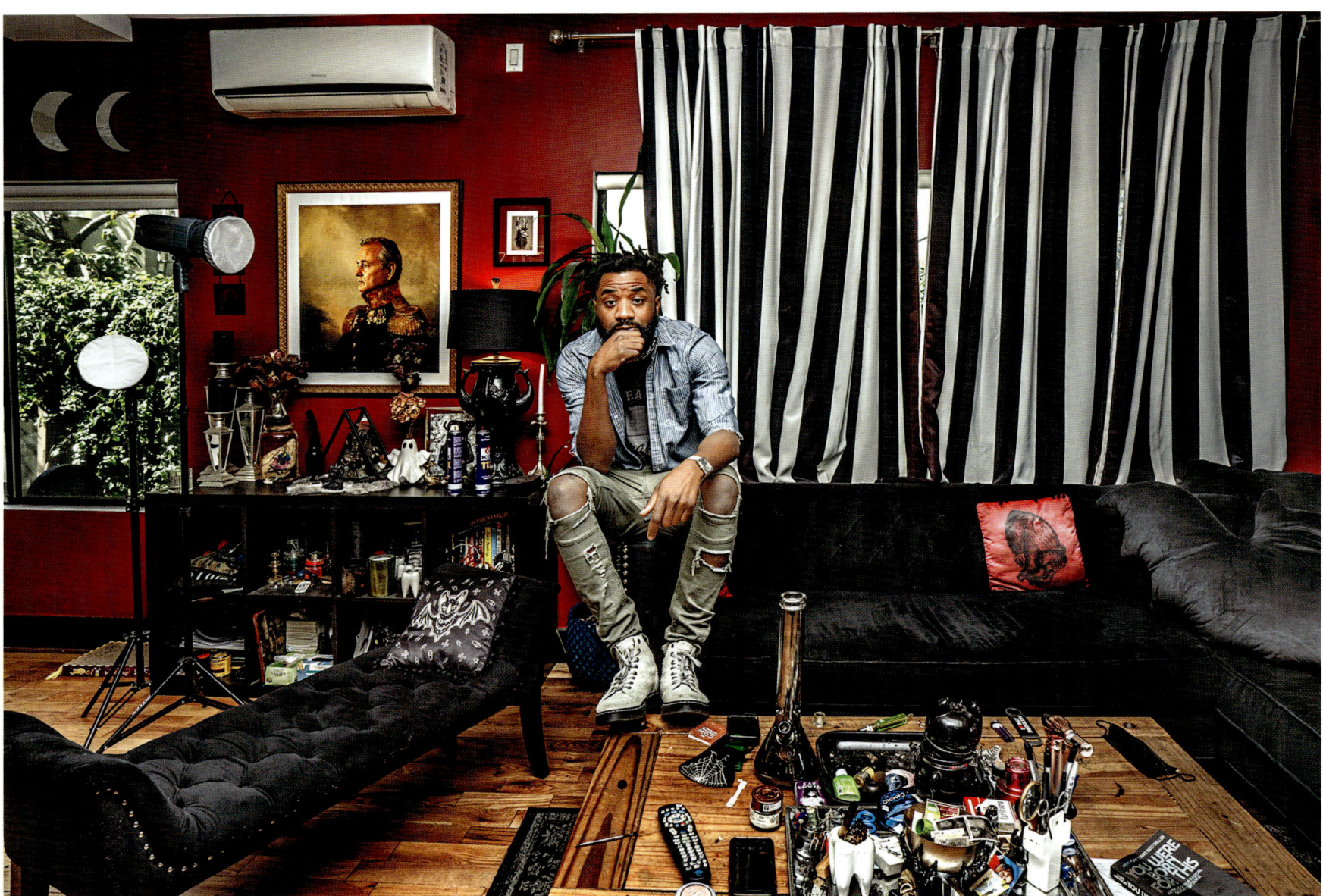

BLAIR SEBASTIAN TOLES

Photographed at home in Los Angeles on March 11, 2022.

Blair was born in 1990 in Canton, Ohio. He was the sixth of eleven kids for Vernon and Alecia. Dad was a steelworker and Mom worked at a grocery store. He grew up with his dog Duke in Canton, singing and tapping his way through life. His mom and dad split up when he was five. Dad wasn't that great a guy, and Blair ran away from home numerous times. He made friends easily, excelled at dressing well in school, and got mediocre grades. When he was 14 he left home and moved into his best friend's house. He worked at a fast food restaurant, in retail, and sold weed and Adderall while he was a pizza delivery driver. It was 2015. Blair was 25 years old and he headed west for Los Angeles. He got a job at the Starbucks at Universal Studios straight away, and is now a bartender and a band manager. Blair moved into this house in 2021 and lives there still.

"Love the people! There's such a clusterfuck of different cultures that come here from all around the world. You can learn a lot if you keep an open mind. Traffic will forever be terrible. Get used to it. Gentrification sucks and will always suck until we figure out some way to make it not suck. This city will kick your ass and make you forget who you are sometimes. You gotta stay grounded for sure! It can be as fast or slow-paced as you want it. Just make sure you keep moving. Don't get complacent."
—Blair

NILS GREVILLIUS

Photographed in home in Santa Clarita on March 6, 2022.

Nils was born in 1963 in New York City. He was the last of five kids for Norman and Enid. Dad was a journalist and Mom was a lawyer. Nils spent his young years in Indiana and then in Pasadena, California. He was a serious and brainy kid growing up with a dog and a Schwinn ten-speed bicycle. He wanted to be an architect when he grew up, but he wasn't very good at abstract math, so that was that. He was good at English and reviewed books and articles. Nils was in the Air Force reserve in high school, but was absent often because of his father's moves and his mom's being in law school. He was an honored football player and track-and-field kid in high school even though he lacked ability. He took these on as a way to self-improve, and it helped prepare him for his life later on. He started a cleaning company and cleaned three bars in the area. When Nils was 17 he left home and served in the US Army for the next seven years. During that time and after, he went to several colleges, studying a wide variety of subjects including abnormal psychology, government, history, English and Korean, and law and political science. After college was done, he lived in Iowa and Oregon, working as a private detective for the Pinkerton Service. Nils has been a licensed private detective since 1992, and has held licenses in Iowa, Oregon, Washington, Canada, and South Africa. He got married in 2000 and had a son Aldo. In 2010 they split up and Nils and Aldo moved back to Pasadena. In 2018 they moved into this house, and live there still.

"My thoughts on Los Angeles, specifically, are parallel to those of the Spanish in the 1700s: it is often glorious, but most of the time it is a City of Devils for the corruption, ineptitude, programmed strife, and stratification. I love this state, but it needs help. The Beat artist John Kelly Reed, once associated with the Ferrous Gallery in the 1950s, who lapsed into derelict alcoholism in the 1970s, once stated: 'Pasadena, California is the only city in the United States where a man could freeze to death under a rose bush in full bloom.' Believe it."
—Nils

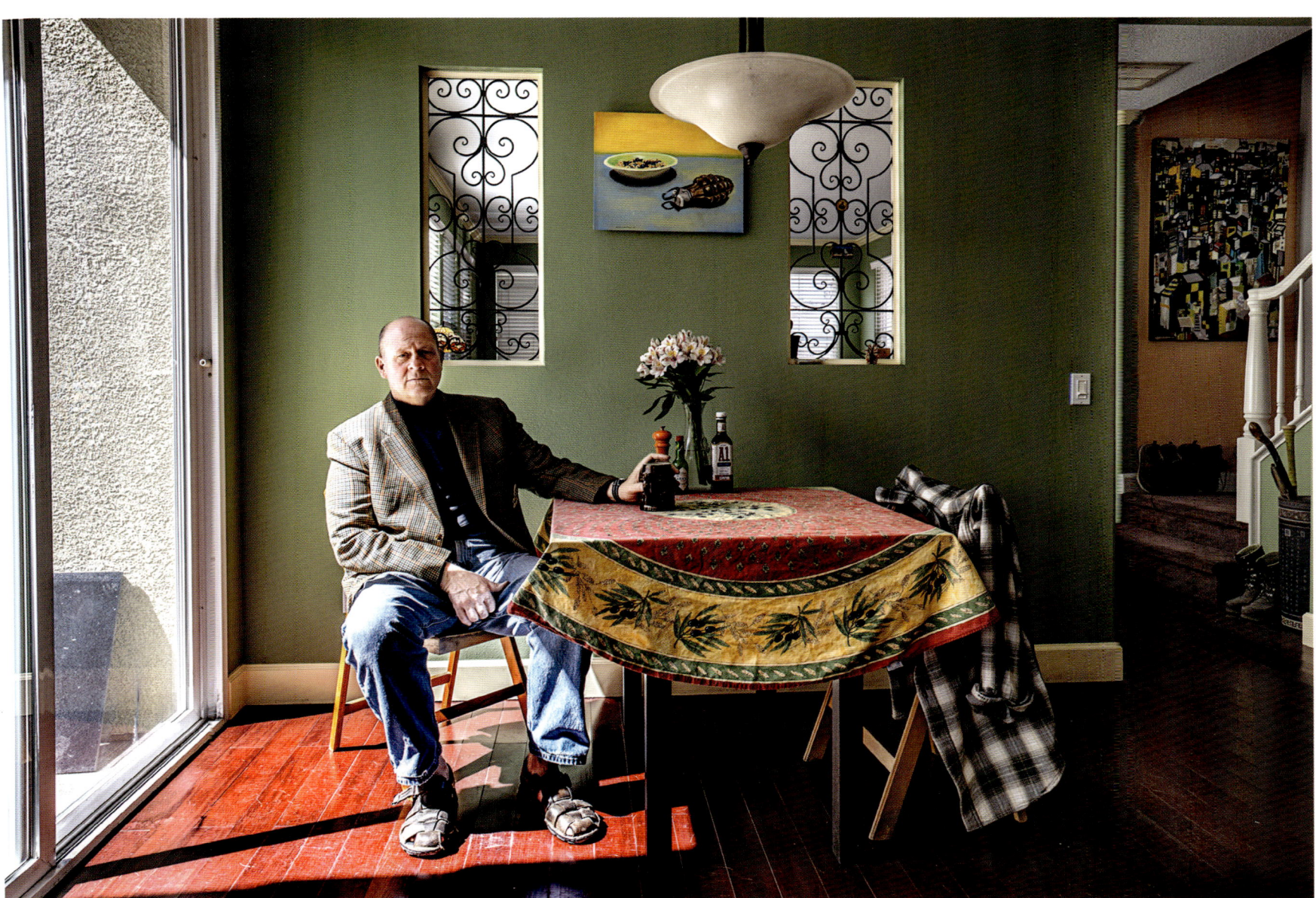

NATHAN GALLIGANI AND LILY POLSTEIN

Photographed at home in West Hollywood with their new puppy Otis on February 25, 2022.

Nathan was born in San Francisco in 1992. He was the oldest of three for Rob and Jennifer. Dad was a lineman for the gas and electric company and Mom worked in advertising. Nathan spent his young years in Pacifica, California. He was well liked and was an organized little boy who lined up his toys facing the same direction. After a career assessment test in seventh grade suggested he should be an aerospace engineer, school sent him to Moffett Airfield for a day. He met a rocket scientist there and held a moon rock. He played soccer until he was 13 then quit to skateboard instead. Nathan was on the swim team in high school too. He worked as a dog walker, at a skate and surf store, at a pizza place, a pet store, and for a plumber. When Nathan was 25 he left home and moved to LA. He went to college and left with a film degree. Nathan works at Apple's advertising agency as an assistant producer.

Lily was born in Los Angeles in 1995. She was the oldest of two for Claire and Jay. Mom was a film producer and Dad was a lawyer. Lily spent her young years in Los Angeles. She wanted to be a fashion designer when she grew up, then later a photographer. She did pretty good at school except for math. She spent time after school taking photographs and volunteering at local food banks. She babysat, was her grandmother's driver, assisted costume designers, and interned with photographers. When Lily was 17 she headed to the east coast for two years of college, then came back to San Francisco to study urban agriculture. She worked at a general store that sold ceramics and vintage stuff. In 2018 Lily started her own landscape design and edible garden business. She installs edible gardens in homes and commercial spaces, and loves that her office is outside.

Nathan and Lily met in San Francisco on a dating app in 2015 and have been together ever since.
They moved into the apartment in 2019, and in 2021 they brought Otis home.

"I love the LA geography: the cities, the beaches, the mountains, the snow, and the desert. California can be laid back or it can be fast paced. I love that we have that option. Living in West Hollywood is great. It has a neighborhood feel, it's close to the beach, and very walkable. I love that everyone is friendly, and that it feels safe. When I first moved to LA it took some adjusting. Growing up in the Bay Area I thought: 'Well, it's home, and it's kinda nice,' but when I moved to LA I realized how beautiful the Bay Area really was. Part of me really regretted leaving that for strip malls and palm trees. (I hate palm trees.) Gentrification is a charged subject for a lot of people, especially where I am from. At this point San Francisco/Oakland are the pinnacle of gentrification and it is easy to see why it is so hated. I have seen it personally affect my friends, and I have also seen it ruin portions of SF, with the city quickly losing all of its flavor it once had."
—Nathan

"I love LA. You can go to the snow, beach, and desert all in one day. I can't imagine living anywhere else. Developers and business owners can gentrify neighborhoods without displacing individuals but they need to conceptualize strategies to better the community, rather than tearing it apart."
—Lily

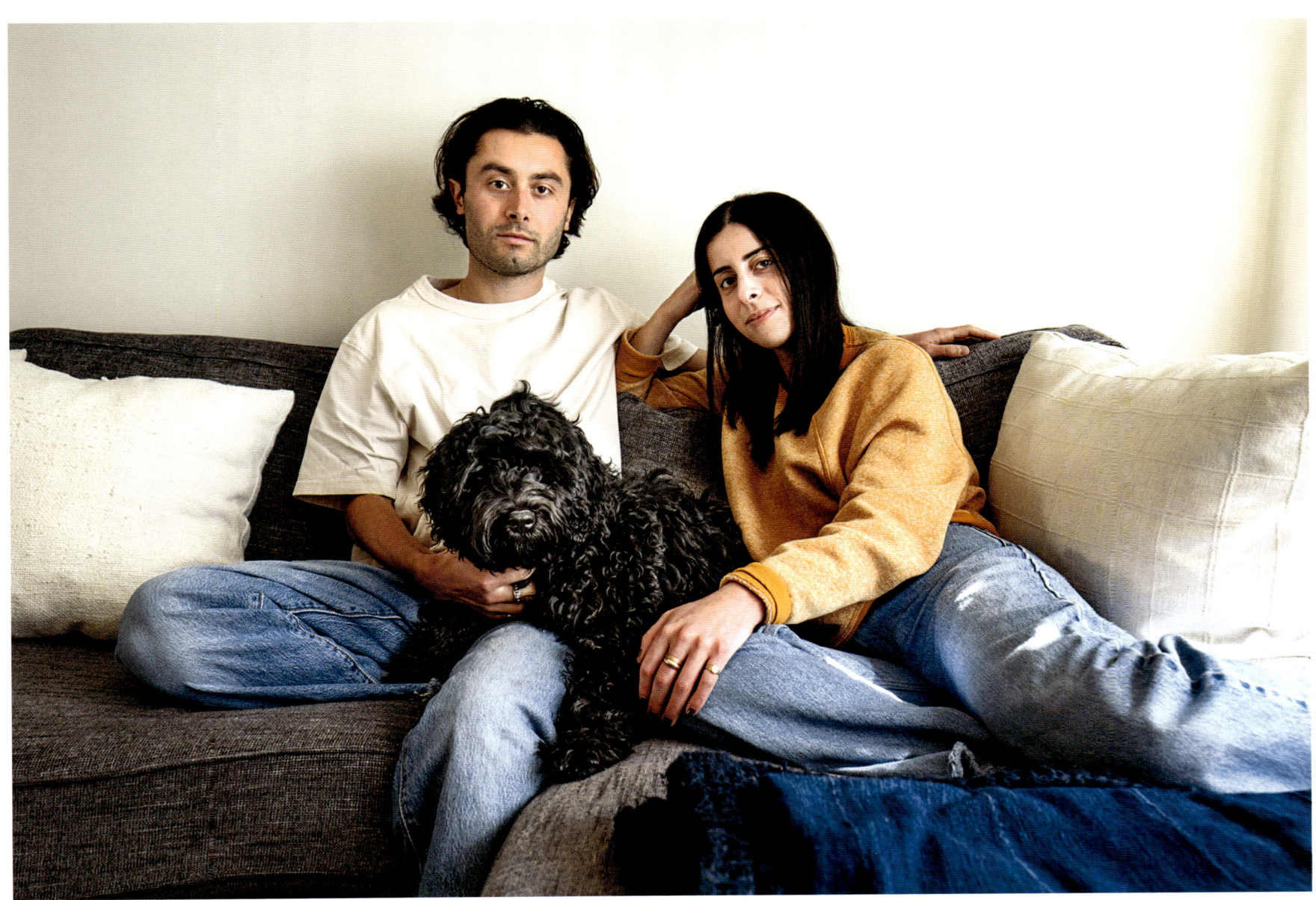

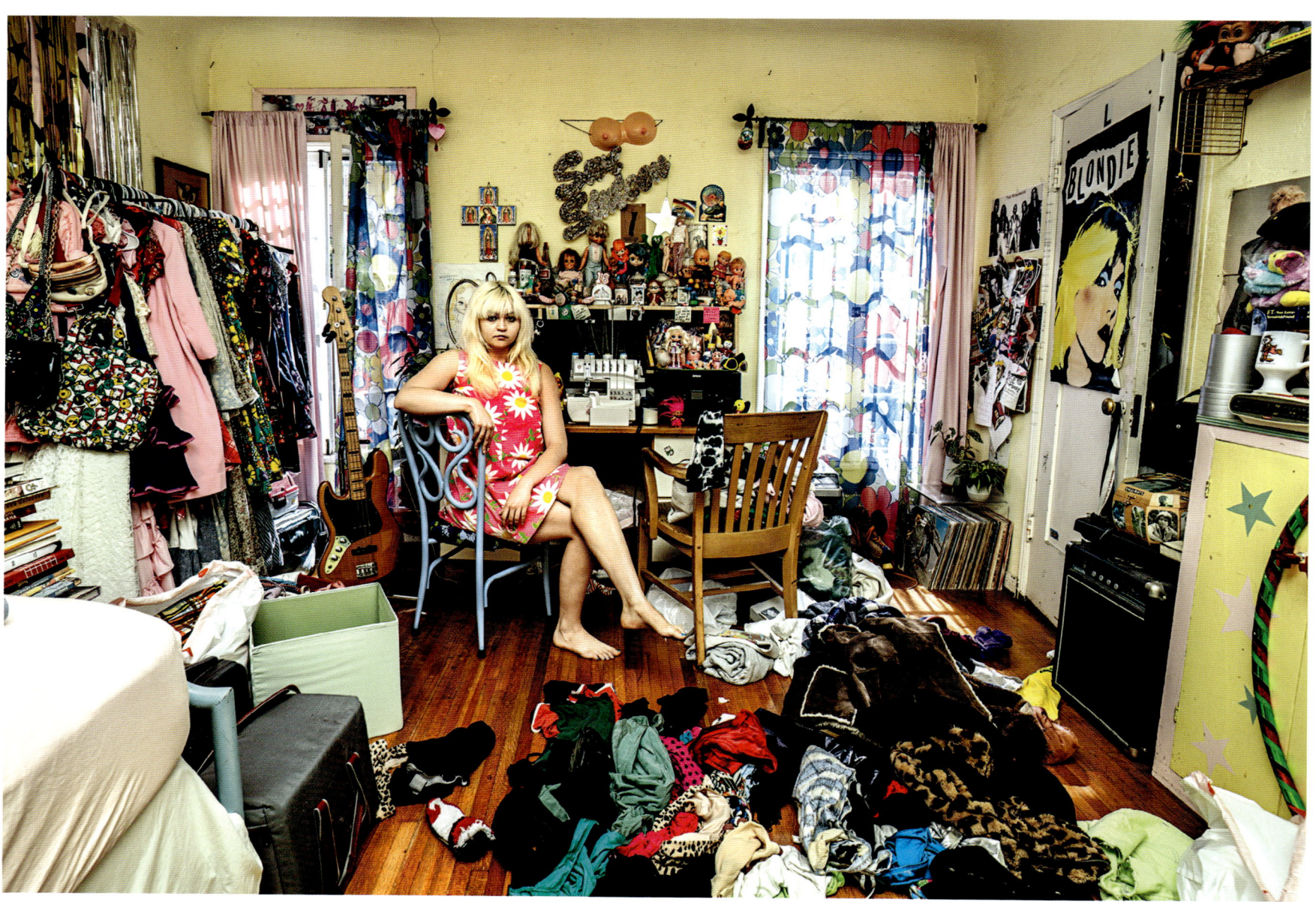

LILY NOYES

Photographed at home in Los Angeles on February 26, 2022.

Lily was born in 1997 in Los Angeles. She was the first of two for Phil and Lisa. Dad produced TV shows and Mom acted and taught nursery school. Lily was a very outgoing kid who was a self-described chatterbox, towering over the boys because she was so tall. She started going to concerts when she was 11 and she collected Hello Kitty stuff. She grew up with lots of pets: dogs, cats, chickens, and a goldfish she named Britney Spears. She wanted to be a fashion designer, a princess, and also a circus performer when she grew up. She learned to sew during the Covid quarantine and now she designs her own clothes. She did well at anything arty and not so good with math. Later she attended college and studied film and experimental video. She worked as a babysitter, a dog walker, a camp counselor, a hand model, and as a production assistant. Lily's goal is to move out of her parents' house by her next birthday.

"I love living here, and am always prepared to defend LA with an iron fist. People love to say: 'LA has such dark energy,' but yeah, that's exactly why it's cool. Our pastel-colored 1950s apartment buildings, Googie diners, and dingy strip malls alongside our sordid history of cults and scandal and murder. Home to the biggest movie and music stars but also to people like Charles Manson and Jack Parsons. I love that dichotomy. Joan Didion, Eve Babitz, and Kenneth Anger represent it the best. It's pure magic. It's a strange place to grow up. Girls in small towns are competing with the head cheerleader, girls growing up in LA have to compete with daughters of movie stars or girls who are movie stars themselves. It's all a little Less Than Zero-esque. You go to a modeling casting and they make you write down your Instagram follower count. But I wouldn't trade it for the world."
—Lily

DENNIS KEELEY AND VERONICA COTTER

Photographed at their home in San Pedro on March 28, 2022.

Dennis was born in 1952 in Newark, New Jersey. He was the third of four kids for Robert and Audrey. Dad was an accountant and Mom was a homemaker. Dennis spent his young years growing up in New Jersey with his dog Milo. He was sick a lot and was often at the hospital. He collected comic books and wanted posters. He was a creative kid, drawing and taking photos, writing poetry, and eventually he started playing the drums. He also bowled a 181. Dennis was thrown out of Catholic kindergarten because when they gave kids scissors, he gave everyone haircuts. In high school he played in bands and was also in a bad car accident. Because of that he was home schooled for his senior year and his marks got super good. He worked in a men's clothing store every day after school and on Saturdays. He also drove a truck delivering air freight from New Jersey and New York to Kennedy Airport every day. He worked for Otis Elevators, and was a janitor. When he was 17 he left home and moved to California where he went to art college in Valencia for five or six years. After college was done, Dennis moved to Los Angeles. He worked on a top-secret military graphic project, as a photo editor for a magazine, and as a photographer. In 1982 he quit working at the magazine because T Bone Burnett asked him to join his touring band with David Bowie's guitarist Mick Ronson. They opened for The Clash and The Who. For the next 25 years, Dennis photographed famous musicians, mostly for album covers and publicity. As the nineties rolled along, music took a turn that Dennis no longer found interesting. He started teaching kids at risk at the Watts Towers, and did workshops at colleges. In 2013 Dennis became the Chair for Media Arts at the Art Center, and did that job until 2021 when he retired. He built study away programs, worked on projects in Mexico, India, and China, and he spoke at the United Nations about the power of photography in peace building. He met Veronica at a camera store in 1991 and in 1994 they got married. They moved into this house in 1992 and live there still.

"I have a book published by Getty Research, entitled: Looking for a City in America: Down These Mean Streets a Man Must Go. (Essay by Andre Corboz; Photographs by Dennis Keeley). It's a city of many cities. The Pacific Rim is a reality for a new kind of community life. The freeways were a new way of life, and now a nightmare. I have a 20-year photo project on freeways. This country is not looking at the future for healthcare, early education, jobs, technology, justice, diversity, economic opportunity, infrastructure, and especially transportation."
—Dennis

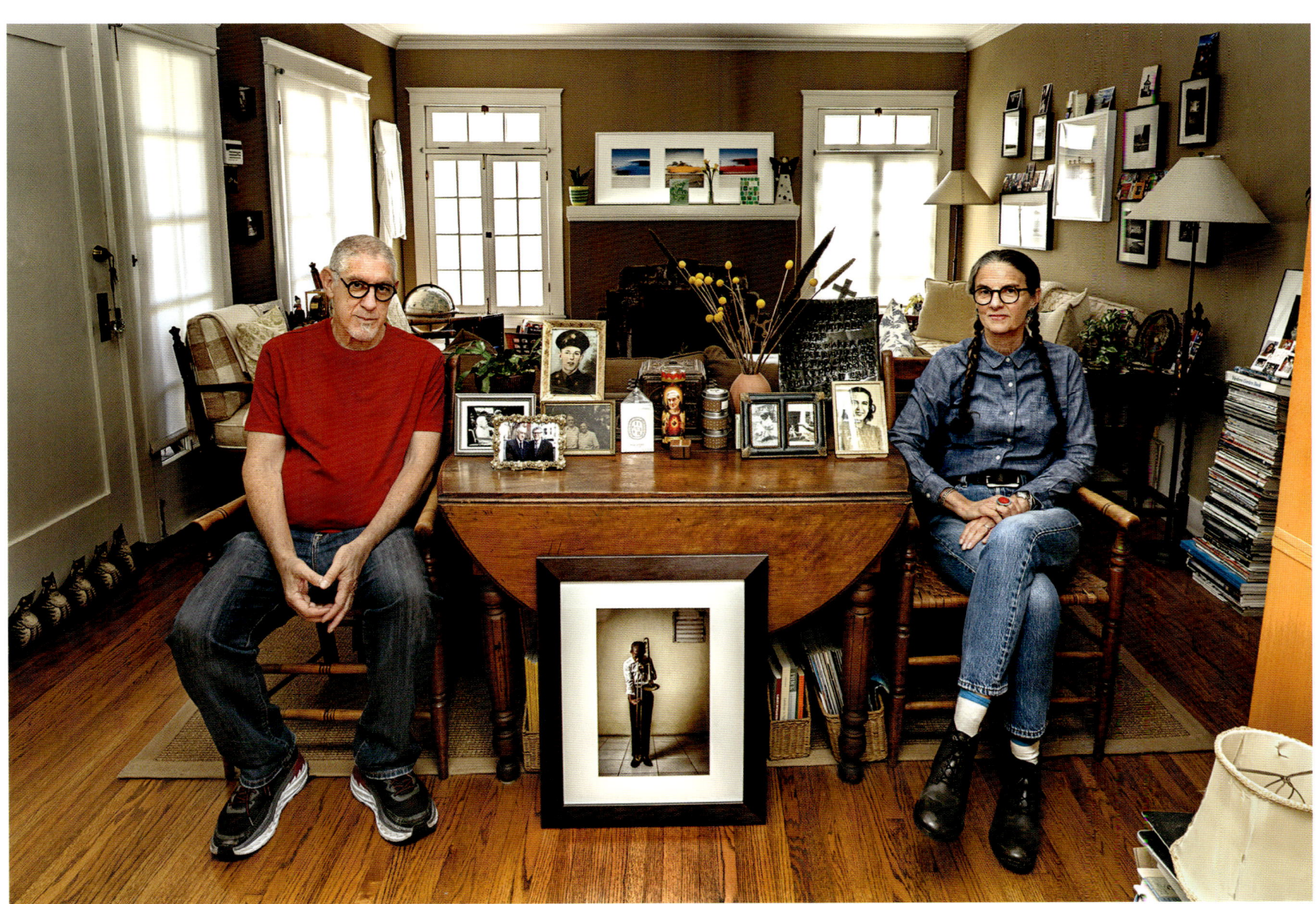

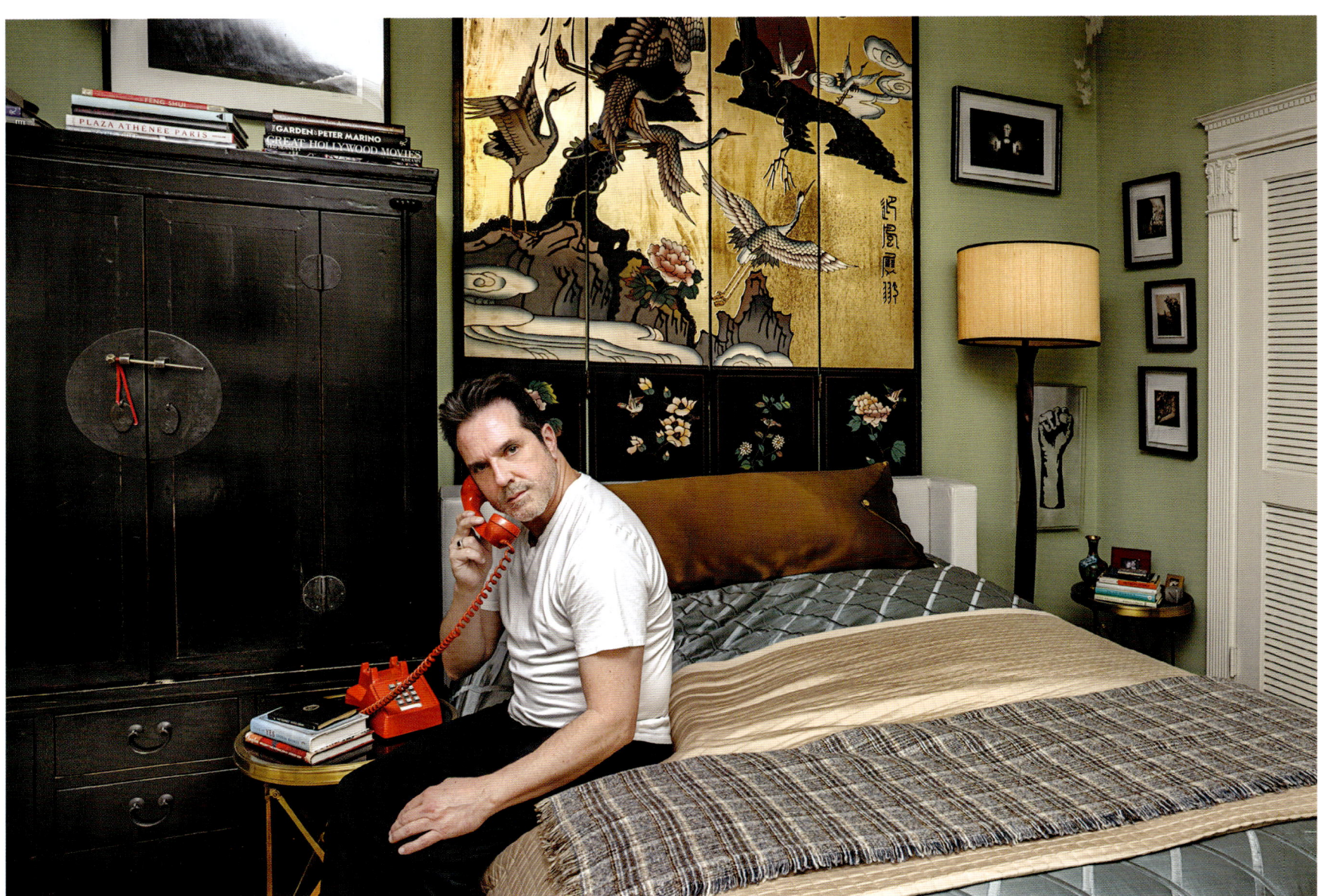

ED SOLÓZANO

Photographed at home in Beverly Hills on March 12, 2022.

Ed was born in Boyle Heights, Los Angeles in 1963. He was the third of four for Edward and Erma. Dad was a lawyer and electrical engineer and Mom taught English as a second language. Ed spent his young years in the suburbs of Montebello. He was a smart kid with a good sense of humor, attending Catholic school up to grade eight. He wanted to be a talent agent or a movie producer when he grew up. He did really well at English and history and not so well at chemistry and astronomy. He was student body president and everybody liked him. Ed went to a private all-boys high school, but being gay, he found it strange to not have all his female friends nearby as a buffer. He got involved with the drama department and that became a good social outlet. He worked as a stock boy at the local pharmacy and also for an Armenian catering company on the weekends. Later, Ed went to college and studied communication arts. His goal at the time was to work in the TV and film business. During college, Ed lived at home with his family and worked at a medical clinic. When he was 25 he moved into his own apartment. Pretty much straight out of college, Ed was hired as a page at NBC, going on to work in the biz until 2018. His last job was senior vice-president of movies and mini-series, at a well-known company. During that year he also got his real estate license. His TV career lasted 15 years but his real-estate career far surpassed that. Ed spent eight years in a relationship with a man who shared his love of houses. Together they decorated, fixed, and flipped houses, moving around a lot. Eventually they went their separate ways and Ed moved into this apartment on his own in 2003.

"I love LA. I don't think I could ever leave. I love the weather, and the proximity to the beach. And the food scene is incredible. We are surrounded by amazing, eclectic, world-class cuisine and I never tire of finding new and innovative places to eat and enjoy. I consider this a walking neighborhood, and it's been a godsend to be here during the pandemic, because I never felt isolated. As a real-estate agent, it's hard for me not to be in favor of gentrification. There's not enough housing to accommodate our growing population, so something has to give. But with that being said, I do prefer a blend or melting pot of ethnicities and differing socioeconomic backgrounds sprinkled throughout neighborhoods; it fosters a broader point of view and is way more interesting to me than sameness. It may be why I've tended to gravitate toward cities on the east side of town. Ludicrous from a man living in the heart of Beverly Hills? You can take the boy out of Montebello, but you can't take the Latino out of the boy."
—Ed

ADAM NORMANDIN AND HIS WIFE ALLISON

Photographed at their home in Downtown LA on February 27, 2022.

Adam was born in 1965 in East Meadow, New York and he spent his young years growing up there. He was the second of two boys for John and Edith. Mom worked in corporate finance and Dad was a painting contractor. Adam was a shy kid, and wasn't much for group activities after school, but he did like to ski. That he could do alone. He did well at art and was average at most other studies. Immediately after three years of political science at college, Adam left for Los Angeles. It was 1987. Adam worked in insurance sales, in investment banking, at a frame store, and painted toy prototypes before he decided to try his hand at being a full-time painter. Adam met Allison in 2005 at a party and in 2012 they got married. They lived in Miracle Mile and the San Fernando Valley before moving into this converted loft in Downtown LA in 2013. Adam is now a very successful painter and exhibits his work in art galleries from coast to coast and beyond.

"LA feeds my creativity. It has a light quality, unlike anywhere else I know. There is also an odd, quirky history that I enjoy. As for gentrification, I think LA has always been rapidly changing. My current neighborhood (Arts District, DTLA) has been gentrifying at warp speed since I arrived. What started as an industrial warehouse district, with dilapidated buildings, rife with prostitution and drug deals, has quickly transformed into high-dollar real estate. My wife and I laugh that we first felt out of place, not having neck tattoos and facial piercings. Now, we don't fit in because we don't dress in Gucci!"
—Adam

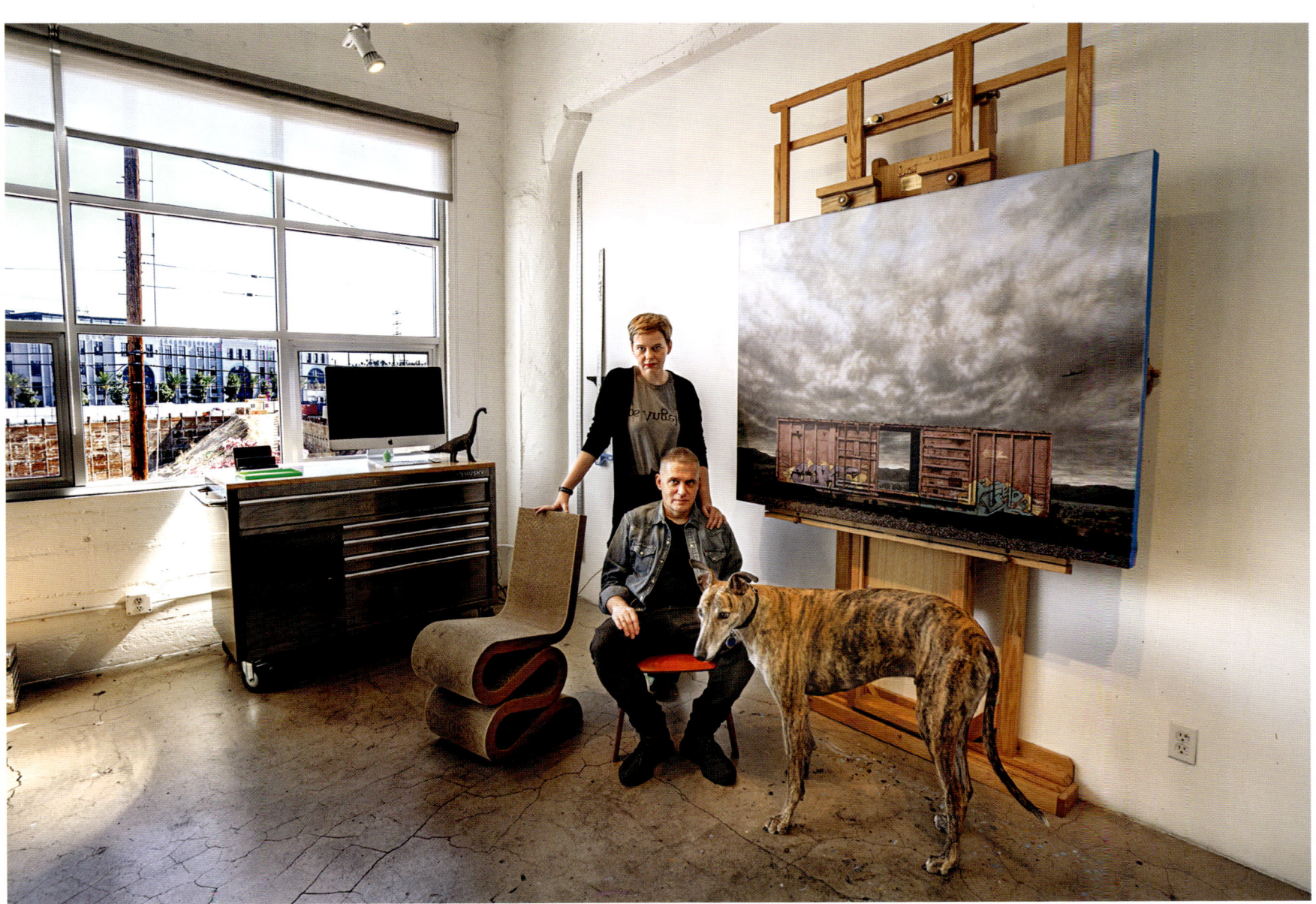

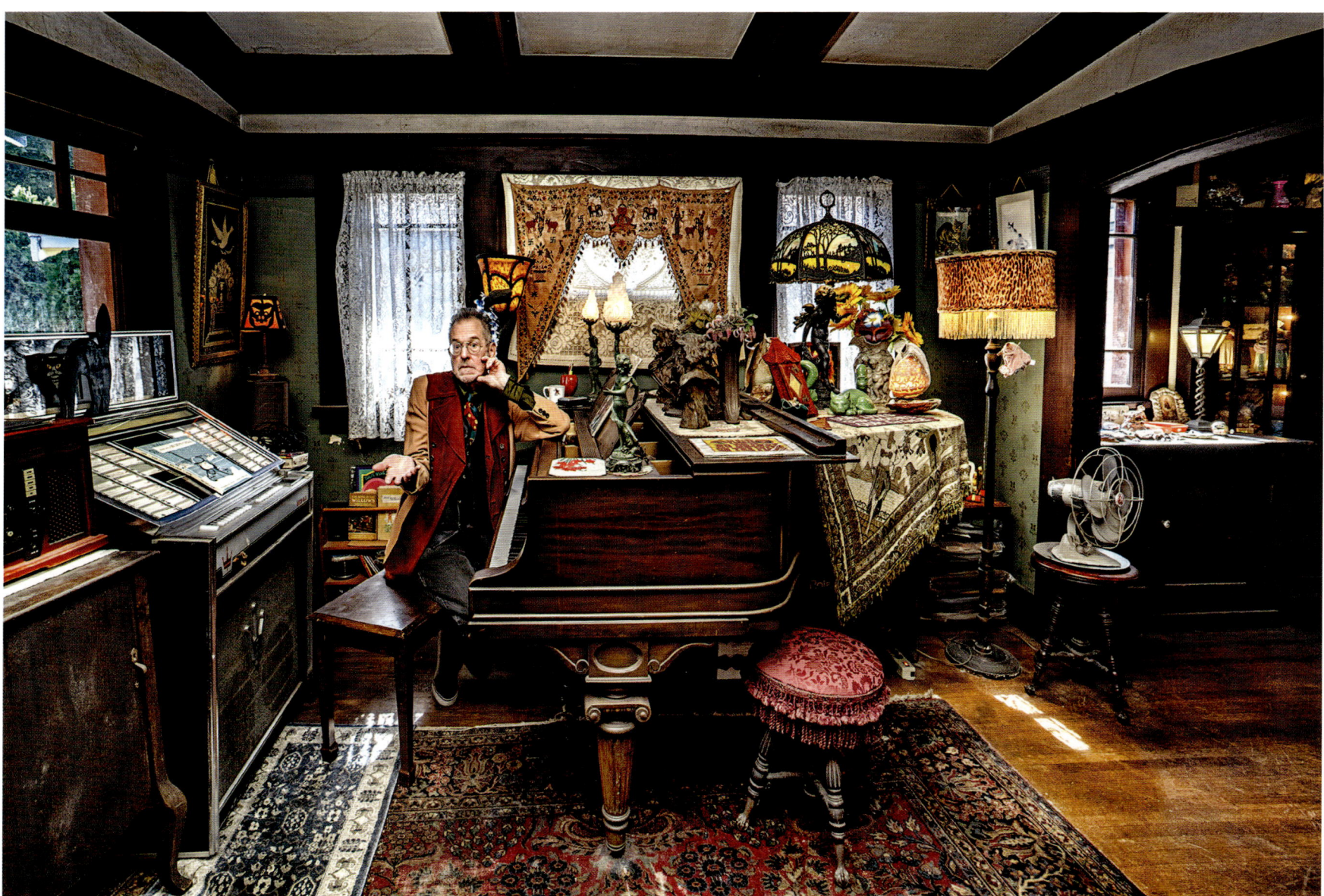

KRISTIAN HOFFMAN

Photographed at home in Highland Park on March 8, 2022.

Kristian was born in San Gabriel, California in 1952. He was the fifth in a lineup of seven kids for Hallock and Gene. Mom was an actress who also read vintage fairy tales on the radio, and Dad worked as executive secretary for a liberal think tank. They were Quakers and raised the kids as such. As religions go, Kristian thought this was a good one. They were anti-war and anti-violence and they didn't believe in churches or priests. The family moved around a lot and the kids loved living in the old houses. Eventually Mom and Dad built their dream home in Santa Barbara, but it burned down a year after. They divorced when Kristian was about 17. Sometimes the kids all got along, but sometimes they did not. Kristian's brothers made fun of his music taste; he liked The Monkees. All the kids were very artistic—drawing, painting, and playing musical instruments. Kristian accomplished a few odd things in high school. He got an award from the Bank of America for achievement in art, and one of his posters was hung in the beautiful downtown public library and was also featured in the local newspaper. Sometime around 1970 Kristian went to Cal Arts on a scholarship; the first of two times he enrolled. He met Paul Rubens there, better known as Pee-Wee Herman. He had fun playing piano in the practice rooms, watching some of Paul's hilarious films, and going with him to some gay bars in Los Angeles. He did that for a bit off and on and started moving back and forth to New York. There was some travel to Denmark and Paris too, and by 1973 he was living in Christopher Mako's apartment in New York City. Christopher was a really good friend of Andy Warhol's. Kristian worked at the Cinemabilia bookstore in New York. He also played in bands: The Mumps, the Swinging Madisons, Contortions, Dave Davies, Rufus Wainwright, and Ann Magnuson. Finally in 1985 when he was 33, Kristian moved back to Los Angeles. He met his husband Justin Tanner and 20 years later they got married. They have a band called The Roswell Sisters. Kristian thinks he's lived in this house at least since the Northridge earthquake of 1994.

"I resisted liking LA for years after I moved here. I thought of it as a temporary respite before I was able to move back to Manhattan. I totally hated driving, and I still do. I detest it. But you just can't get around it here, even though they say you can. I always wanted to be driven, and not drive, and I still do. But I was seduced over the years by so many interesting historical neighborhoods, all stretched out from downtown and east to Pasadena, and west to the beach. Every place we lived had an amazing neighborhood vibe, and I've come to love the neighborhood I now live in the best of all."
—Kristian

MARY K HUMFELD AND SONIA MANGANARO

Photographed at home in Palm Springs with their dog Cleo on February 22, 2022.

Mary K was born in Holyoke, Massachusetts in 1955. She was the youngest of two for Jen and Bus. Dad was a Major General in the Air Force, and Mom worked as a military wife, volunteering and representing the officers' wives in addition to raising two kids. Mary K spent her young years all over the country on Air Force bases. She was a well-liked little girl with lots of friends. She loved The Monkees and The Beatles. She swam and ice skated, and played the guitar and piano too. She wanted to be a musician or a director when she grew up. In high school, she got her first job so she could save money for a study trip to England. She loves England to this day. Mary K worked at an ice-cream restaurant performing musical numbers. After studying theater for three years at college she did some summer stock and then worked in Los Angeles as an assistant in the TV business. Ultimately she decided the ups and downs of Hollywood were not for her. She moved to New York and went back to college, taking theater education. Mary K worked at PanAm Airlines and then at American Express for the next 25 years. She got very, very ill in 2013 and left American Express. The cold winters of New York did not feel like a good place for her to recover, so she and Sonia headed west to the California desert, to Palm Springs.

Sonia Pina Manganaro was born in Sydney, Australia in 1964. She was the youngest of three for Giovanni and Diana. Dad worked for an airline company and Mom worked at a department store. Sonia spent her young years growing up in Australia and traveling often to Italy to visit her relatives there. She was a happy kid who loved school, doing well at math, art, and theater, watching old movies on her off time. She wanted to be like Judy Garland when she grew up and started rehearsing her Academy Award speech when she was five. She also wanted to be an interior designer. In high school, Sonia worked at McDonald's, then at a supermarket where she announced the daily specials. In college, she worked at a TV station as a production assistant and later worked at Australia's version of Off Track Betting, placing bets on horses over the phone. She had to quit that job because she was spending all her earnings on horse bets. Sonia went to college for a few years in Australia, studying theater, and when that was over, moved to England for two years. She worked at a stationery store and then for jewelry designers. On her way there she stopped off in New York and fell in love with the city. In 1993, back home in Australia, Sonia met the love of her life—Mary K, who was visiting from New York. Sonia moved back to New York to be with Mary K and stayed for 17 years. Sonia worked as a buyer for the Alphabets retail chain, and on a buying trip for that company, she discovered Palm Springs. Sonia fell in love with the desert the first time she visited.

In 2015 Mary K, Sonia, and Cleo moved into this house. They divide their time between Palm Springs and New York City.

"I love it here. I love the outdoors, the warmth, the natural beauty, the cactus, the palm trees, and the mountains are extraordinary. I love hiking, taking pictures, and hosting friends who visit us here in Palm Springs. I love the fact that it is not too big or small and very, very different from our home in New York. I love the magic light that shines on these mountains, the architecture of the homes, the landscaping. "
—Mary K

"I love it here and hope that it always maintains its character, architectural beauty, and lifestyle. I love our home and the magic of the mountains. The light is extraordinary."
—Sonia

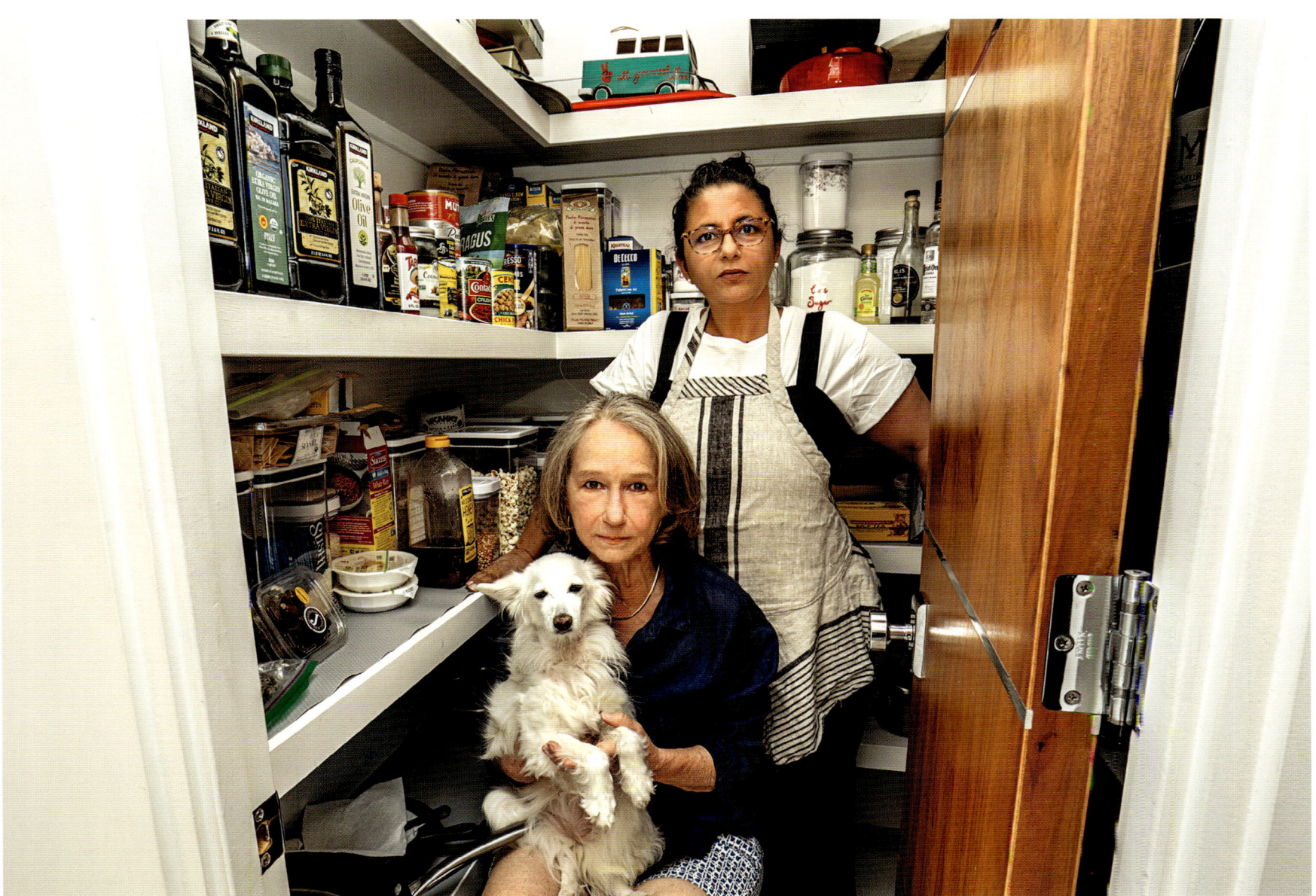

JONATHAN PALEY

Photographed at home in Lebec on March 6, 2022.

Jonathan was born in Alexandria, Virginia in 1954. He was the fourth of five for Henry and Cabot. Dad was a union organizer and later chancellor at a university, and Mom was a high school teacher and a psychologist. Jonathan spent his young years on the east coast … first Crescent, New York and then Brooklyn. He wanted to be an astronaut when he grew up. He did really well at school until high school, and then did really badly. He studied music and photography in his after-school hours. He worked at the Traffic Department in a clerical job, as a groundskeeper, and in a toll booth. When he was 19 he left his Brooklyn home, Manhattan bound. He did one year of college, studying film and writing before dropping out. He got his start in the New York punk scene around 1975, first in the band Mong, then with The Paley Brothers and the Nervous Eaters. Later he moved to Boston and played in bands until 1986. He worked at a record store, as a taxi driver, then three and a half years at sea as a deck hand. When the sailboat he was working on finished its final voyage in Los Angeles in 1990, Jonathan got off the boat and stayed. He found work as an extra in the movie business, as a body double, an actor, a musician, and a songwriter. Jonathan got married to Janelle, who passed away in 1997. Later he had a daughter with Bambi Conway. Jonathan works as a hospital emergency room technician, a nurse, and as a set medic for movies. He moved into this house in 2013 and lives there still.

"Until very recently LA has been the lead that America has followed since the early 20th century, like the promised land. For me, as a kid in Crescent, living in ten-foot snow drifts, I'd see images of sunny, warm California on TV, beautiful blonde girls in bikinis and surfboards. It is where so much music and TV came from. The left coast 'movement' was an unacknowledged and unstoppable tsunami of societal upheaval. Life in rural California is near-idyllic looking, like a tourism pamphlet. However, the quality of life in the cities has been in rapid decline since the 1970s and 1980s. Too much development, too many people, poor municipal planning, terrible traffic, and a huge, rapidly expanding homeless population. Too many redundant agencies and programs throwing our tax dollars away. The power grid and the power companies are crumbling dinosaurs. The collection and distribution of water is chaotic and there will soon be severe mandatory rationing. The state government spends billions on 'studies' of California's problems instead of putting the money into fixing the problems. I hate the airport and I hate the traffic."
—Jonathan

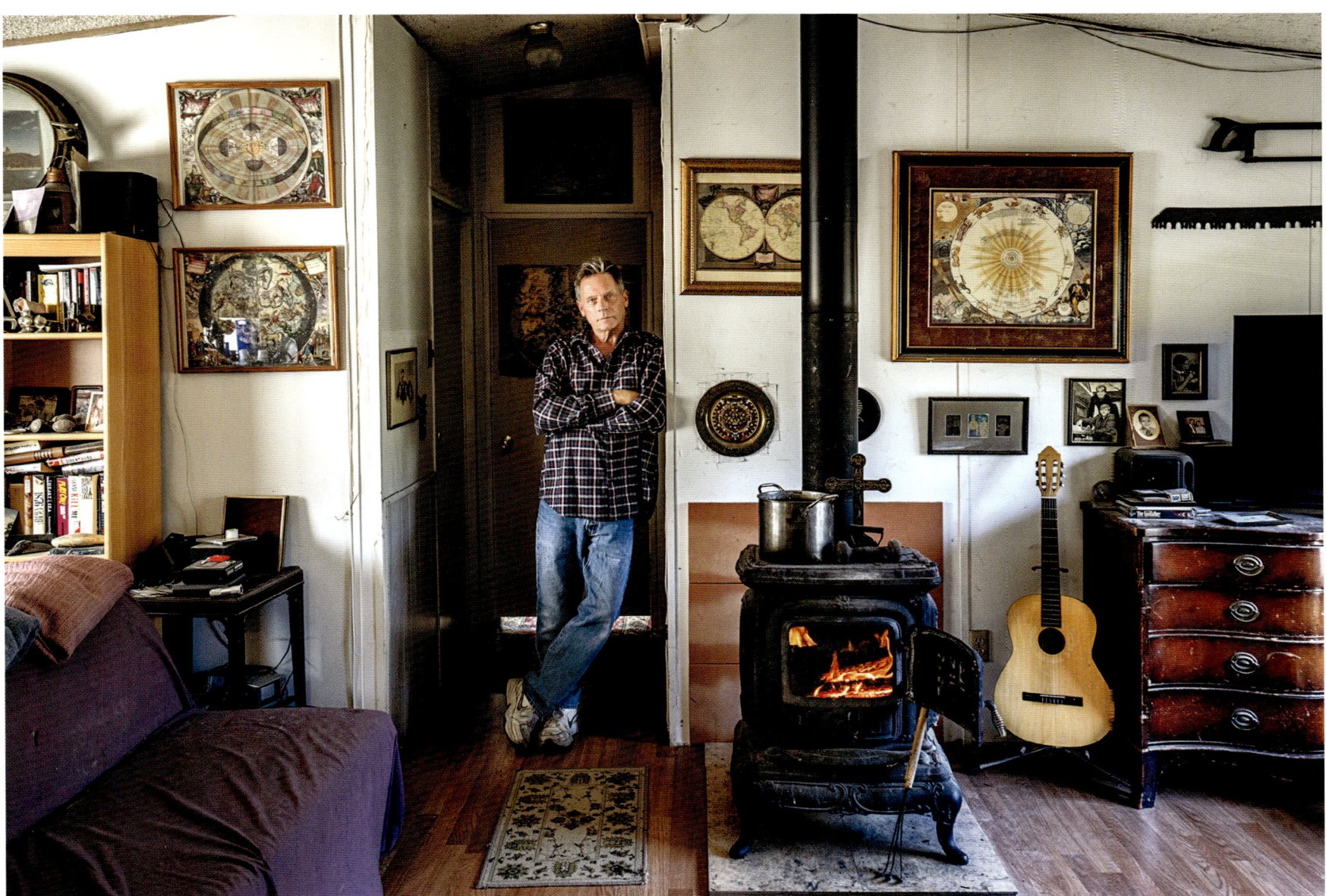

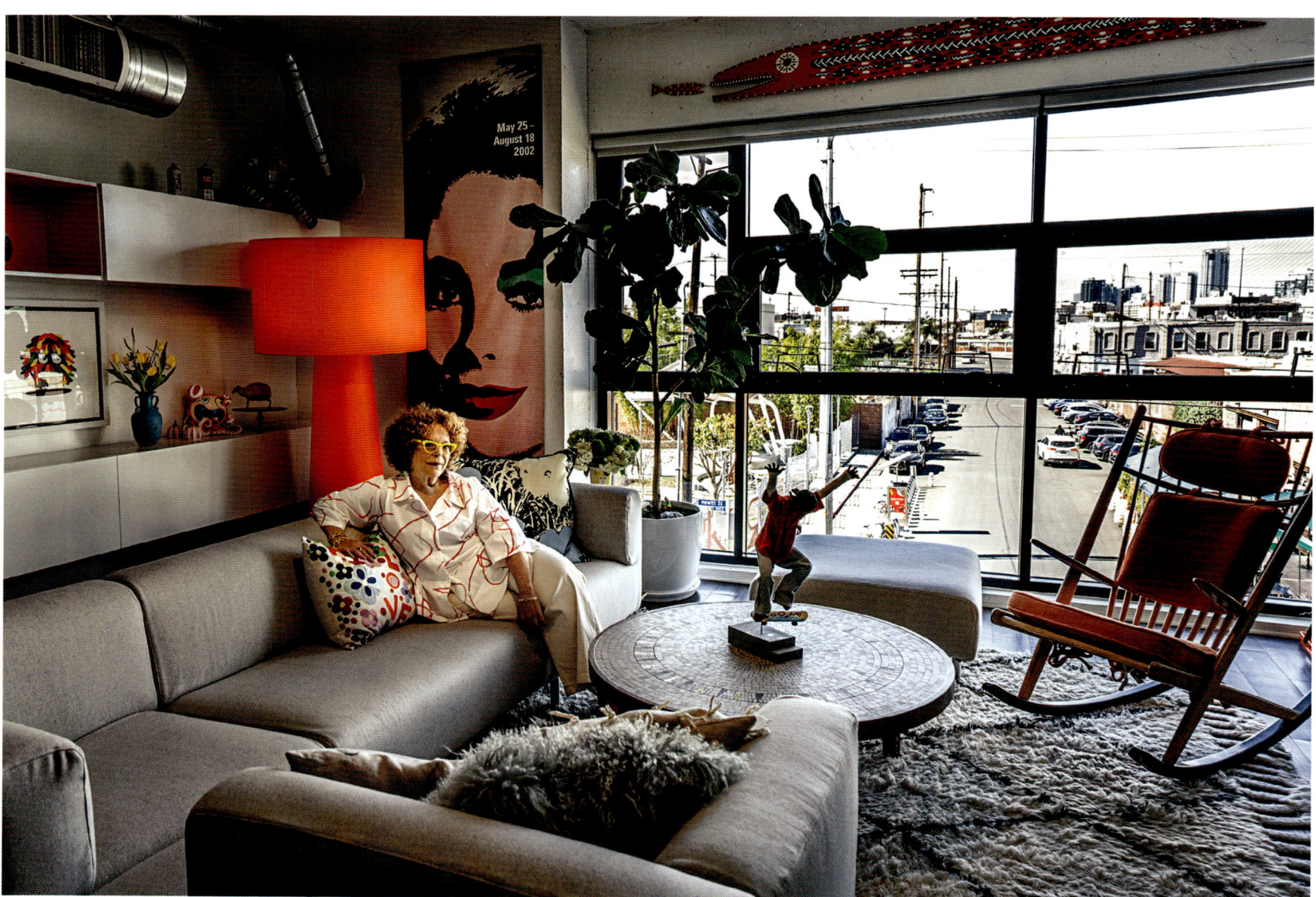

ANDREA TAYLOR

Photographed at home in Los Angeles on February 27, 2022.

Andrea was born in 1957 in Mount Vernon, New York, the first of two for Nadia and Bill. They lived in Irvington, New York until she was four, then they moved to Hartsdale, New York. Dad was a labor lawyer and Mom was an artist. Andrea was a chatty kid who always loved beautiful things and she had a dog named Promise. She wanted to be a back-up singer when she grew up, but gave that up after one audition. She was a discipline problem in high school so they put her in the area at school for problematic students. Andrea thought school was boring and she hated the suburbs, so she went into the city often. She babysat, raked leaves, and wrapped Christmas presents at a Hallmark store, until she got a cooler job at a record store across the street. There she saved up enough money to go to Europe the summer before she moved to Boston for college, where she got a degree in film and advertising. She returned to New York right after college and started working as a junior copywriter for an ad agency. She lived in New York until 1995, moved to Atlanta for five years for work, and then headed to Los Angeles to work for the Disney Channel. It was 2000 and Andrea was 43. She worked in entertainment, advertising, and marketing for years and years and then became an interior decorator. Her motto is: the client is the star, not her. Andrea lived in Beachwood Canyon for 17 years and in 2018 moved into this house.

"If there's happiness with a place, then I'm happy here. Unlike some New Yorkers, I think LA is filled with beautiful places. When I lived in New York, I thought living somewhere for the weather was the dumbest thing I ever heard. While there is traffic and annoyance here, and great disparity between wealth and poverty with basically no middle class in LA, there is also an ease of life here that I enjoy. I like the brightness that goes with that sunshine and the optimism that I feel because of it. Gentrification happens everywhere in the world. It's happened throughout history. I will quote my father's father who lived with his nine brothers and sisters in a tenement on the Lower East Side. When people would talk about how the neighborhood was changing in a bad way, he would say: 'This neighborhood was never good. It's the memories of a neighborhood that are good.' Moving people out isn't always good, but keeping crumbling, rat-infested buildings isn't always the best solution either. And don't get me started on the homeless situation because it's dire and it's at its worst just a few blocks from my amazing apartment. It's not about housing, it's about mental heath, human services, and an overhaul of our whole system."
—Andrea

CLAUDE HALL

Photographed at home in West Hollywood on February 23, 2022.

Claude was born in Brooklyn, New York in 1968. She was the middle of three kids for Myreille and Jean. Mom was an accountant and Dad worked in a bank, both were from Haiti. Claude spent her young years in Queens, New York. She was a well-behaved little girl who got good grades and never made waves. Her parents taught her to not ask questions and to do as she was told and because of that, she never really expressed herself. She wanted to be a flight attendant when she grew up because she wanted to travel; she wanted to be a teacher too, and secretly she wanted to be a model. Sometimes Claude would hike with her church group. She also did track and field and took dance classes. She worked in a shopping mall selling handbags and went to the Fashion Institute of Technology. When college was done, and Claude was 20, she left home and moved to Paris where she stayed for 17 years. Claude got married and divorced twice during that time. She worked in fashion and then in interior design there. In 2007 when she was 39 years old, she left Paris and moved to Los Angeles. She worked in men's fashion when she first arrived and now she works in a furniture showroom and is a jazz singer. Claude moved into this apartment in 2009 and lives there still.

"LA is a town that will take you down if you don't know what you want, and it has a lot to offer. If you can get past its top layer, you'll find people of value with interesting lives. And its beauty lies in Mother Nature. It's so easy to disconnect from life and reconnect to yourself here. And since it's so spread out, if you're the curious type that likes exploring, it can be an adventurous place to live. Gentrification saddens me. Many neighborhoods are losing their flavor and horrid architecture is replacing buildings with soul. I feel that the balance between growth and honoring the past needs to be found. I love how LA is a mix of grit and glamour (drive east on Beverly Boulevard all the way to Downtown and you'll get what I mean), big city and small town, concrete and Mother Nature. You can be anything you want here ... just make up your mind fast!"
—Claude

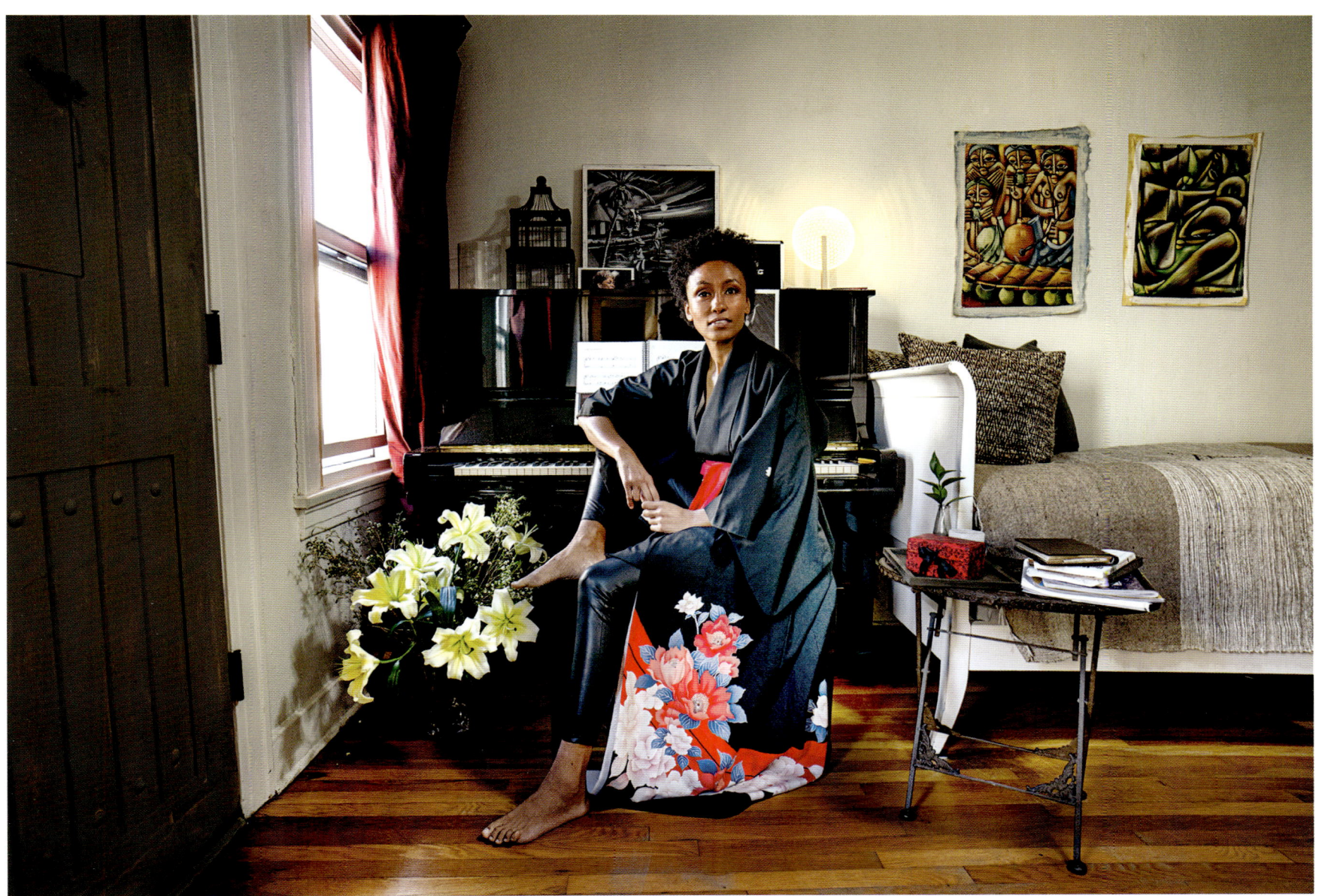

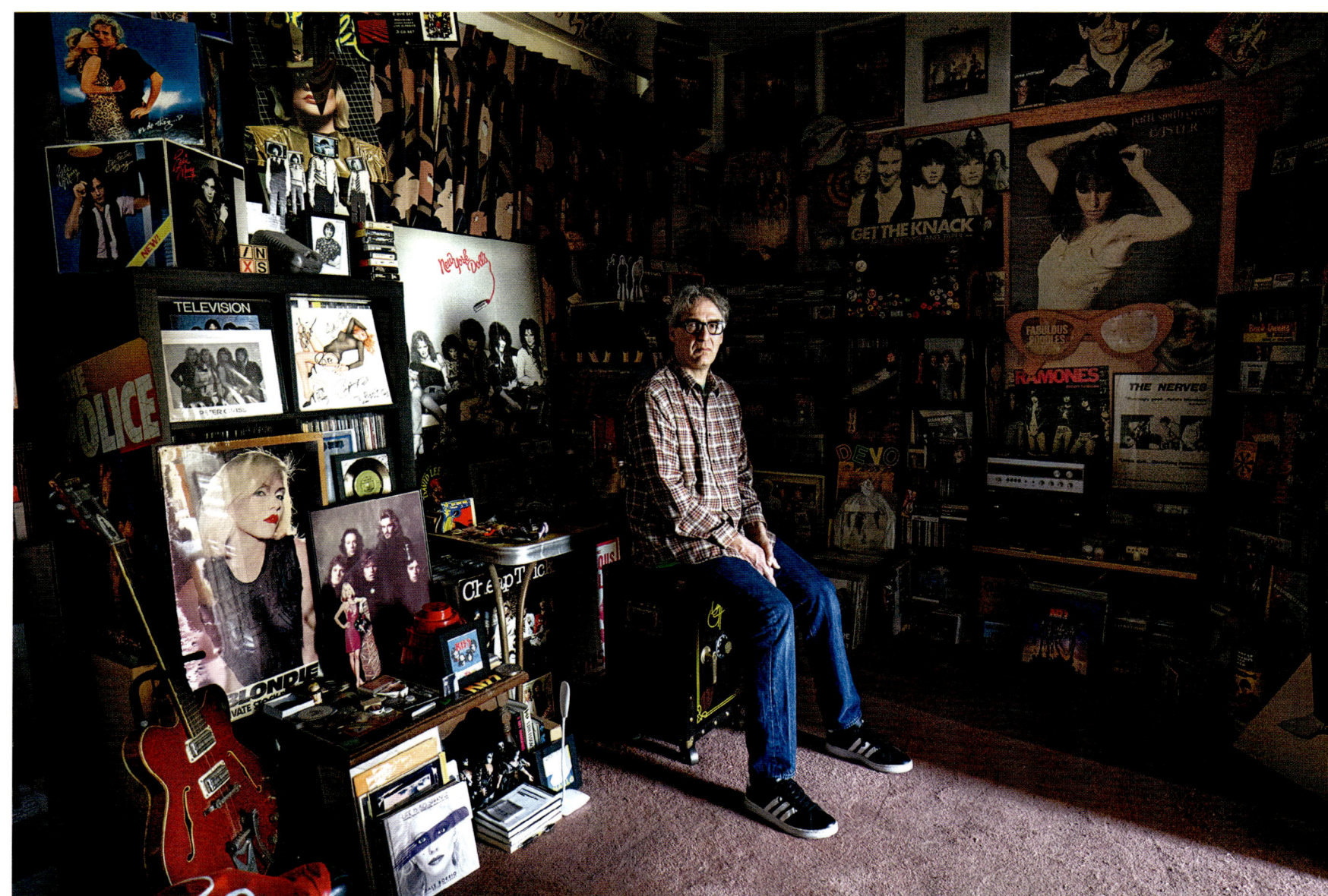

RONNIE BARNETT

Photographed at home in Los Angeles on March 16, 2022.

Ronnie was born in Houston, Texas in 1965. He was the last born for Jack and Jerri, and had four half-brothers. Dad owned a flange company and Mom became a dental assistant later in her life. When Ronnie was eight, his parents split up. He spent his young years with his dogs in rural Texas, then at five they moved to Houston, Texas. He knew when he was little that he wanted to do something with music when he grew up. He took journalism and typing at school and both those skills came in handy later in his life. In ninth grade Ronnie got a bass guitar and he formed a band. When he was 18, he moved away to Austin, Texas and started community college, but his hopes were dashed only three months later when his dad died in a plane crash and he had to move back home. Ronnie worked at a record store and as a valet car parker in Houston. Once he moved to California he worked for a company that made videos of tourists singing pop songs. He fell in love with Kim Shattuck and in 1989, when Ronnie was 24, he followed his heart and together they moved to California. A year later they formed a band and called it The Muffs. Ronnie and Kim split up romantically, but the band continued and did really well. By the end of that year they had a recording contract with Warner Brothers. Later on, in 1995 Ronnie married Lisa Marr. They split up in 2002. The Muffs lasted almost 30 years until 2019 when Kim died. Ronnie continues to work in record stores, as he has done for most of his life. Ronnie moved into this house in 2000 and lives there with his friend Kelly.

"I love this house. It was built in 1895, which is almost year zero in Los Angeles. It sits elevated on a hill above Echo Park Lake and is centrally located a block away from the 101 Freeway. It's very close to Dodger Stadium and hundreds of places that serve tacos. The weather is consistently beautiful as is the view of Downtown from my backyard. As far as annoyances, it is the city after all so there's occasionally a loud party next door, someone tagging walls in the alley, and the horrific New Year's Eve/4th of July fireworks—including the days leading up."
—Ronnie

BARRY BLINDERMAN

Photographed with his dog Elvis at home in Silver Lake on May 17, 2021.

Barry was born in 1952 in Bethlehem, Pennsylvania, under an auspicious star. He was the youngest of three kids for Abe and Etta. Dad was a pharmacist who painted on Sundays, and Mom was a homemaker who was also a community volunteer. Barry spent his young years in Bethlehem. He wanted to be a doctor when he grew up, then as a teenager, a rock star. He did well at school but did get in trouble for talking too much. He loved art and music. He had a band that recorded a single in 1969 that got played on the local radio. In 1970 when Barry was 18, he left for college to get a master's degree in art history, and never returned. Barry played folk music and flipped burgers. He worked as a short-order cook, in a pharmacy, and was a lighting technician at a disco. He wrote songs, was a courier, a video-surveillance equipment installer, a poster roller at Pace Editions, and was a lounge musician. In 1980 he moved to Manhattan. Barry wrote articles for art magazines, eventually opening Semaphore East Gallery in the historical East Village, showing important emerging artists. In 1987 he closed the gallery and moved to Normal, Illinois to be the Director of the Gallery at Illinois State University. There he continued to show important artists: David Wojnarowicz, Keith Haring, Jane Dickson, Jeanne Dunning, Martin Wong, and many more. Barry was married twice and has two daughters—Gabriel and Leah. Barry retired and moved to Los Angeles in 2019, buying this house in 2021.

"I've dreamed of living in LA since around 2008, having deeply enjoyed my curatorial visits here since the mid-1980s. Work and raising two kids had to come first, but when I retired and my daughter graduated college I began seriously pursuing the move. I came here for the art, the music, and the weather, and I don't think any other city in the US can compare in this particular trifecta. Even though Covid befell us five months after I began living here, I've enjoyed every moment and have met new people every day. Everyone is involved in art, writing, music, and film/TV! Having my cute, friendly dog Elvis helped keep me sane during the worst of the pandemic. On the downside, of course I'm appalled by the economic disparity that has hit people of color ever harder due to Covid, and I've never seen homelessness on such a scale before."
—Barry

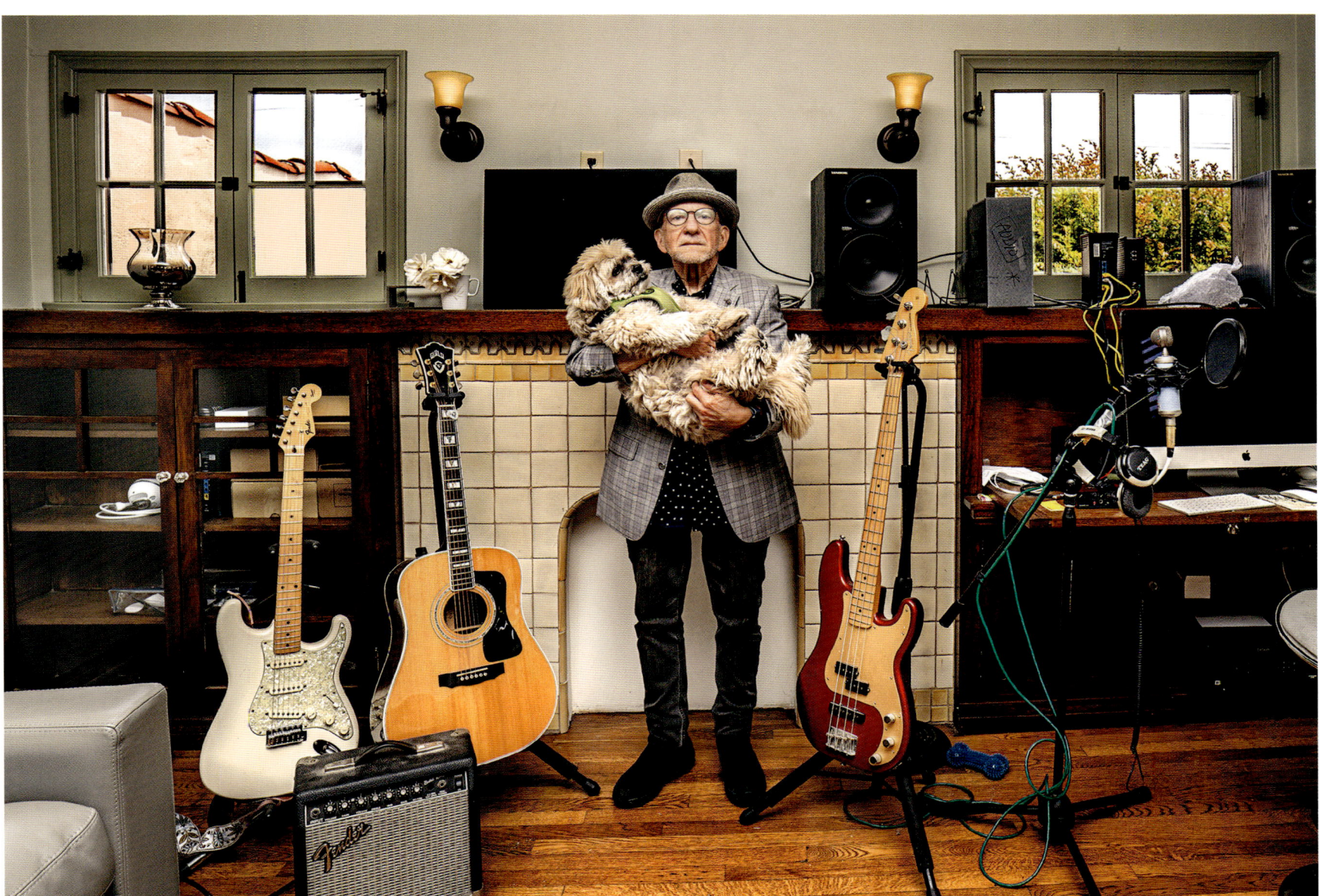

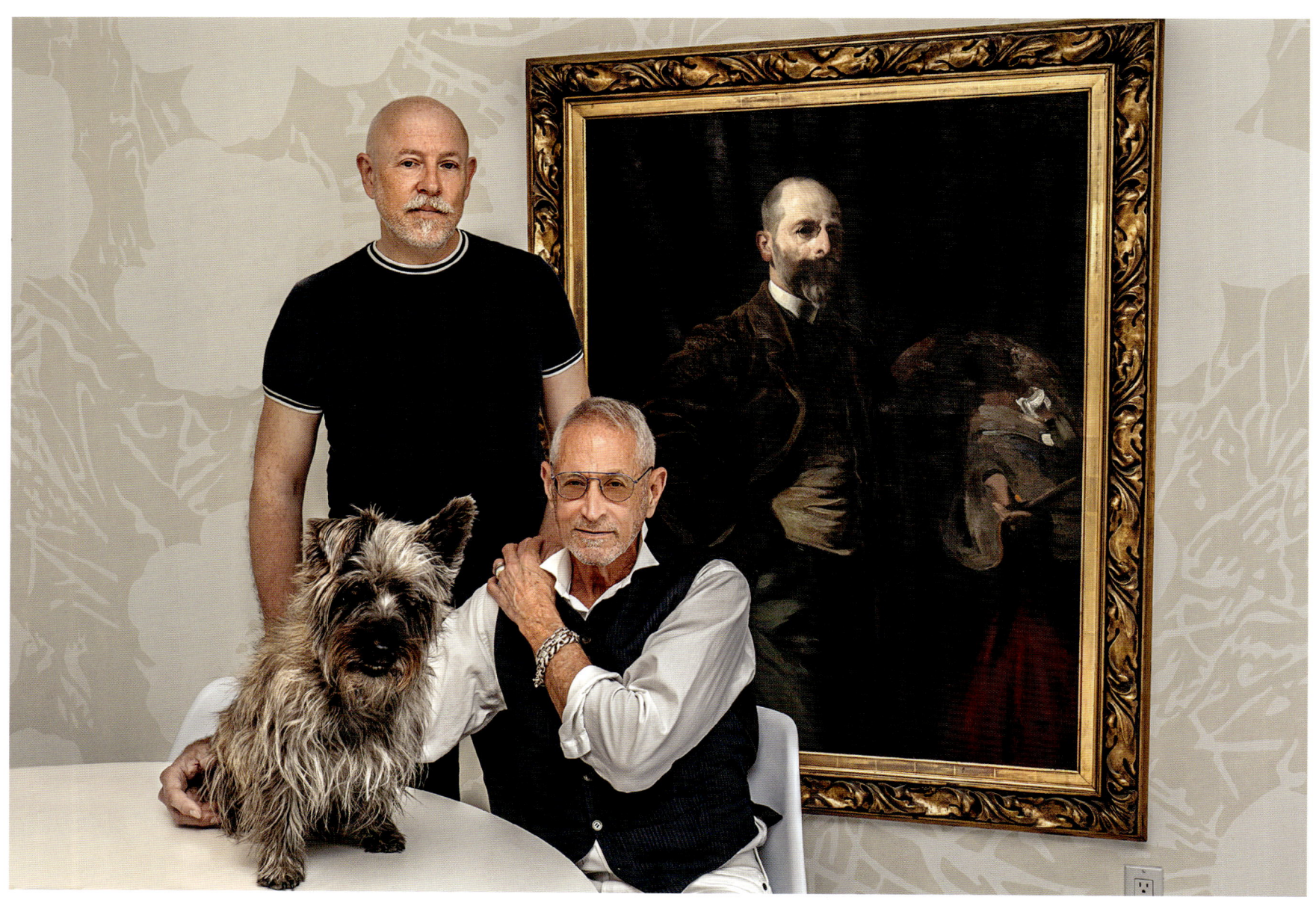

RICHARD HAYMES AND MICHAEL DEJONG

Photographed with their dog Atticus at home in Palm Springs on April 7, 2022.

Richard was born in Brooklyn, New York in 1953. He was the youngest of two kids for Anita and Marvin. Dad owned a restaurant where he was sometimes the chef, and Mom was a credit manager. Richard spent his childhood growing up in Brooklyn. He was an outgoing boy, studious and artistic. He wanted to be a doctor when he grew up, but having never heard of a gay doctor, he thought an artist might be a better choice. He was a super smart kid who even skipped the third grade. He did lots of art and theater and played in little league too, even though he wasn't very good. At 12, he worked at a local department store in Brooklyn, where he learned that women's stockings came in a color called "glacé taupe." He sold magazine subscriptions door-to-door, worked as a bagel baker, in a record store, and later as a movie projectionist at the New School. Richard got an art degree, a master's degree in administration, and a certificate in communications. After college, still living in New York City, he designed textbooks, graphics for all the top fancy art galleries, museums, and some dance companies too. Eventually, though, the New York City winters proved just too hard, and so in 2011 Richard and Michael headed west to Palm Springs. Richard is working on the genealogy of his mother's side of the family and does pro bono design work.

Michael was born in Chicago Heights, Illinois in 1962. He was the youngest of three for Ruth and Floyd—his twin sister arrived ten minutes before he did. Dad was a carpenter and a mechanic and Mom was a homemaker, both hailing from the Netherlands. Michael was a quiet kid who wanted to be an artist when he grew up. He spent his childhood in Lansing, Illinois with lots of pets: an alligator, a piranha, a squirrel, a rooster, guinea pigs, mice, a dog, and a cat—not all at the same time. Michael was band president, played the clarinet, excelled at art, and was very active with his church. He tutored special needs kids, was an after-hours grade school janitor, and worked at a local vegetable stand. Michael left home when he was 20, college bound. During college, he was a clerk in a women's shoe store, and he worked in a refrigerated fur storage facility. Leaving college with a master's degree, Michael moved to Chicago for one year before heading east to New York City's East Village. He worked in galleries, wrote books, and worked as a photo stylist. He had his first solo art exhibition in 1988 only a few months after moving to New York, and wrote his first book in 1995. He was a contributing writer at two online newspapers and wrote a weekly advice column. Michael is a successful artist and is working on a new book.

Richard and Michael met in 1988 in New York City on a phone sex line that was advertised in the back of the *Village Voice*. They became domestic partners in New Jersey in 2004, and got married in 2013 when gay marriage was legalized in California. In 2012 they moved into this house, where they still live.

"Having always been a city boy, surprisingly, Palm Springs has been a wonderful place to call home. Prior to Covid, it was easy to make friends with similar interests through the Palm Springs Art Museum, modernism, the film festival, the dog park, or the gym. Gentrification has actually brought the median age of the population down and it's nice to see more young people moving here. The summers have been getting increasingly hotter and unbearable, but we work around it and go from air conditioning to air conditioning."
—Richard

"Palm Springs is beautiful. Filled with creative folks set on discovering the next phase of their lives."
—Michael

LEIGH WISHNER AND BRIAN LIGHT

Photographed at home with their dog Satchmo in View Park on February 2, 2022.

Leigh was born in 1975 in San Pedro, California. She was the oldest of two kids for Marianne and Stanley. Mom was a grassroots organizer for women in politics and Dad was a doctor. Leigh spent her youth as a tomboy in Palos Verdes, California, always taking in stray cats and dogs. She wanted to be an archeologist when she grew up. Other than math and physics, Leigh did well at school. She was an athletic kid, who played a lot of volleyball, some basketball and baseball, and even fenced a bit later on. In 1993 she moved east to study art history and archeology at Barnard College. After college Leigh stayed in NYC for 20 more years. She worked for a company that sold fake fur coats, as a sales person at Liz Lange Maternity, and for an antique business that worked in historic fashion and textiles. It was 2011 and Leigh was 36 years old. Her mom had recently passed away and she was tired of the harsh east coast weather, so she moved back to Los Angeles to be closer to her dad. She worked as a curatorial assistant in the textile department at a museum, and then at the Fashion Institute of Design and Merchandising, where she still works as a digital media manager.

Brian Light was born in New York City in 1954. He was the third kid in a lineup of four for Muriel and John. Mom was a waitress and Dad was a tile layer. He spent his childhood years in Queens, New York. He was an average student who played basketball, football, and hockey too. He wanted to be a psychologist when he grew up. When Brian was 21 he left home and moved into his own apartment. He went to college for one year but had to quit so he could get a job and help support his family. He worked as an electric meter reader, a UPS driver, and at a tennis club. He stayed living in Queens for about 15 years before he moved to Westchester, New York. He worked for the New York Sanitation Department for 28 years, retiring as Executive Officer in the Bronx Borough. After that, he wanted to start a new chapter in his life and so he moved with Leigh to Los Angeles in 2011. Brian is a freelance writer for the Film Noir Foundation and a researcher.

Leigh and Brian met in New York City in 2000 at The Rodeo Bar and they got married in 2013.
They lived with Leigh's dad for a few years then they bought this house in 2015, where they still live.

"I love LA—cliché but true. I don't love driving, but I love exploring all the different pockets in this huge, sprawling city! For a fairly 'young' city, it has a surprisingly rich and fascinating history. How can you beat this weather? And the natural beauty—you get beach, chapparal, desert, mountains, and more. I love the CA frame of mind—laid-back, multicultural, sophisticated, a little kooky, and open to new things. It really took me living in NYC for almost 20 years to really, truly appreciate my hometown, and once I came back, I haven't looked back ... as for gentrification, it's sometimes a misunderstood term related to economics and not exclusively to race/ethnicity. It's complicated!"
—Leigh

"I enjoy life in LA very much and the transition was easier than anticipated. I love the weather, the movie culture, the music scene, and museums—nothing I actually hate—gentrification is a problem in certain areas of LA, but I think the term is occasionally misapplied."
—Brian

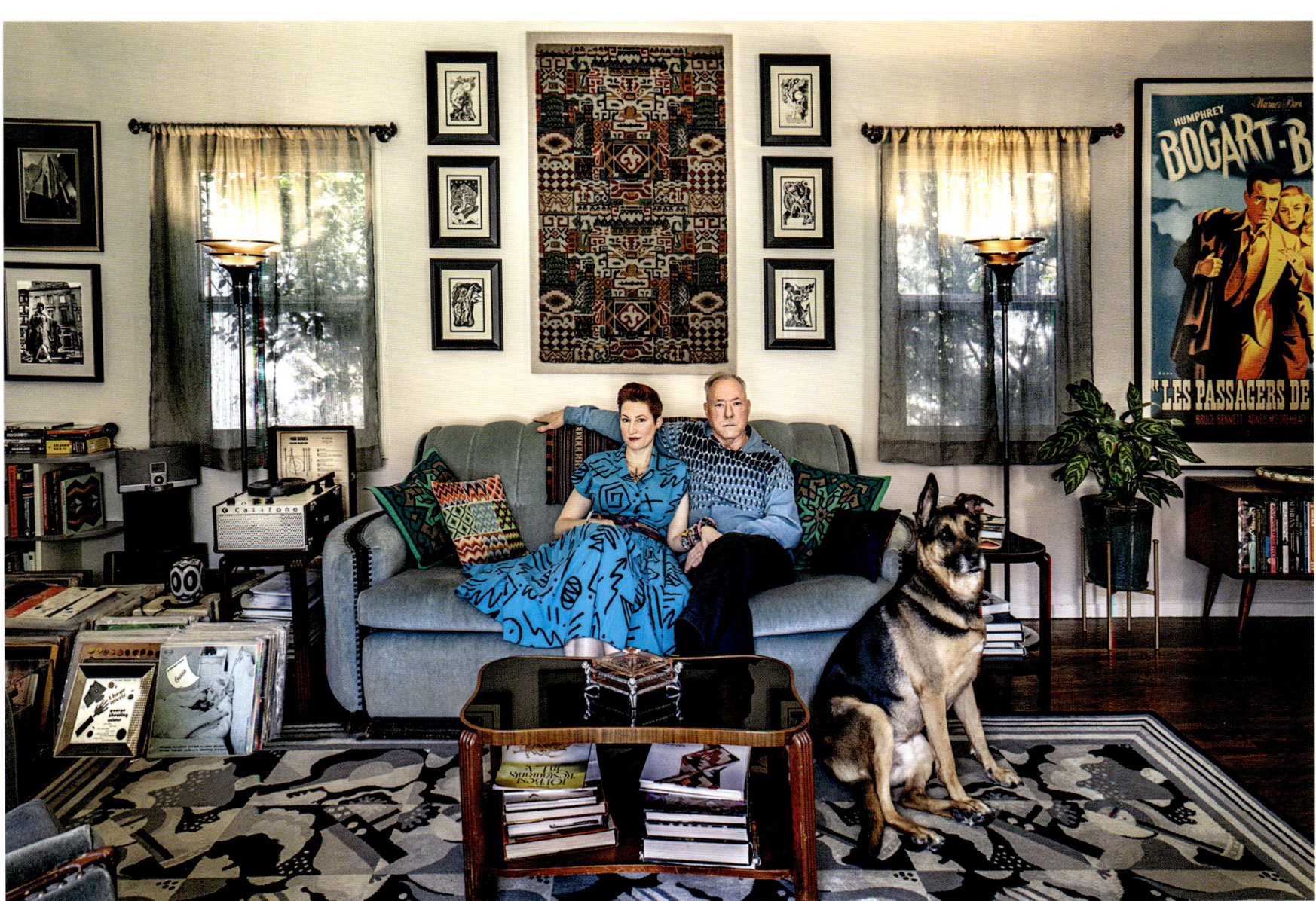

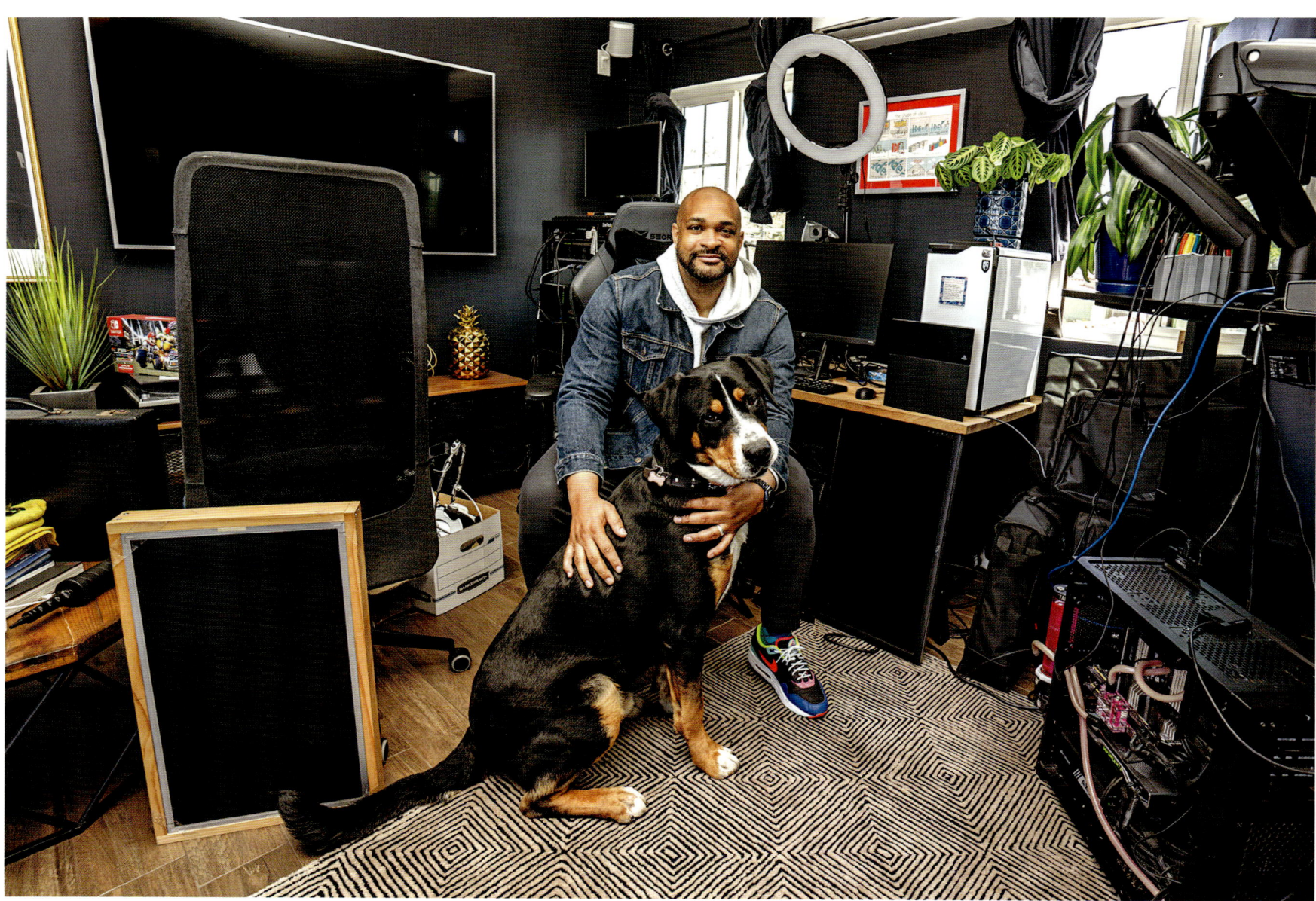

CARL BOGEN

Photographed at home in Los Angeles with his dog Frank on March 20, 2022.

Carl was born Carl Davis Bogan III, in 1983 in New Haven, Connecticut. He was the youngest of two for Eileen and Carl Jr. Dad was a shoe repairman and Mom was a teacher. When he was one, the family moved to Decatur, Georgia and Carl spent his young years there. When he was seven, his parents split up. He wanted to be a race car driver or a motorcycle racer when he grew up. Carl was never the star of the show, but was popular just the same, with lots of friends. He did really well with art and music and not so good with math. He played basketball and was in the band and orchestra. Carl went to three colleges in Atlanta studying motion graphics and 3D design. He worked as a busboy, as an electrician's assistant, as a bellman at a hotel, as a valet driver, as a computer repair person, and he also installed home theaters and car sound systems. Carl was 23 and college was done when he moved to Los Angeles. He worked in post-production, as a visual effects supervisor, as a lighting person on some films, and in the artificial intelligence field. Now Carl is a chief tech officer for a tech company. In 2011 Carl met his wife Lauren on a dating site, and in 2014 they got married. Carl moved into Lauren's house in 2012 and together they live there with their two boys.

"I love living here because it's right in the middle of things without feeling like I'm in the middle."
—Carl

XIAO LIU AND JOHN WINTER

Photographed at home in Los Angeles with Violet and Willow on February 26, 2022.

Xiao was born in Beijing, China in 1976. She was the first and only daughter for Liu and Xie, and was the first of two daughters for her dad Xie. Mom was a journalist and photographer and Dad was a music professor. When Xiao was three years old her parents split up. She spent her childhood growing up in Beijing. Her mom was very busy and moved a lot, so Xiao often lived with her relatives and friends. She wanted to be an artist when she grew up. She was good at art and attended an all-art high school. When Xiao was 18 she left home for college. She first moved to Switzerland to go to hotel management school, then moved to San Francisco to study art. She worked at a fabric store, at vintage stores, as a makeup artist, and as a shoe designer. After college, Xiao moved to Los Angeles—it was 2004 and she was 27. She eventually started working as an art director on movies then worked at a talent agency. Xiao got married for two years and had her daughter Violet. In 2013, Xiao started her own entertainment company, Chinawood, which helps Chinese companies develop projects with American talent and entertainment companies.

John was born in St. Paul, Minnesota in 1970. He was the youngest of four kids for George and Nancy. Dad worked for the IRS and Mom was a schoolteacher. John spent his young years growing up there. He was a popular kid with a big personality. He loved comic books and later collected art. He played tennis, acted in school theater, and later made videos too. When John was 18 he left home for college in Madison, Wisconsin, where he studied TV and film. He worked as a waiter, a bartender, in a comic book store and an ice-cream shop, he babysat, shoveled snow, and delivered newspapers and flowers. After college John moved to New York. He stayed there for 15 years working as a production assistant and eventually as a producer. In 2010, when he was 40 years old, John headed west for Los Angeles where he continued working as a producer.

John and Xiao met in 2015. In 2016 they got married and in 2020 their daughter Willow was born. In 2017 they moved into this house and they live there still.

"I love living in LA. Sometimes traffic gets to me, but overall I love it. I know gentrification may not be fun for some people but it gives other communities such as Asians a chance to make LA home as well."
—Xiao

"LA is my home. Although I have other properties, this home is my favorite yet. I get to express my creativity in our home design—inside and outside. LA is an easy place to poke fun at and point out all that's wrong—traffic, segregation, and homelessness. But there is beauty in the grime and grit, and humor in all the nonsense. LA has some of the best and most diverse food options of anywhere in the country. The weather is absolutely perfect. LA is so huge it continues to expand, and the options are even more here than in New York."
—John

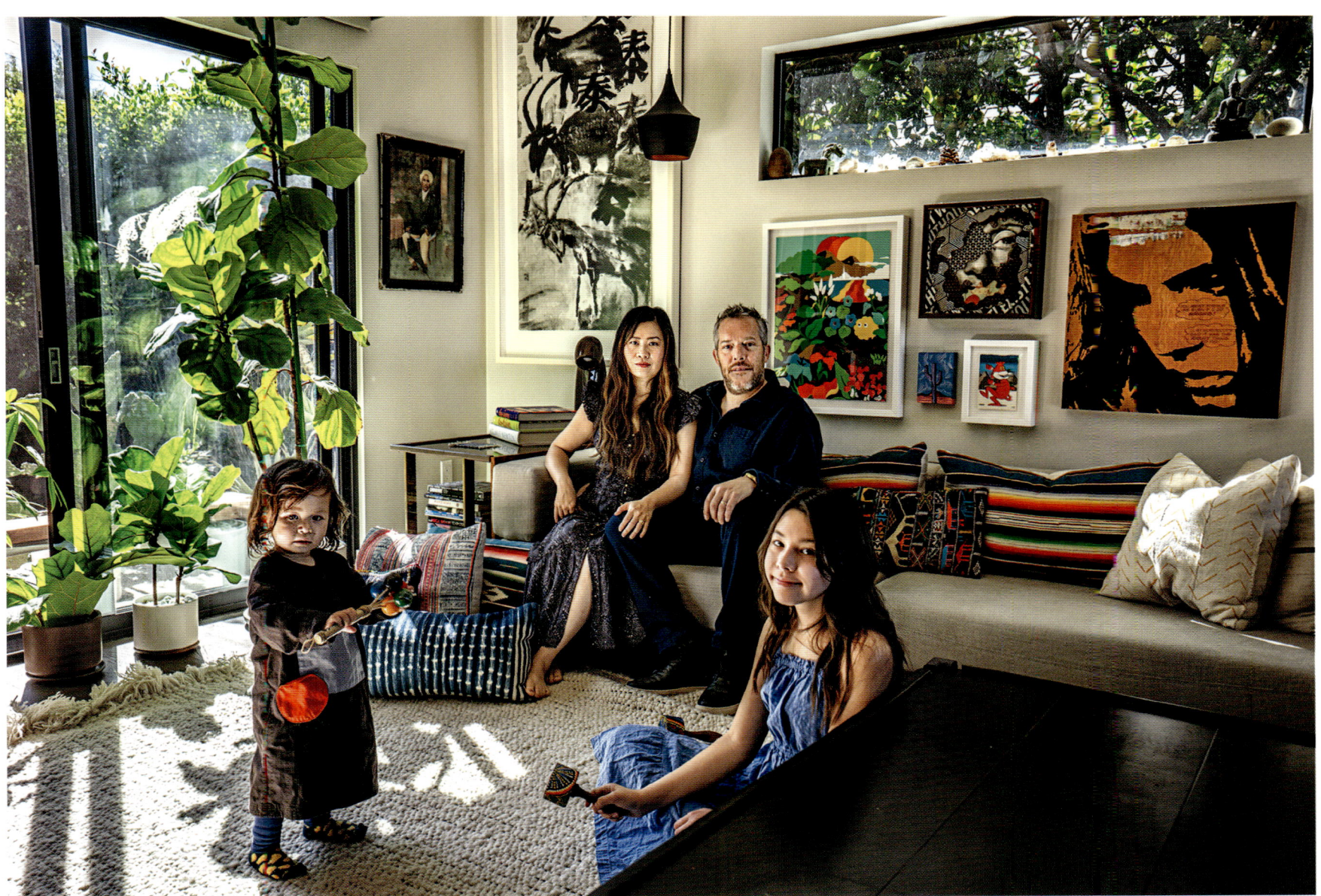

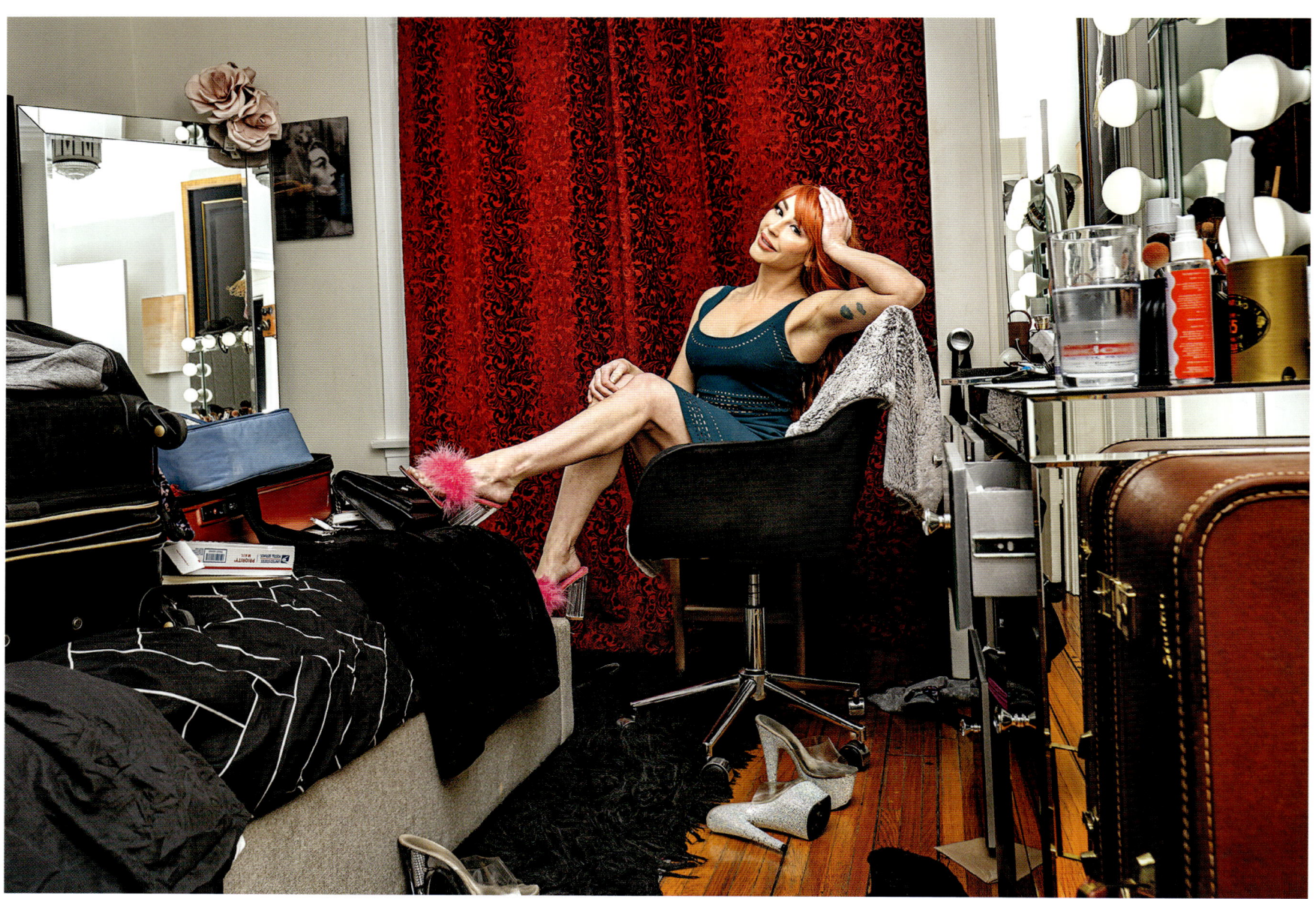

CINN

Photographed at home in Los Angeles on February 22, 2022.

Cinn was born Leia Christiana in 1989 in Laguna Niguel, California. She was the only child for Betty and Roger. Mom was a homemaker and an artist and Dad was a civil engineer. She spent her young years growing up with her dogs in Lancaster then later moved up to Hollister. Once in the eighth grade, Cinn stood up and announced that she wanted to get paid to dance around in her underwear. She excelled at drama and the performing arts, and failed math. She learned to do back handsprings and the splits when she was a cheerleader, and performed at statewide competitions, and she studied dance in high school too. Her mom passed away when she was 18. That same year she left home and got a degree in cosmetology. She sold hair straighteners at the mall and worked as a go-go dancer too. She lived in San Francisco for a while and then San Jose. She was a nude model, and a promo model for SVEDKA Vodka at every gay club in the Castro. When Cinn was 24 she made the move to Los Angeles. She started web-camming and also appeared on Playboy TV and music videos. Cinn is a content creator, a performer, and an artist. She moved into this house in 2020 and lives there with her boyfriend.

"It's not surprising to me that health and wellbeing are so promoted here because LA is not a particularly healthy place to live. With the dry weather, heavy pollution, low air and water quality, we've got to make up for it somehow. Although eating healthy here is a breeze, easier then anywhere I've ever lived. LA is so rich in resources—you can become whatever it is you dream of: any type of entertainer from any genre storybook or far stretch of the imagination."
—Cinn

NANCY AND SPENCER HUNT

Photographed at their home in Santa Monica on May 25, 2021.

Nancy was born in St. Louis, Missouri in 1952. She was the youngest of three for David and Louise. Mom was a high school teacher and Dad worked for the Post Office. She spent her childhood in the suburbs but when summer came along, she was with her grandmother in El Paso, riding horseback to Mexico. She wanted to marry George Harrison and be an Andy Warhol Superstar when she grew up. She was really good at sewing and made all kinds of unconventional clothes. She was always waiting for the next new group to arrive from England and read a lot of fanzines. Nancy left home at 18, college bound to study theater. She moved to LA in 1975 after college. She worked nights at the Cinerama Dome, and opened a store called NaNa in 1976. She sold clothes that she sewed and other things too. NaNa stores were all over the country coast to coast. Nancy got married, had two kids, and divorced. NaNa stores closed in 2000. In 2001 Nancy opened another store called Brat that she still runs, and she teaches fitness classes too.

Spencer was born in Wiesbaden, Germany in 1970. Because Dad was in the Air Force, they moved back to the USA within a year of Spencer's arrival. He was the oldest of four kids for Arthur and Mary. Mom was a computer programmer and Dad was a software program manager for various companies. Spencer spent his childhood in the coastal town of Guilford, Connecticut. He wanted to be an architect when he grew up. He excelled at computers in school. He studied photography, loved thrifting and record shopping. He shopped at a store that carried Nancy's clothes line. Spencer programmed a data entry system for the local police department when he was 14. He also worked at a department store for exactly the number of hours it took to purchase a trench coat. Spencer left home at 17 to study architecture at Carnegie Mellon. In 1990 he moved to Los Angeles. He continued his architect life for about five years then started working in the gaming business.

In 1986 Nancy bought this house. Spencer and Nancy started dating in 1994. Spencer moved into the house when they got married in 2000 and they live there still.

"Everything is here, why would you want to live anywhere else?"
—Nancy

"It took me six years to love LA, mostly getting past my east-coast bias. LA is a rhythm that is easy to embrace ... from neighborhoods that are rediscovered, waves of traffic that you learn to avoid, and people coming and going ... LA is an easy love with its climate, endless variety, and creative optimism."
—Spencer

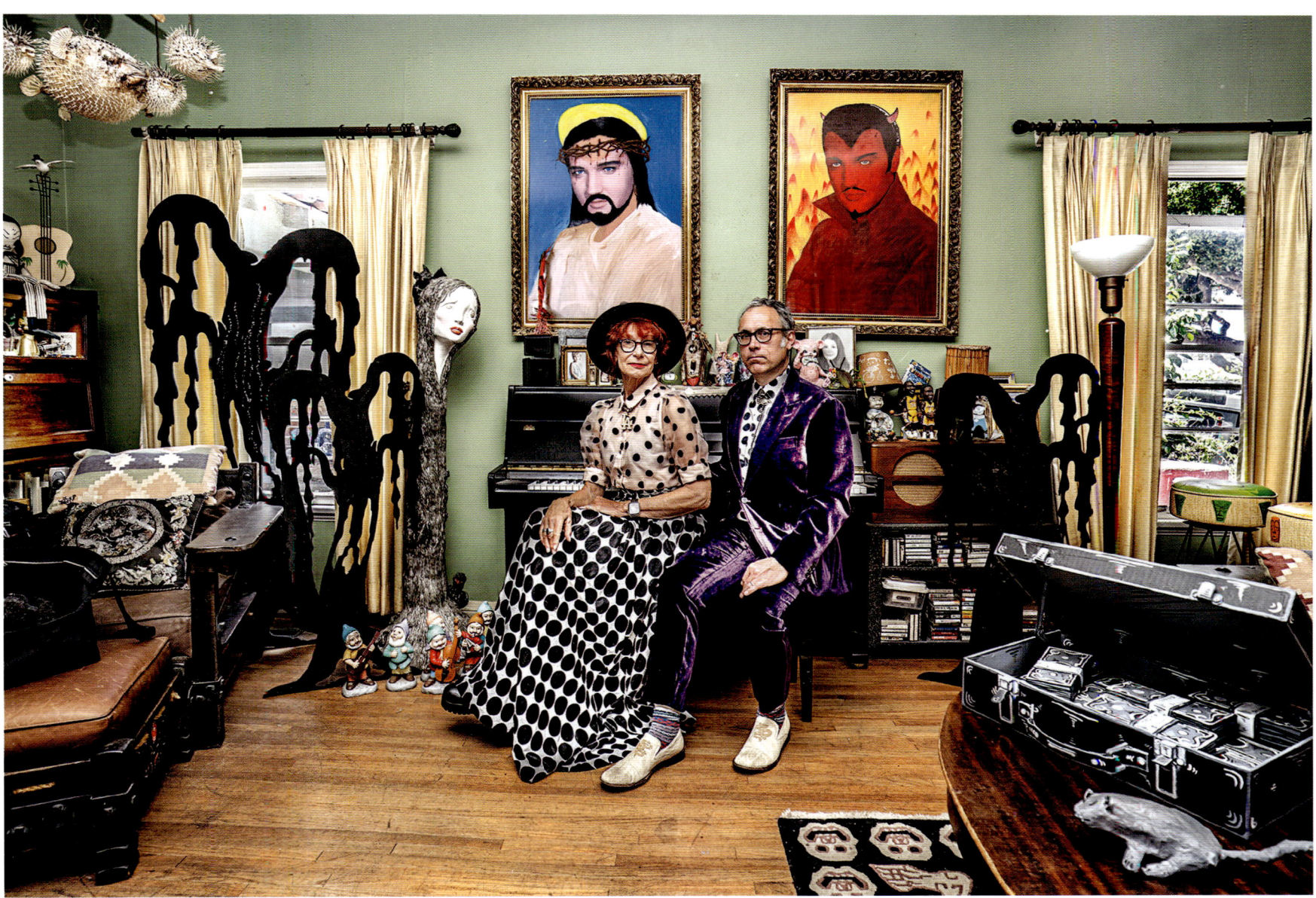

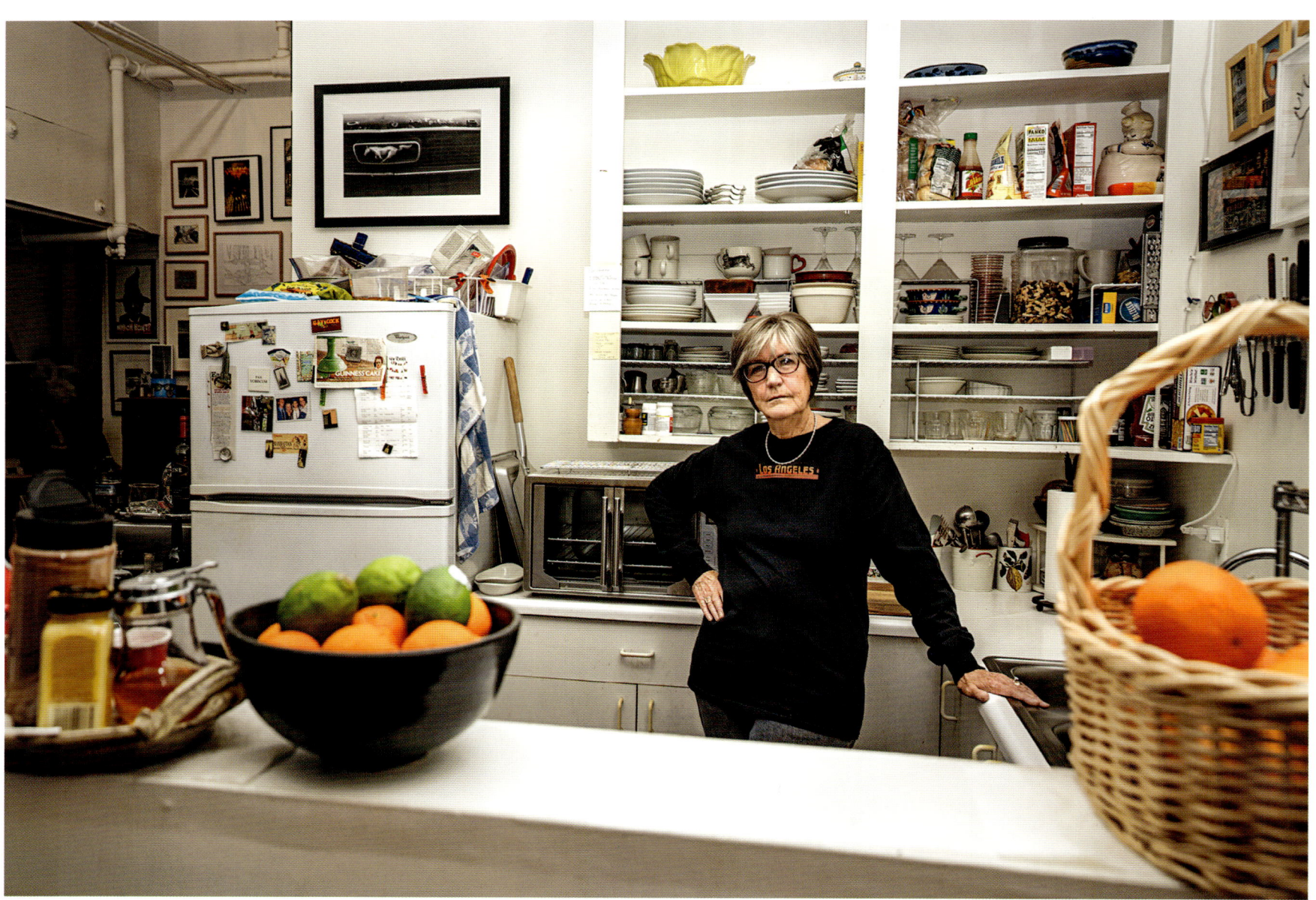

DIANE COCKERILL

Photographed at home in Los Angeles on March 5, 2022.

Diane was born a fourth-generation American in 1951 in Los Angeles, California. She was the youngest of two girls for Randy and Alice. Mom was a homemaker and dad was an insurance broker. Diane spent her childhood years in Mid City and then in Westwood, Los Angeles. She did well at school, organizing ping-pong tournaments and chemistry clubs on her off time. She wanted to be a Motown back-up singer when she grew up, or a photographer. When Diane was ten her dad bought her a camera. She graduated from high school and then studied fine arts at the University of California. After that she was a freelance calligrapher, taught tennis, and was an assistant to a designer. He made her carry a Pantone color chip when she went to get his coffee to be sure she put the right amount of cream in. Finally in 1979 Diane began a career in advertising. While working in design at the Hollywood Park Racetrack in the 1980s, she met a graphic artist named Bruce, and in 1989 she married him. Bruce is a photographer now too. When they moved to Downtown LA in 2016, she started shooting street photography. They lived in Westwood, West LA, and Bel Air before moving into this art studio in 2017, where they still live.

"LA is a challenge—I have a love/hate relationship with the emphasis on love; alternately exhilarating and frustrating, beautiful and mundane. Since I have a long history here, the changes have been overwhelming, with many favorite institutions demolished with unremarkable buildings replacing them. There are many exceptions, with exciting and innovating architecture but the old buildings hold the history, glamour, and intrigue of old Los Angeles that I miss. I have spent the past five years photographing as much of downtown Los Angeles as I can to preserve memories of this grand city. My great-grandfather's stationery company, founded in the 1880s, was replaced with modern lofts, my other great-grandfather's hardware building is unrecognizable, my father's insurance company was in the storied Carthay Circle Theatre building, built in 1929 and demolished in 1969. The predominate problem today is the homeless issue. The local government can't quite agree on a solution, but we have the Olympics coming in 2028, so ..."
—Diane

CYBILL

Photographed at her Arts District dungeon on March 5, 2022.

Cybill was born in 1986 in New York City. She was the youngest of two for Joseph and Angel. Joseph worked at the New York City Transit Authority and Mom worked with databases. When Cybill was 16 her parents split up. She spent her young years growing up in New York with dogs and a few parrots. When she was little, she wanted to be either a dominatrix or a zoologist. She did well with art and science at school, spending her free time making things and writing. During the summer between high school and college, she worked as a clerk in a hospital records office. When college was finished, Cybill spent a year or so archiving her art prints, before becoming a dominatrix full time. In 2012 when she was 26, she moved west to Los Angeles to open a dungeon. She got married in 2016 and divorced two years later. In 2019 she moved into this space and lives there still.

"I've never enjoyed California and have actually been trying to move away for the past three or four years, but health issues and then the pandemic have delayed that. The 'gentrification' in California is mostly a false one, sped along and based on the aspirations of the property owners who, while initially wishing to replicate the Brooklyn boom, have mostly just achieved the tax breaks given for vacant units based on an imaginary market value."
—Cybill

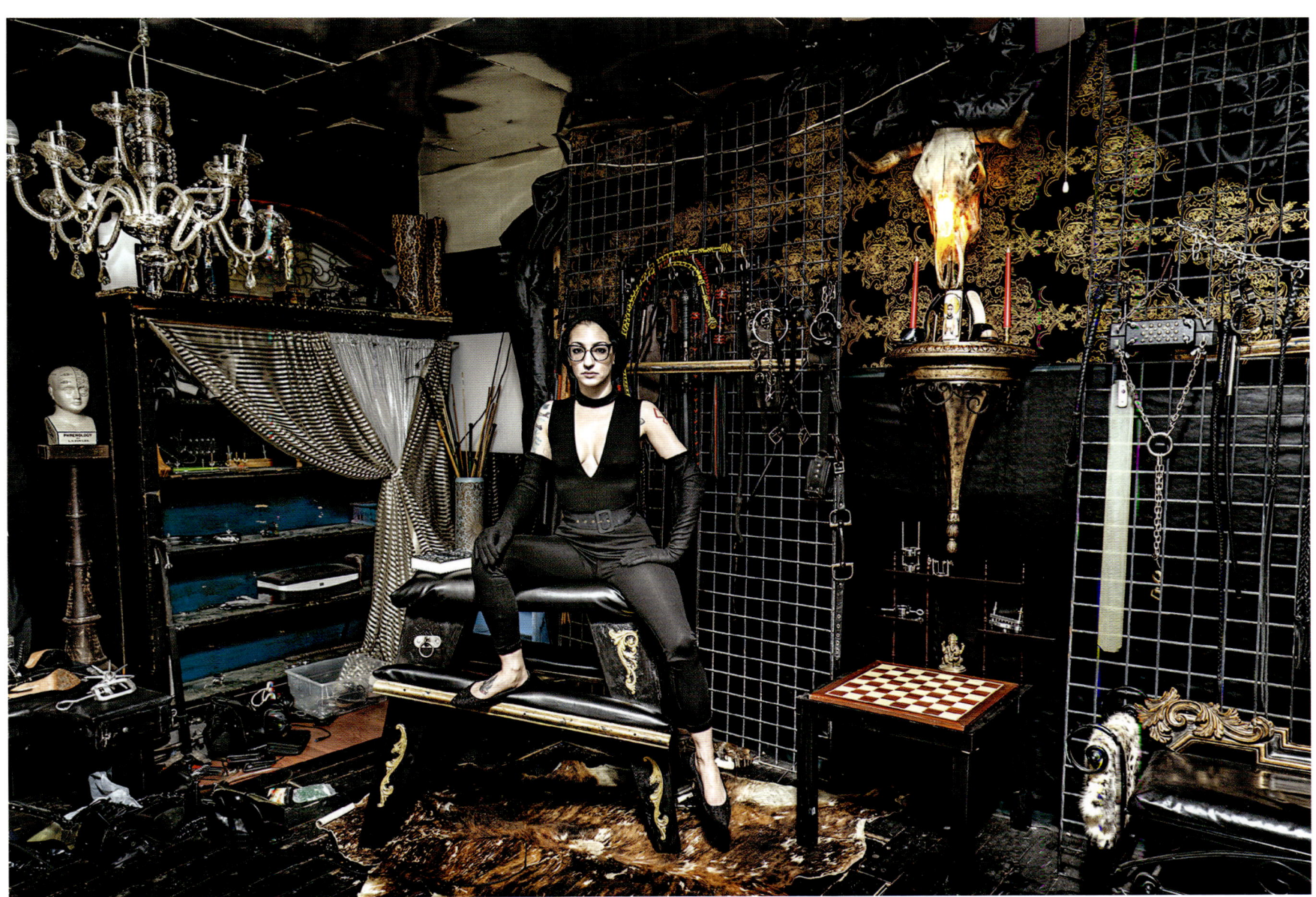

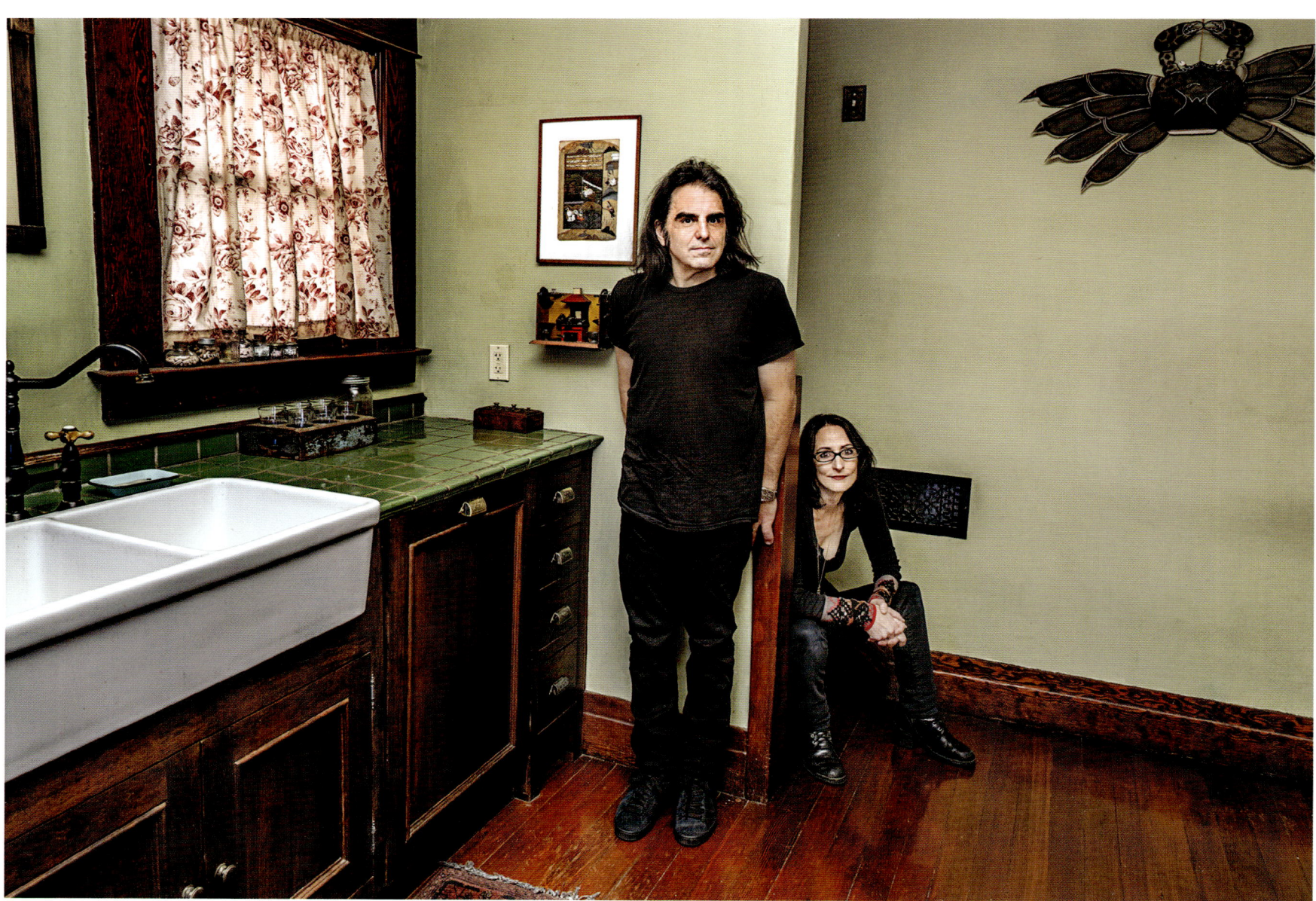

MICHAEL HILF AND ALYSON SOUZA

Photographed at their home in Silver Lake on March 22, 2022.

Michael was born in 1967 in Detroit, Michigan. He was the oldest of three kids for Marvin and Carol. Dad owned an appliance store and Mom was a homemaker. Michael spent his childhood years in Detroit and its suburbs. He wanted to be a filmmaker when he grew up. His mother took him to see *Willy Wonka & The Chocolate Factory* and he fell in love with movies. He was a set builder and part of the crew with his high school theater. When Michael was 17 he left home and went to Eastern Michigan University for two years then to New York University to study film. He graduated college in 1989 and decided to stay living in New York. Michael worked as a DJ and opened the landmark Ace Bar in the East Village with his partner Jim Abraham; he owned a film company, he directed TV commercials and music videos, and has made five short films that have won 20 awards. He has rebuilt classic cars, restored a 1909 Victorian home, plays guitar, and is a writer too.

Alyson was born in Bridgeport, Connecticut in 1968. She was the oldest of two kids for Anne and Al. Dad was a conceptual artist and Mom was a graphic artist. They lived on a farm in Massachusetts until Alyson was seven, then they moved to Northampton and Amherst, Massachusetts. When she was 13, her parents split up. Alyson did well at art and science in school, but hated physical education. She spent her free time drawing and making things. It was 1986. Alyson was 18 and she left home, headed for New York City's infamous East Village. She studied fine art at college there on a full scholarship. Alyson worked as a printmaker, a bartender, and when she moved to Los Angeles, she became a painting conservator. Alyson is a successful artist, and exhibits throughout the United States.

Alyson and Michael met in New York City in 1994. Michael had just opened the Ace Bar and Alyson needed a job. He hired her to be a bartender and the rest is history. They stayed living in the East Village until 1999, then headed west for Los Angeles. They got married ten years later. Michael and Alyson lived in the Fairfax District, then Koreatown, before moving into this house in 2008.

"LA is surreal—disconnected perfection, which is somehow harmonious. I love being in the epicenter of Hollywood history and I hate that the city is constantly destroying its own history."
—Michael

"I loved NYC and didn't want to move. Michael convinced me that we should try something new so I reluctantly followed. LA took me some time. The two cities couldn't be more different and I didn't have a driver's license when we moved here. I don't suggest anyone get their license at 30. Eventually it all worked out. We bought a dilapidated 1909 craftsman at the bottom of the real estate crash and the two of us spent four years bringing it back to life. We both love fixing old things and our skill sets complement each other. Between the two of us there isn't much we can't fix. There is a lot of beauty here but very little on its surface. All the real gems, you seek out or stumble upon. LA is a giant unknowable amoeba. I am always learning about new things in this city, 23 years here and I know I have only scratched the surface. That's pretty cool."
—Alyson

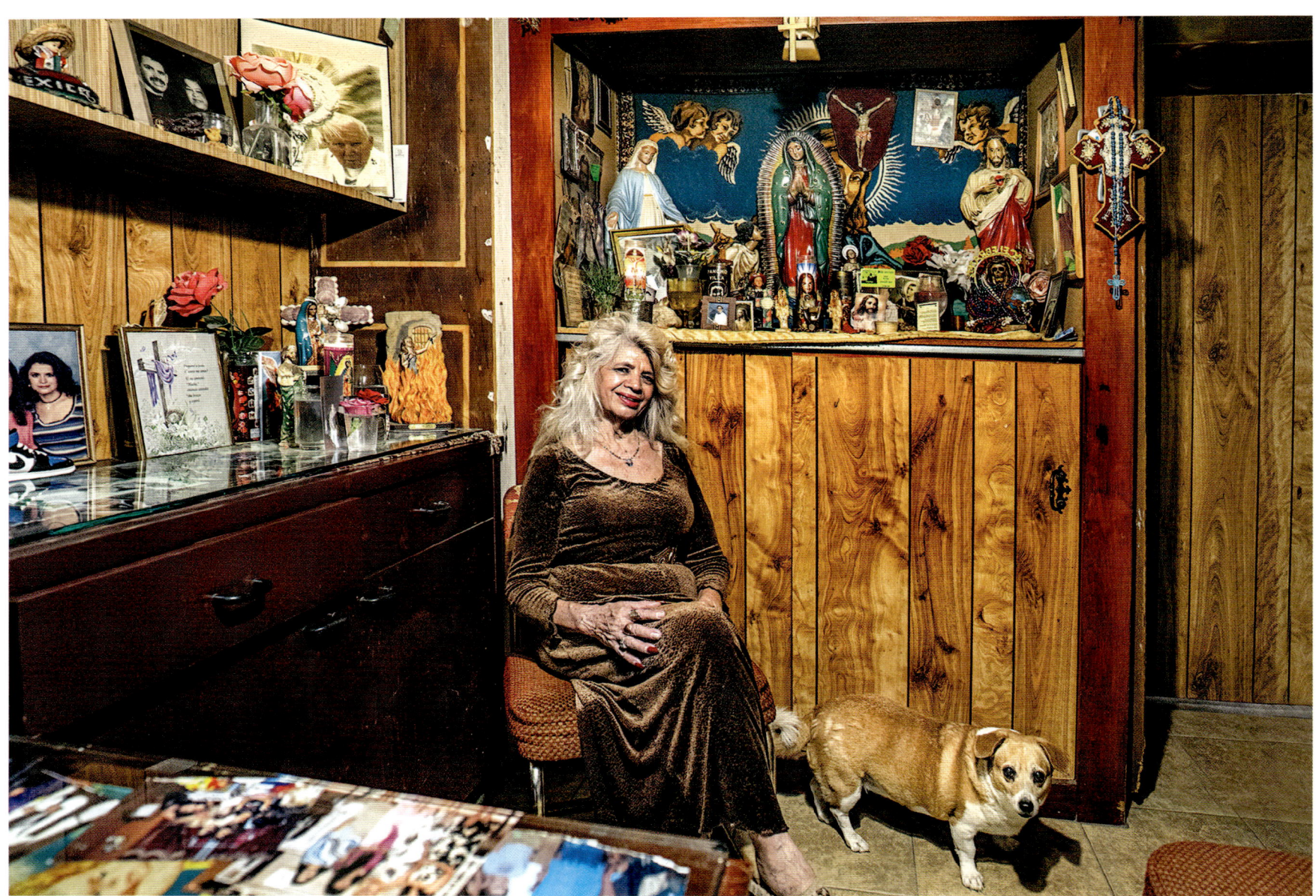

SARA REYNA

Photographed at home in Cathedral City on May 4, 2021.

Sara was born on April 1, 1951 in Acambaro, Mexico. She was the third of six kids for Narciso and Porfiria. Dad owned a large successful bakery and Mom was a homemaker. They were from Acambaro too. When Sara was five her dad was murdered in a robbery and when she was eight her mom died. With no one left to care for her, she was sent to live with her uncle in Reynosa. Sara was an average student and wanted to be a doctor when she grew up. She would visit her grandmother Carmen after school rather than do school activities because Carmen was teaching her how to read tarot cards. That's a skill she shines at to this day. Carmen was a doctor, who learned how to read cards from her mother, too. When Sara was 14 she left her uncle and moved back to Acambaro. There she met Antonio. She married him when she was 15 and got pregnant straight away. They stayed together for seven years and had five children together. She says having that first baby was the happiest thing that ever happened to her. When she was 23 she left Antonio and moved to Alamo, Texas. She left two of the kids with him and she took the other three with her. She worked as a dishwasher, a janitor, a cook, and as a produce packer. She also worked as a nurse's assistant. She was so good at that, the company offered to send her to medical school, but she was supporting all her kids so she had to keep her two jobs instead. She continued to build her clientele reading cards. She also met and fell in love with a man named Geraldo in Texas. They stayed together for 16 years. As a family, they traveled all over the United States. In 1990 they took a trip to the California desert, where Sara had always dreamed of living. Geraldo didn't like it and Sara loved it. He left Cathedral City and returned to Texas without her, where he was murdered a few years later. Sara and the kids stayed. Seven years later she met and fell in love with Martin. They got married, and eventually moved into this house, where she lives still. Martin passed away recently, and Sara is redecorating her house.

"I came to Cathedral City and fell in love with it. In spite of the changes, I still love it. Life can be beautiful but sometimes we go through very hard times. We have to stay strong and keep going. It doesn't matter what happens, we have to keep going. If we fall down we have to grab onto something we love and pull ourselves up. I love myself a lot, I love my job, I love my family, that's it. Despite all the times I have failed, I rise up again."
—Sara

JANET AND ERIC MCCORMACK

Photographed at their home in Toluca Lake on May 27, 2021.

Janet was born in Dawson Creek, British Columbia, Canada in 1965. She was the youngest of three kids for Allan and Carol. Dad owned his own catering business, serving up for the oil industry in northern Canada. Carol and Allan were both from northern Canada, and were married for 54 years. Janet spent her childhood in northern Canada, moving to Edmonton when she was four, and then in Yellowknife for a year when she was eight. She wanted to be a horse when she grew up. She was a pretty good student and loved to read. Janet was a tomboy who played baseball and tap danced until she was 12. She wanted to be a camera operator and studied radio and television at college. Janet realized pretty quickly that her dream of being a camera operator was not what she had hoped. She started working as a production assistant in the movie biz and never looked back, ending up an assistant director. Janet sold vacuum cleaners, worked in a Western store, learned how to steam hats, sold shoes, and worked for her dad's partner in the catering business.

Eric was born in 1963 in Toronto, Canada. He was the oldest of three for Keith and Doris. Dad was a financial analyst and Mom was a homemaker; both were from Toronto. They were married for 52 years. Eric spent his childhood mostly in his bedroom, occasionally venturing out onto the streets of Scarborough. When he was six he wanted to be a garbage man when he grew up. By the time he was seven he wanted to be an actor, hopefully playing a garbage man on TV. He wasn't all that good at sports but was really, really good at theater. Eric left home for college when he was 20, moving downtown to study theater. By the early nineties he was coming to Los Angeles for pilot season, and by 1996 he took up residence there. Early on he worked as a waiter, sold menswear, and managed an ice-cream store. Eric has worked as an actor since 1984, and might be best known for his portrayal of Will, America's gay sweetheart on the hit TV show *Will and Grace*.

Janet and Eric met on the set of *Lonesome Dove* in 1994. In 1997 on a boat in English Bay, they got married, splitting their time between Vancouver and Los Angeles. They had a son Finnigan who was named after the dog on the TV show *Mr. Dressup*. They moved into this Toluca Lake house in 1999 and have lived there ever since.

"It took me a long time to feel comfortable in Los Angeles. What saved me was volunteering for Project Angel Food delivering meals to people living with HIV/AIDS. I learned to drive here and got to know different areas. We were blessed to find our neighborhood and our friends next door. It's a real community. My mom came down to live with us and she loves it here. Even though my heart will always long for Canada, my belief is that you can find beauty anywhere."
—Janet

"We love our neighborhood, and our house. Made some great friends here. Best sushi ever, just down the street. And I loved shooting Will & Grace *around the corner, for 11 years. And I love driving my Vespa on Mulholland. But despite being here for 25 years, it's never really felt like 'my town.' I think we're too Canadian that way. The lure of our Vancouver life is strong."*
—Eric

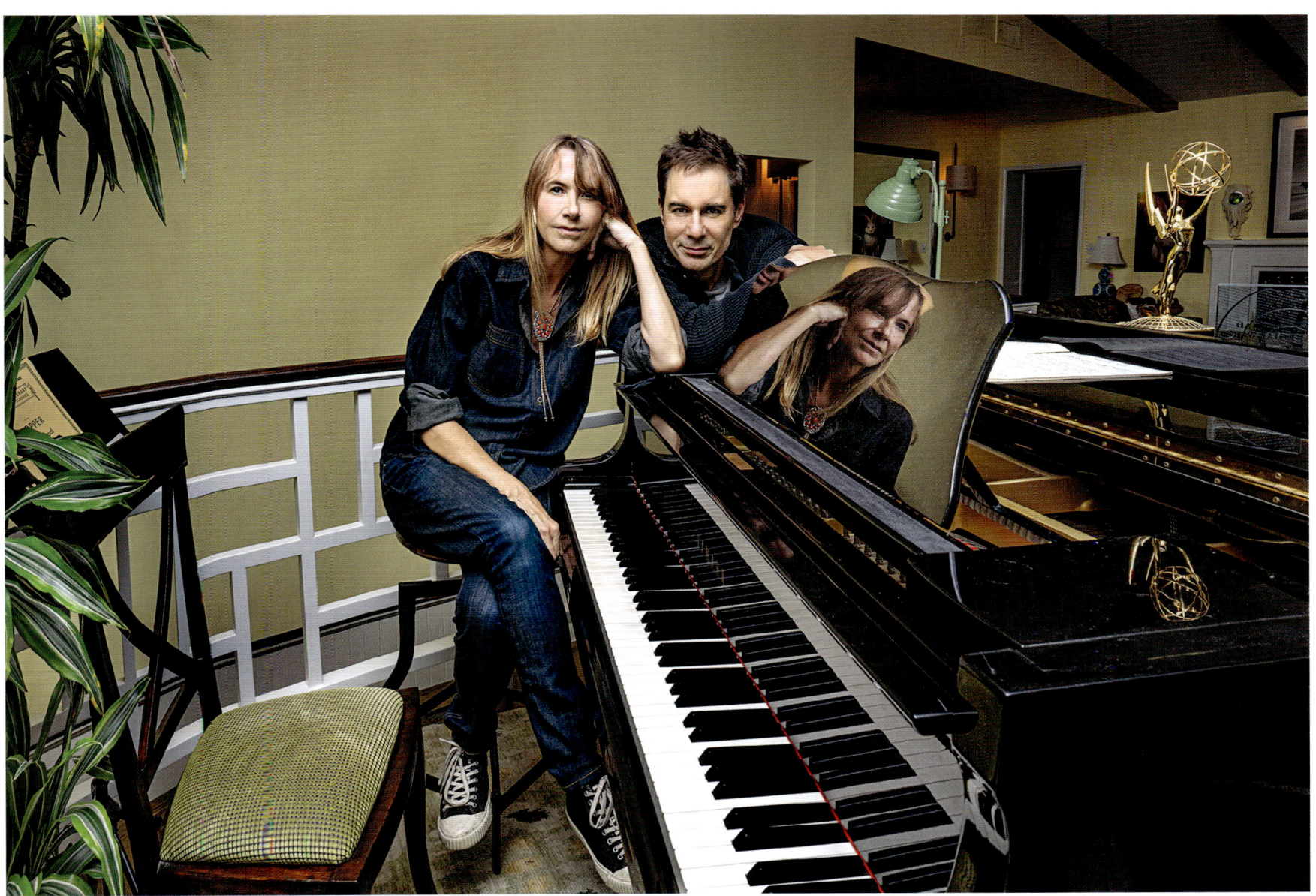

JOHN LANSING

Photographed at home in Marina del Rey on March 19, 2022.

John was born in 1949 in Rockville Center, Long Island, New York and grew up in Baldwin, Long Island. He was the second of four kids and the only boy for John and Loretta. Dad taught reading at school and Mom taught dance in the basement of their house. John wanted to be a doctor when he grew up. Later, in high school, he wanted to be a pilot until algebra got in the way. Working as a newspaper boy, a golf caddy at the country club, and as a retail clerk in a clothing store, John saved enough money to buy a used Corvair. While attending college he discovered and fell in love with theater, and he started spending time in Manhattan where the action was. John played Danny Zuko in a touring production of *Grease* and then was hired to play Zuko on Broadway. Sometime in his thirties John segued from acting to writing and directing. He closed down his New York digs and moved to Los Angeles. He was writing now, finally creating the story and not acting in someone else's. John got married in 1985 and got a divorce 23 years later. Not long after that, he met Vida, a woman who grew up in his home town of Baldwin, and they live together still. John lived in West Hollywood, Laurel Canyon, and Sherman Oaks before moving into this loft in the Marina in 2007.

"When I moved to California it was love at first sight. One of the joys of living in Los Angeles has always been the different lifestyles you could experience in one sprawling city. From Downtown, to the Hollywood Hills, to the Pacific Ocean, there's something for everyone."
—John

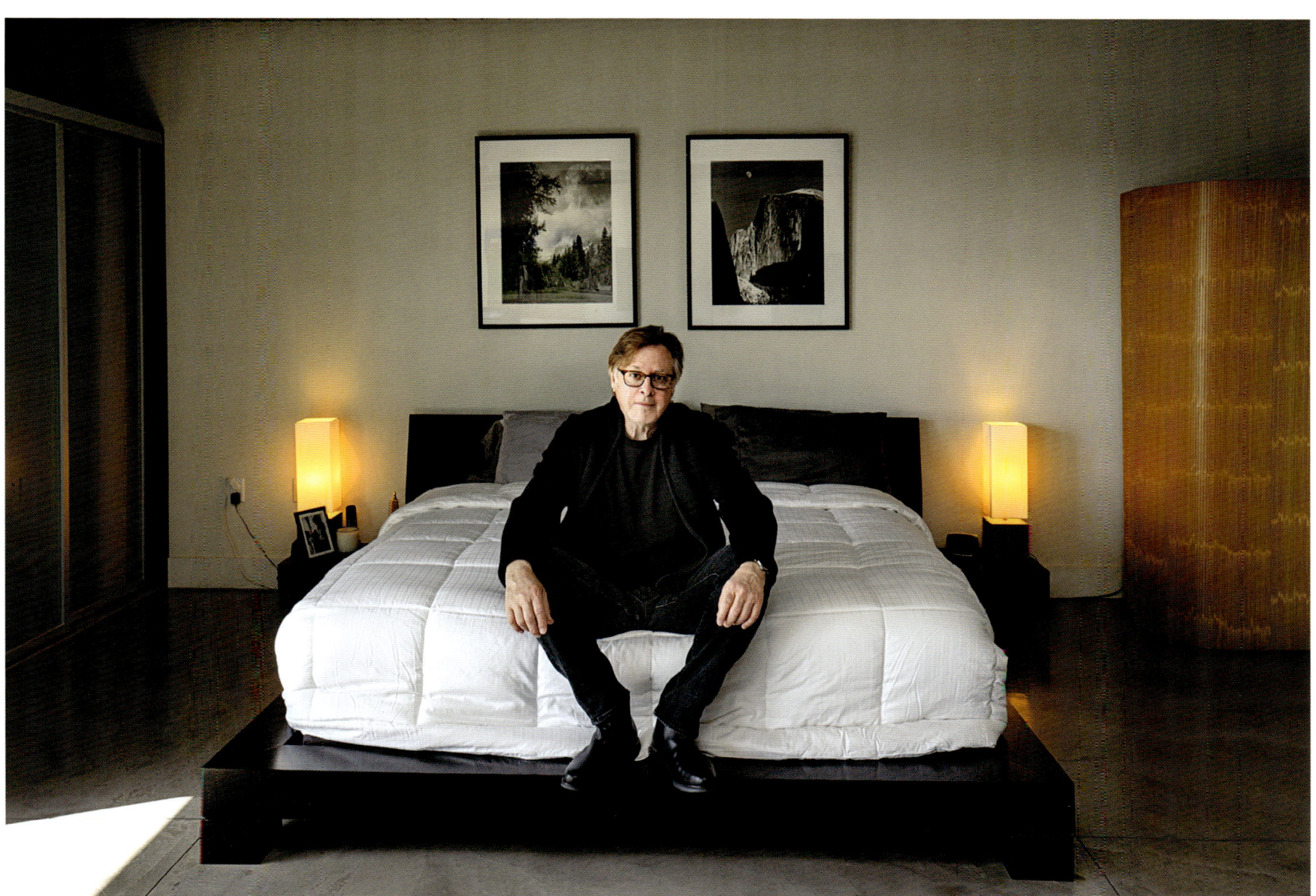

LOUIS JACINTO AND KENE ROSA

Photographed at their home in Beverly Grove on March 29, 2022.

Louis was born in Bakersfield, California in 1955. He was the oldest of four for Harriet and Catalino. Dad worked for the Santa Fe railroad and Mom was a homemaker. Louis spent his young years in Bakersfield. He wanted to work in the Empire State Building when he grew up, or be the Pope. He was a Boy Scout who stood up for himself and others, always fighting against things that were wrong. He did well at school, and took Mexican folk dancing. He worked selling newspapers after school with the other boys in the neighborhood and he worked at a butcher shop during high school. Louis moved to Los Angeles for college and when that was finished, he stayed. He worked for the local welfare department helping people get medical insurance who had psychiatric problems. During college he worked at the faculty lounge. The professors came in and got drunk during the afternoon and the more they drank, the more they tipped. When college was finished, Louis worked in social services, did photography, worked at a stock brokerage firm, as a photojournalist, as a grade-three teacher, and is now working in social services again. During all this, he continued to take photographs, which have been shown at galleries and museums. In 2020 Louis was named a Cultural Trailblazer by the city of Los Angeles and opened an online gallery to show the work of other artists.

Kene was born Kenneth Jacques Rosa in New York City in 1954. He was the 13th of 14 for Rafaela. Dad was a plumber and Mom was a seamstress. Kene spent his youth in the housing projects of Brooklyn. He wanted to be a shopkeeper when he grew up, then later he wanted to be an architect. He did well reading and writing at school and not so good with math and gym. He hung out with other artistic kids and was a member of the yearbook staff. He left home when he was 17 to live with his sister in Crown Heights until he graduated from college. He worked in a liquor store in the East Village. It was one street down from The Electric Circus and the famous Fillmore East, where he saw all the hippies. He also worked at an auction house. After college was done, Kene moved to the Bronx where he stayed for almost 20 years. In 1999, when he was 45 years old, he moved to California. He was offered a job at a fancy gallery but he was also really tired of the east coast weather. He worked for five years as the chief curator for an important gallery in Beverly Hills before retiring for health reasons. Now Kene is an art consultant.

In 2001 Kene and Louis met through a voice ad in *Frontiers* magazine. In 2009 they moved into this apartment together, where Johnny Lange, the famous Hollywood songwriter, lived for over 60 years.

"I enjoy that this is a walkable neighborhood with an abundance of amenities, including access to museums."
—Louis

"There is nothing bad to be said of the year-round 'vacation' weather we enjoy. Folks are flaky and looking to get something for nothing (old story!). The fact that 365 days of the year something is green and something is blooming is a godsend. Home is where YOU make it. Happiness is a choice! Things come to you when you make the space in your heart and soul. We all meet for a reason."
—Kene

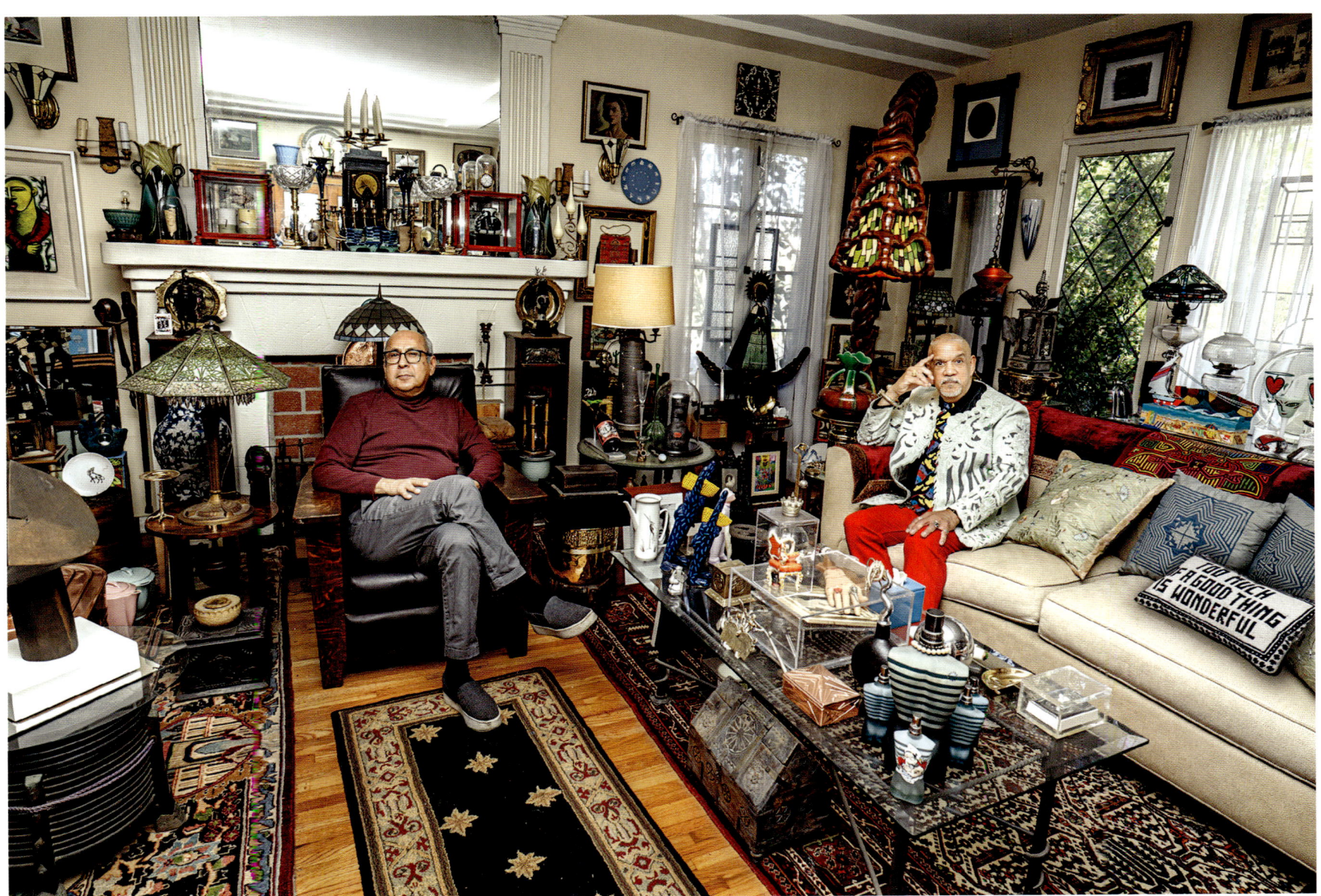

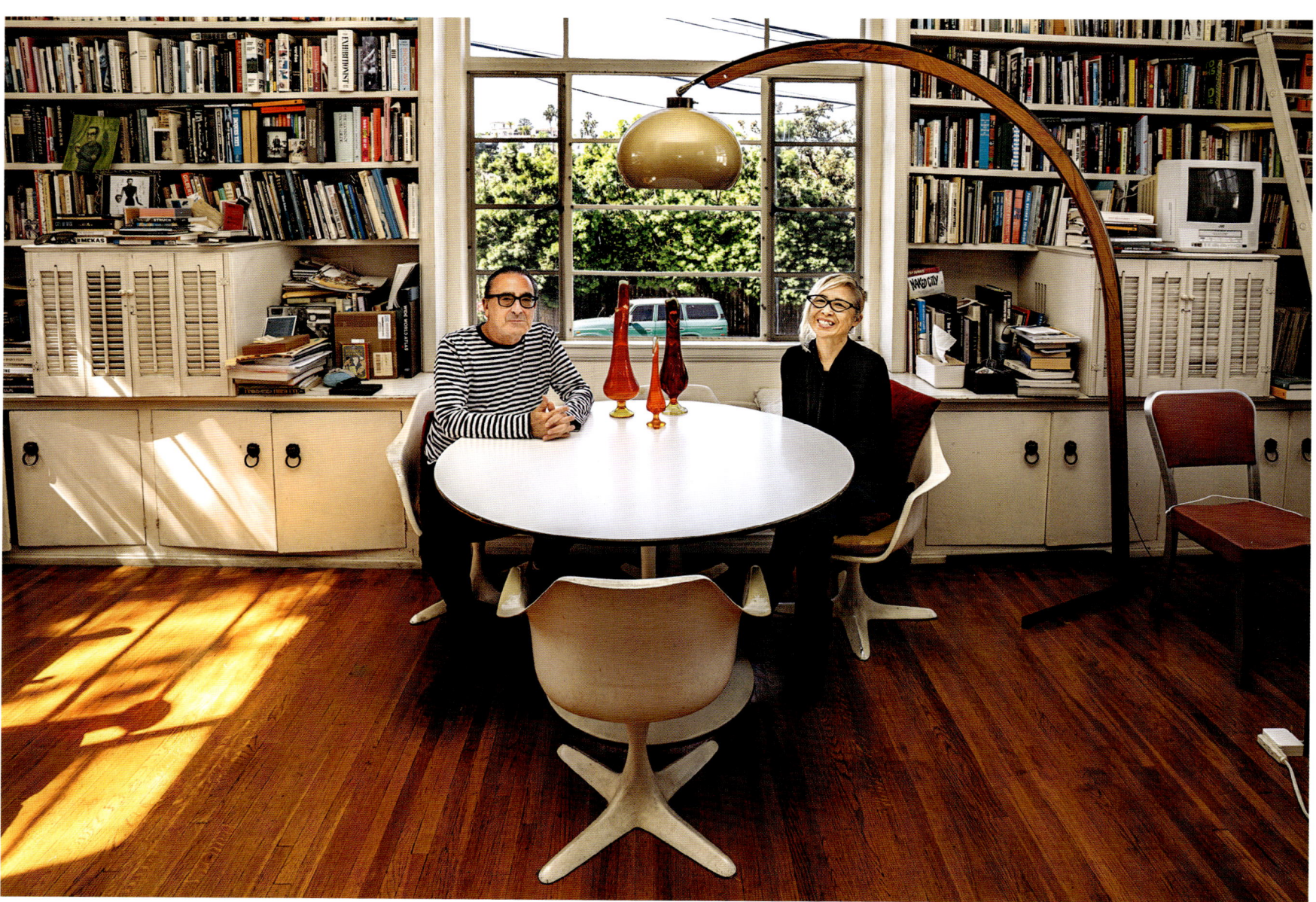

TOSH AND LUN*NA BERMAN

Photographed at their home in Silver Lake on March 18, 2022.

Tosh was born in 1954 in Los Angeles, California. He was an only child for Wallace and Shirley. Dad was an artist and Mom was a shopgirl. Dad died on his 50th birthday in a car accident. Tosh spent his young years in LA. He wanted to be an assassin when he grew up; he saw that on TV. He was bullied by his gym teachers and, generally speaking, didn't like school. When Tosh was 21 he left home and moved in with his girlfriend. He worked at the famous record store Licorice Pizza, at a bookstore, and was a publisher too. Now he mostly just writes, and has published three books. Tosh met his wife Lun*na Menoh at an opening for her artwork in 1988 and the same year they got married. They went to Japan on their honeymoon and a year later they went back and stayed for a year. They still return to Japan every year and Tosh thinks of Japan as his second home.

Lun*na was born in 1956 in Kitakyushu, Japan. She was the oldest of three for Ichiro and Hiroko. Both Mom and Dad were teachers. Lun*na spent her young years in Mojiko, Japan. She was a smart kid who wanted to be a dancer when she grew up. She excelled at looking good in early school years and then later in high school, at art, music, and gym. She swam, played basketball, and played the piano. When Lun*na was 18, she left home and moved to Tokyo to go to college. She studied film and fashion. After college was done, Lun*na stayed living there for several years. She made clothing sculptures and did performance art. In 1988 she and a fellow artist went to Los Angeles to do an exhibition. While she was there, she met Tosh, and they married that same year. Lun*na worked in Los Angeles as a wardrobe stylist, a designer, a driver, a writer, and a translator. She was a painter, a performance artist, and is now a musician. They moved into this house in 1997 and live there still.

They moved into this house in 1997 and live there still.

"Los Angeles is a remarkable location for life. I don't drive, so I walk a lot and there are many great neighborhoods to walk through. Silver Lake being one, and I'm very close to the Los Angeles River as well as Echo Park Lake. I enjoy other cities (NYC, Paris, Tokyo) but Los Angeles is unique."
—Tosh

"Everything is chaotic here compared to other big cities. There is no center, which I love. We can go in any direction; whatever we want physically and mentally. I love Silver Lake cos there are hilly parts in this area, gentle up and down around our house, which is unusual in Los Angeles."
—Lun*na

SHEILA SILBER

Photographed at home in Malibu on May 20, 2021.

Sheila was born in Youngstown, Ohio in 1945. She was the last of two kids for Bobby and Sam. Dad was a businessman and Mom was an electrologist who had her own shop. Sheila spent her childhood in Youngstown. She wanted to work with kids who had problems when she grew up, and that wish came true. She ended up being a probation officer for 40 years working with juveniles for a large part of her career. Dad had a large Daguerreotype and antique camera collection. As a little kid, Sheila would go with him to garage sales searching for that stuff. She was hooked way back then on thrifting and hunting for vintage. She was a good student but mostly she excelled at having fun and partying. She was very, very social. Sheila was the one who had the parties and everyone came. Her parents took a lot of vacations, usually leaving an aunt to watch over things. The aunt lived with them, and because she was deaf and mostly blind, she didn't know there were parties going on. Sheila loved golf and played it from junior high school right up until ten years ago, only calling it quits because arthritis set in. She left home at 17, headed for college at Michigan State, where she studied social work. She worked one holiday season wrapping Christmas gifts but she got fired because she was lousy at it. After college there was a ten-month trip to Europe before returning briefly to Ohio. Then in 1968 she headed west to Los Angeles and stayed. Within six months she got her job with LA County as a probation officer working with kids. The Charles Manson girls were there at the same time. They lied and said they were underage. Once the authorities realized they were 18, they were quickly moved to adult prison. In addition to her job, Sheila started buying and selling at flea markets. It was the sixties and Warhol's work was still $125. Her knack for flipping items quickly expanded and soon she was buying and selling art too. As she came to understand art's value, her flipping turned into keeping, and she became a collector. Sheila met her husband David at a flea market in 1994. He sold things that she collected. They got married in 1997, and moved into this house in 2001. They own a mid-century shop in Cathedral City.

"Malibu has not changed in the 21 years we have lived here. The municipality has lots of rules that control visual changes. So it looks much the same as it did when I moved here, which is wonderful. We are still in the Covid mindset—we don't go out that much."
—Sheila

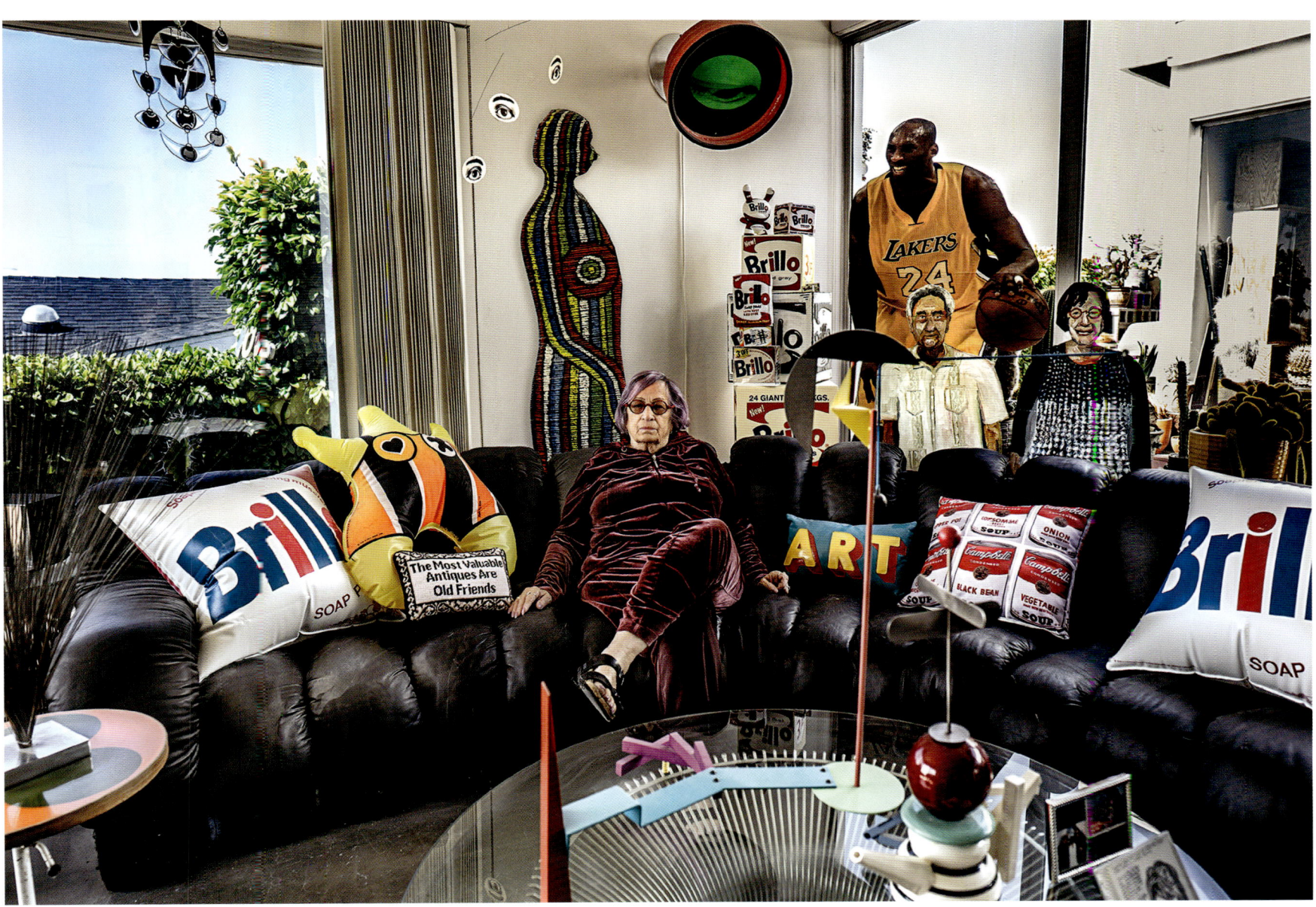

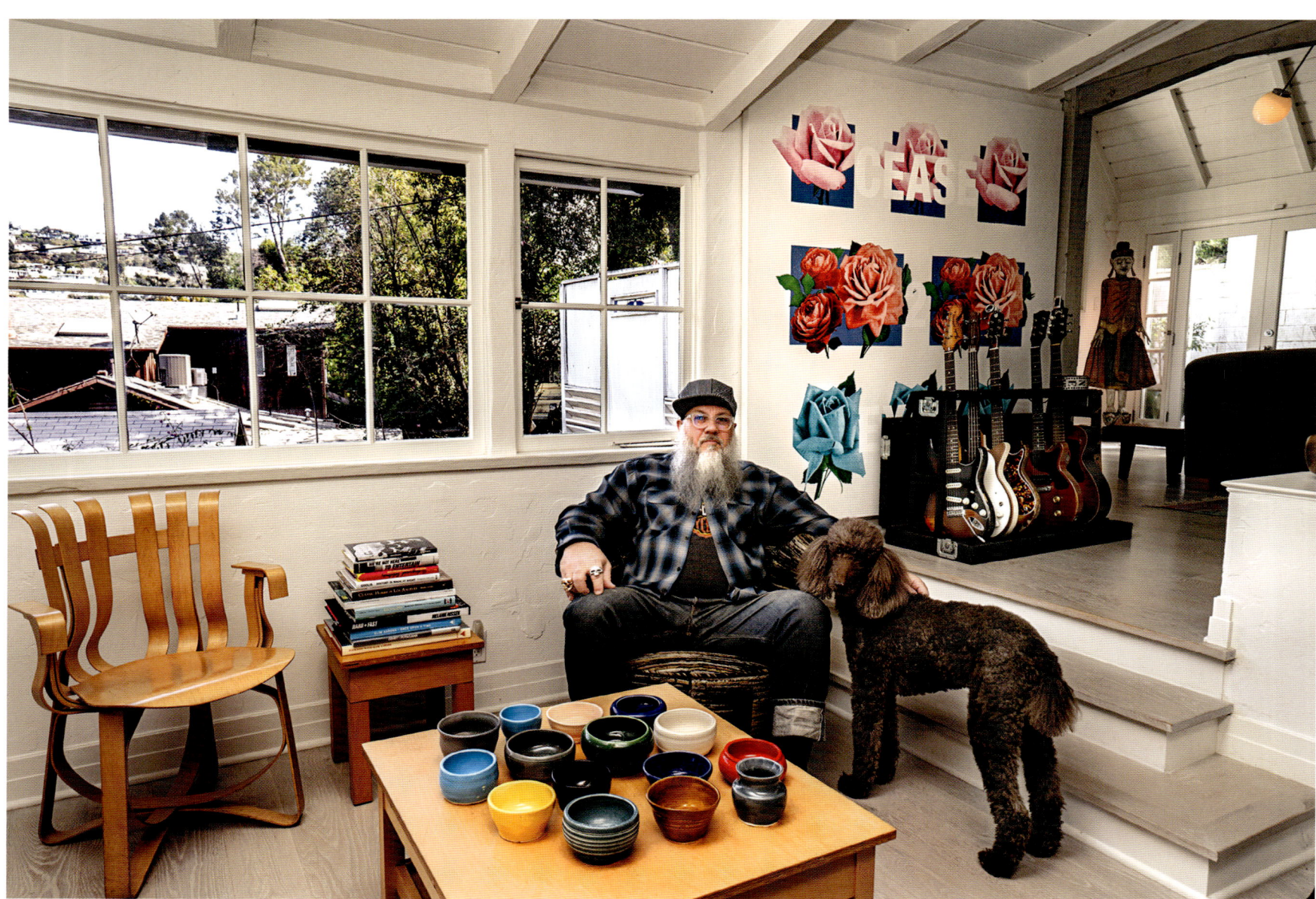

BRYAN RAY TURCOTTE

Photographed at home in Laurel Canyon on March 17, 2022.

Bryan was born in 1967 in San Jose. He was the oldest of two kids for Raymond and Sandra. Dad was an electrician and a bit of a biker tough guy, and Mom was a bookkeeper. Dad was French Canadian and Mom was from San Francisco. When Bryan was nine years old his parents divorced. He spent his young years in Los Gatos, near San Francisco. He wanted to be a marine biologist or a psychologist when he grew up. School came easy for Bryan and he did well there. He played soccer and loved to skateboard. He picked up his first guitar when he was 12 and started playing. Bryan left home when he was 18 for college. For all kinds of reasons, that didn't really work out, so he got a job and his own apartment in San Jose. In 1987 Bryan left there with $300, his guitar, and a little Karmann Ghia, and moved to Hollywood. He worked at a drive-in movie theater, worked as a cook, fumigated houses, was a referee for soccer games, was a line cook, a record store clerk, worked security at a music spot, and as a manager at a vintage clothing store. Bryan interned at a few record labels and then landed a job at Slash Records in 1989, going from mailroom to office manager. He also played bass in the band Black Market Flowers. In 1999 he started Kill Your Idols, an award-winning publishing company that made art books and zines. Then, in 2005 Bryan started a music company that produces music for big companies like Nike, Google, and Coca-Cola. Bryan's collection of punk memorabilia has been exhibited around the world. He writes as a freelance journalist for companies like *Vice* and *LA Weekly*, and is also a film director. In 1995 Bryan met Danya and in 2001 they got married. They have two sons—Ralston and Ford. In 2007 they bought this house and they live there still.

"LA is the best city in the world. Paris, Tokyo, and New York City are a close second for me."
—Bryan

ROB ZABRECKY

Photographed at home in Valley Village on February 20, 2022.

Rob was born in 1968 in Burbank, California. He was the youngest of three kids for Ralph and Renee. Mom was a wedding coordinator and Dad was a carpenter. Rob spent his young years in Burbank, dreaming of being a musician when he grew up. He didn't care too much about school and didn't do that well there. In high school he started a garage band and they did covers of The Kinks and Echo & the Bunnymen. Rob moved to Silver Lake when he was 21 and did four years at a community college. He worked at a paper route, at a restaurant, and at telemarketing, mostly getting fired from every job. After college was finished, he worked in a mail room for an entertainment company and played in bands. Once when he was touring with his band, he wandered into a magic shop in Baltimore, and that was it, he was hooked on magic. Rob met Tommi at a Hollywood party and in 1998 they got married. They moved into this house in 2012 and live there still. Rob is an actor and a magician.

"LA has always been home. I love it here. I love the variety of people and places. I could do without the traffic and sometimes the summers drag out, but you could say that about any city I guess."
—Rob

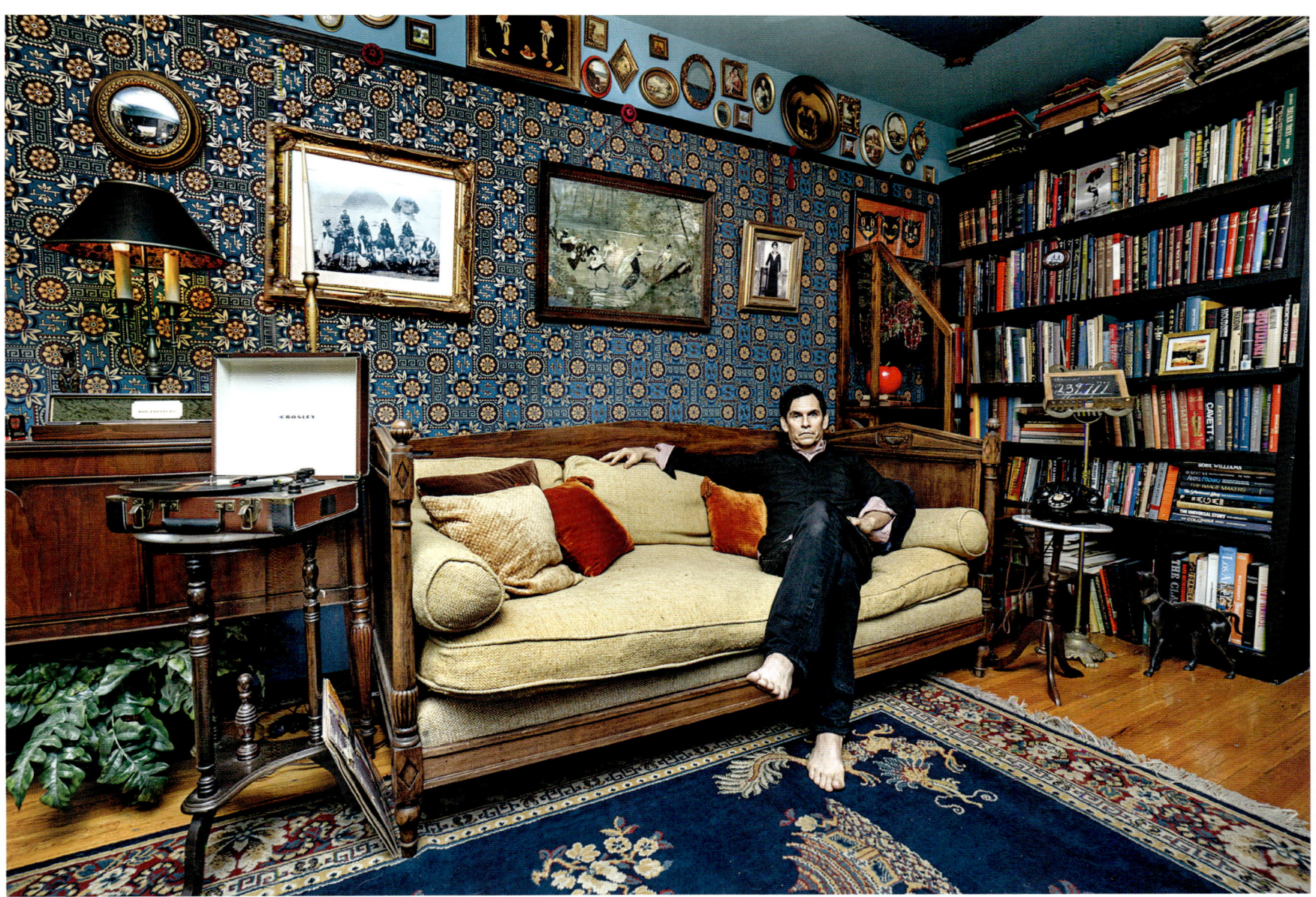

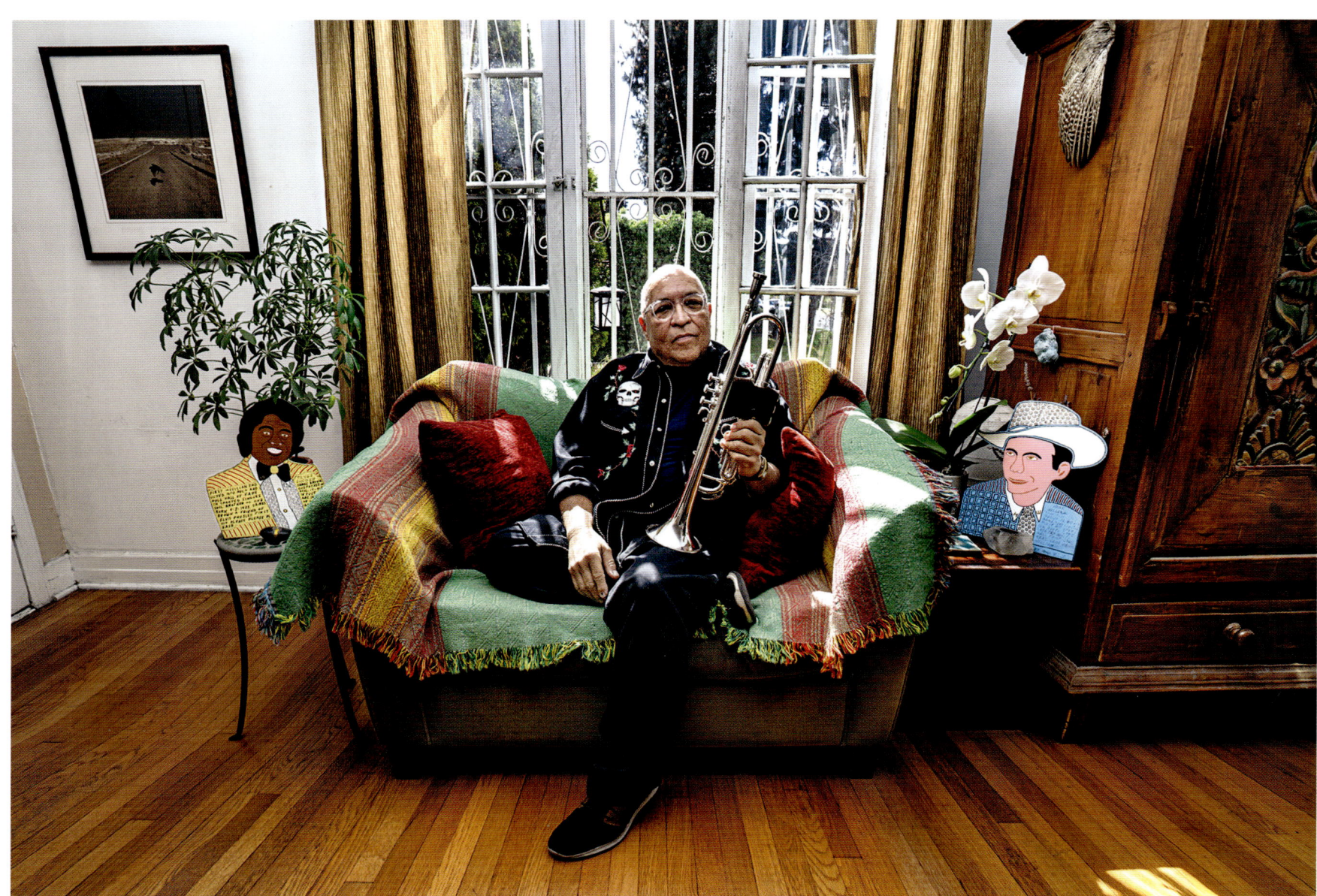

ED VALFRE

Photographed at home in Larchmont on February 22, 2022.

Ed was born in 1950 in San Antonio, Texas. He was the youngest of two boys for Ofelia and Ben. Dad was a postman and Mom worked at the five and dime. At night and on Sunday he played banjo in a New Orleans jazz band. Ed spent his young years in San Antonio. He was a terrible student who wanted to be a drummer and an astronomer when he grew up. During high school, he would play drums in bands until 2am, and still go to school the next day. He played trumpet in the school marching band, but he was happiest on drums. When Ed was 20 he left home for Austin, Texas, where he went to university and studied film for four years. Ed stayed in Austin for another four years, interning as a photographer after college at a local PBS station. He also worked as a projectionist at an art house theater. Sometimes he would let student friends in for free. One night he took mushrooms and went to work. He didn't notice that the movie broke at the end of *Harold and Maude*. Those viewers walked away thinking Harold drove his car off the cliff and died. They didn't see the real ending, which was a lot better. It was 1975 and Ed left Austin. He headed to Los Angeles on the suggestion of an actor friend he knew from school. Once there, Ed met a photographer from Japan who hired him as his assistant. Worried that commercial photography might impede progress on his own art, he segued into sound work for a TV station. He did that for 14 years, working on sitcoms, TV specials, and even the Academy Awards. Ed's brother Ben died in 1991, leaving him an inheritance, and the realization that life does not last forever. That same year, he took a buyout from the TV job and traveled the world for the next seven years. He worked non-stop on his photography, wrote two children's books, got married, and had his son Ben. Ed has exhibited his photography in Los Angeles, Rome, and Bologna. His well-known work "Dreamland" will soon be available as a book. Ed takes photographs every day. Ed and his family lived in Fairfax and Hollywood before moving into this house in 2015.

"What I love about this town is the amazing mix of cultures from all over the world. Art, food, language, and the beautiful faces of people from everywhere on the planet here with the idea of making a new life. I have met artists, actors, and musicians in my time here that make me aware that being creative makes you part of a community. Yes, this is not an easy place, but it is still a place of possibilities. I am living it. What I hate about the city is the homeless situation with rents rising and affordable housing impossible. The traffic is a factor, but I know all the small grids to avoid the worst of it."
—Ed

ALEKSEI TIVITSKY AND LENA MOROSS

Photographed at their home in Silver Lake on March 18, 2022.

Aleksei was born in 1955 in Moscow, Russia. He was the second of two boys for Ludmilla and Konstantine. Dad was a priest and Mom was a seamstress. Aleksei spent his youth in Moscow and wanted to be an artist when he grew up. He did badly at most things at school, but did really well at art. When Aleksei was 16 years old he left home and moved in with his brother and his wife because he wanted his independence. He supported himself by doing illustrations for a magazine. He went to college and studied art for a total of six or seven years. In 1978, Aleksei moved to Los Angeles with his family. His dad was a Russian orthodox priest and it was dangerous to stay there. Aleksei worked at a fiberglass company making swimming pools, and he worked the night shift at the Penny Saver loading newspapers onto trucks. He worked as an art conservator in Russia and Italy and continues that work in the United States. He has been married three times, and the third one was the charm. He lived in West Hollywood and Long Beach before moving in with Lena.

Lena was born in Saint Petersburg, Russia in 1956. She was the youngest of two kids for Nina and Sam. She spent her childhood years in Saint Petersburg. Lena was a quiet bookish kid who knew she wanted to be an artist when she grew up. She did badly at all other stuff in school, often skipping class to go to the movies. She took figure skating and gymnastics. In 1974 the family moved to Los Angeles because it wasn't safe for Jews to be in Russia, and her dad was afraid for his family. They had relatives living in Los Angeles so it was easy to move there and get started. After high school she attended university and studied art. She worked at amusement parks and painted murals during high school and college. Pretty soon after college, in 1979, Lena got married to a musician and had a daughter. Two years later they got a divorce. Lena and Aleksei met in 1981 when they were both married to other people. They met because their parents were close friends. Lena works as a professional artist.

Aleksei and Lena started living together in 1994 in this West Hollywood apartment and they got married in 1995.

"Los Angeles is my home. I don't understand people who live somewhere for so many years and say they hate it. I work here, I live here, my family is here. It took many years to establish myself here. I feel comfortable in Rome, I feel comfortable in Scotland, but Los Angeles is my home (although I can do away with the distances and the traffic in Los Angeles). Every day, I come home and enjoy the view from where we live in West Hollywood on the seventh floor. It is a great city view. Most of all, I enjoy living in Los Angeles to be close to my grandson, Sammy. He is the BEST."
—Aleksei

"LA is not invasive. Not imposing like European cities or New York. I dislike the architecture, I dislike the good weather. I dislike that people put emphasis on material things like cars, bags, etc. I dislike the traffic, to go to my favorite spot in the city it takes God knows how long. I have complicated thoughts on gentrification. The neighborhood our studio is in, is a very good example. When we first moved into our studio, which is located in the West Adams district, there was a great deal of crime, drugs, overall a dangerous neighborhood. And yes, it was cheap. Over the last 20 years, it began to blossom. Black-owned galleries and restaurants populated the street and middle-class professionals began to open their offices. These Latino and African American cultures united and the community feel is strong. Yes, it is more expensive, but overall I think it did more good than bad."
—Lena

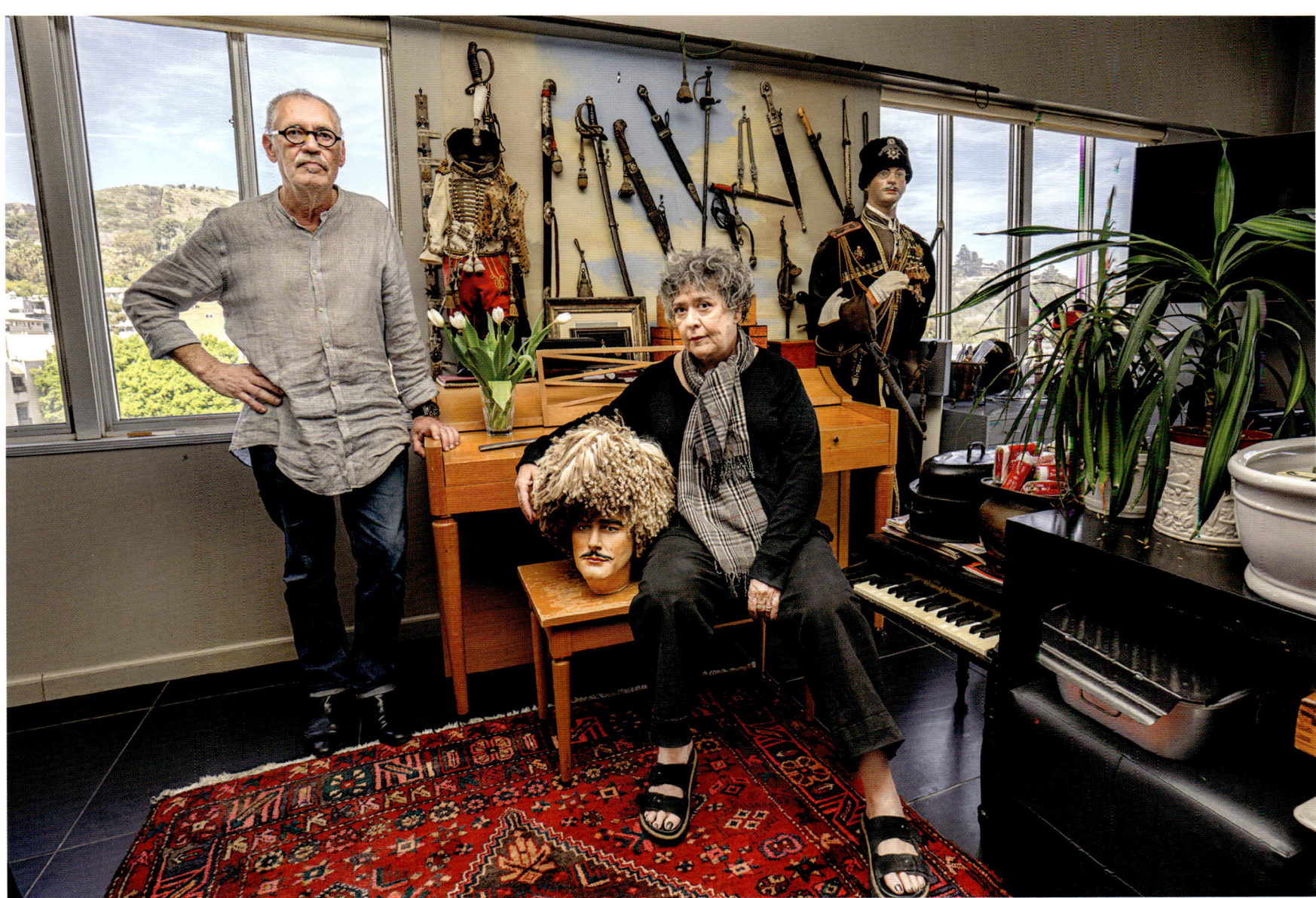

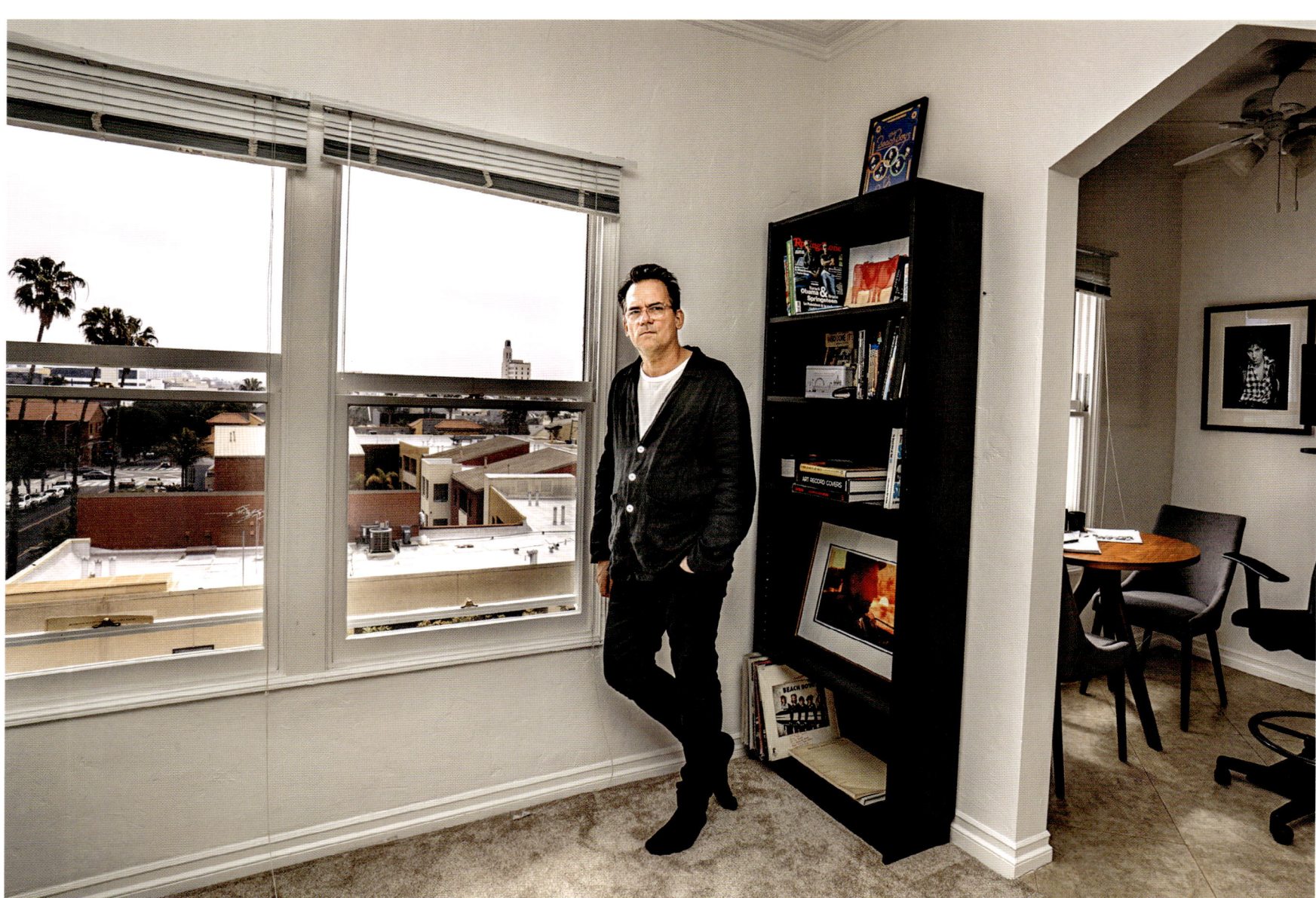

THOM ZIMNY

Photographed at home in Santa Monica on March 26, 2022.

Thom was born in Elizabeth, New Jersey in 1965. He was the second of three boys for Helen and Edward. Mom was a legal secretary and Dad was a carpenter. Thom was a quiet kid who grew up with his dog on the Jersey Shore. He was dyslexic so he didn't do so well at school, except for art—he was really good at that. He loved music, and loved to play basketball and baseball. When Thom was 20 he moved from the Jersey Shore to Manhattan and studied film there for five years. He worked at an Irish tavern, duplicated tapes and cassettes, and he interned at a documentary film company. When college was done, Thom stayed in New York working in film, as an editor for TV shows, and then as an Emmy and Grammy award-winning documentary filmmaker. He has directed films on Elvis Presley, Johnny Cash, and has made seven Bruce Springsteen documentaries. Thom has three kids, and splits his time between Brooklyn and California. He moved into this apartment in 2021 and lives there still.

"Been wanting to live here for a very long time. I find it to be the inspiration reboot that is needed, as cliché as that sounds. It's the perfect environment; I love the light and I love the opportunity to be a stranger. Gentrification saddens me: when the soul of a neighborhood is taken away."
—Thom

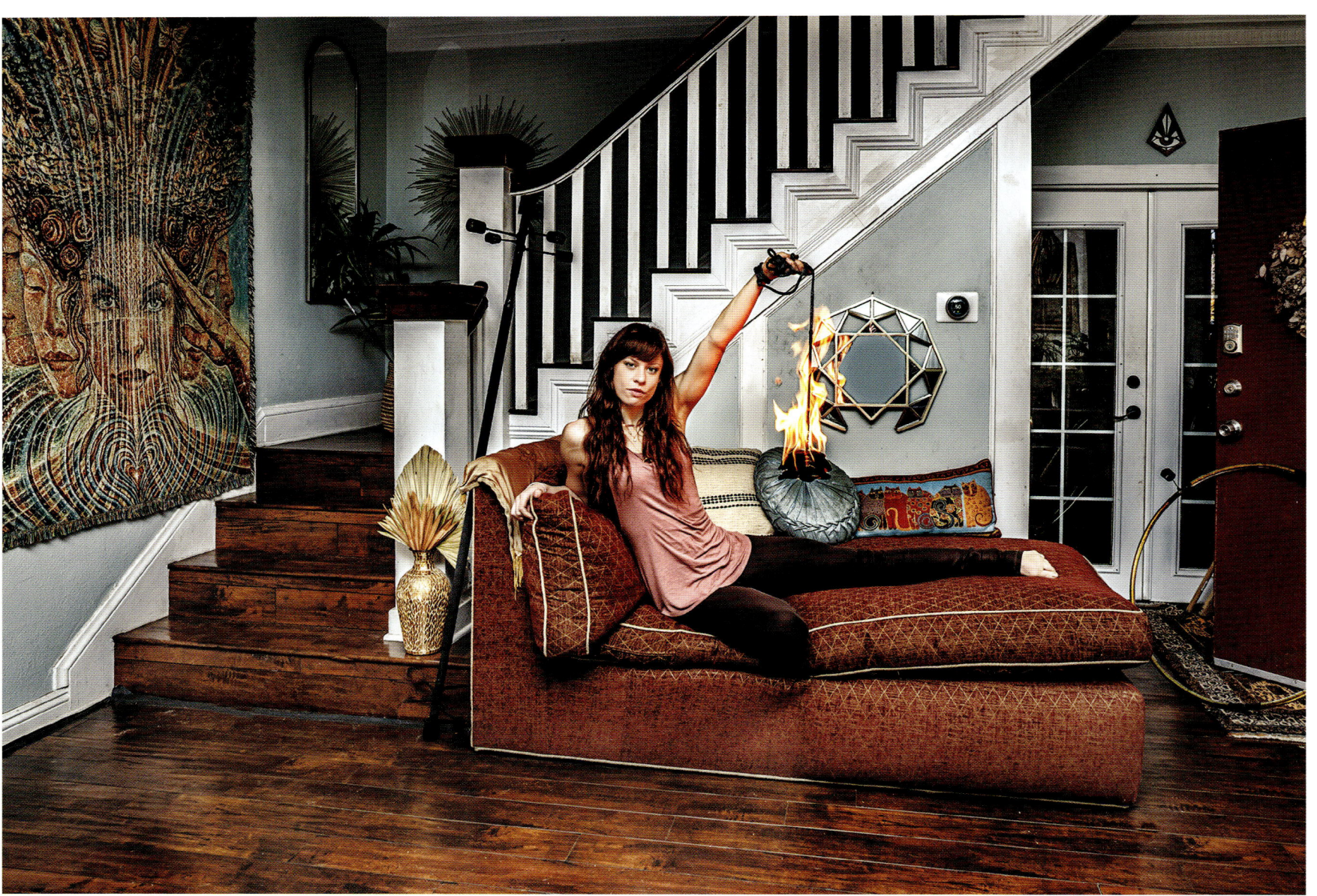

SAM TOBEY

Photographed at home in Los Angeles on March 5, 2022.

Sam was born Suzanne Tobey in Portland, Oregon in 1992. She was the oldest of two for Rebecca and Laurence. They both worked for the Foreign Service. The family moved a lot, living in a different country every three years. Sam spent most of her younger years in French school. Her mom was a fanatic about language and wanted Sam to learn as many as she could. She was an awkward, impulsive kid, with self-described attention deficit disorder. She never spoke the languages well so to compensate she made cat noises and hugged people too much. She did ok at school and wanted to be an artist when she grew up. She was very athletic and found sports to be a great outlet for her aggressive teenage angst. Sam played volleyball and lacrosse and did cross-country too. She went to a New England boarding school for high school, so she was out of her parents' home at the early age of 14. At 18, she moved to Santa Barbara for college and graduated in 2014. She worked mostly at restaurants and bars, even for a while after college was finished. After that she moved to Los Angeles. She lived in her car for a year and a half while learning to fire dance. Sam went to festivals and Burning Man and soaked up as much of the fire dance culture as she could. She trimmed marijuana during the fall seasons, and picked up a number of strange Craigslist gigs for the rest of the year. She also did fantasy wrestling, domination, and other BDSM gigs … interesting, but never illegal. Nowadays, Sam makes her living with her fire-dancing performances. She specializes in a medieval kung-fu weapon called the rope cart. It was featured in *Kill Bill* and in Jackie Chan movies. In 2020 Sam moved into this Mid City house with other festival people. They consider themselves a conscious community. They have house meetings, parties, open mics, and they like to garden.

"I love and adore California. I could not see myself living anywhere else. I feel like I finally found home after all of those years of traveling when I was younger."
—*Sam*

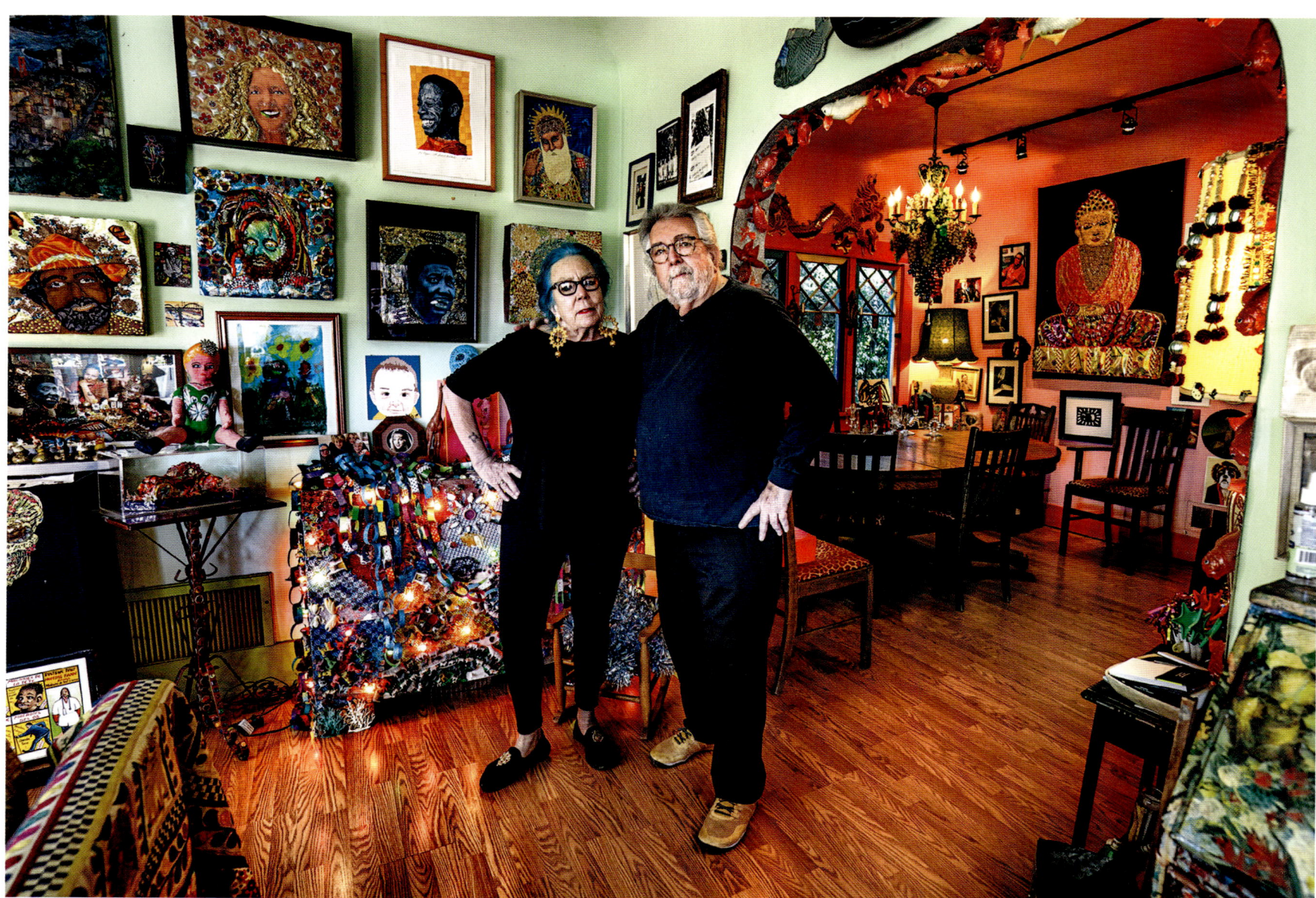

INGRID GRUNEWALD AND HARVEY KORNSPAN

Photographed at their home in Silver Lake on March 18, 2022.

Ingrid was born in Los Angeles in 1942. She was the first born for Natalie and Dietrich. She had a half-brother and one stepsister. When she was six her parents got a divorce. She spent her young years growing up in LA and then when she was five, moved to San Francisco. Ingrid was a fun-loving kid. She had a strong imagination and a large capacity for high jinks. She had dogs and parakeets that she named after people in operas. She thought she wanted to be a nun when she grew up, but later changed that to an artist. When she wasn't in school she learned classical dance, swimming, and tennis. Ingrid went to college right after high school in San Francisco and then returned to LA where she took art classes at night. Next up was a fun year in Europe before returning to New York, working at *Time* magazine as an assistant photo editor. Nine months later she moved back to San Francisco, where she met Harvey. He wanted to break into the movie business so they headed down to Los Angeles. Ingrid is an artist, raised her two daughters, had a catering business, was an art director for the TV show *Dinner and a Movie*, and taught art.

Harvey was born in 1941 in Youngstown, Ohio. He was the middle of three for Sam and Celia. Mom was a homemaker and Dad was a businessman. Harvey spent his young years in Youngstown. He was a very popular kid who wanted to be an engineer when he grew up. He studied violin but wasn't all that good at it. Harvey left home when he was 17 and moved to Madison, Wisconsin for college. He studied philosophy and science. He worked serving food and washing dishes in the cafeteria, and worked summers at his father's used car lot. Harvey headed east after college, to New York City, and stayed there for one year working for the welfare department as a case worker. At 23 he moved to San Francisco to go to law school. That was short lived and he left school after six months. He worked as a counselor at Marin juvee hall, managed a mime troupe, managed the Steve Miller Band, and managed a theater. In 1969 they moved to Los Angeles. He started working as a production manager and then as a director at CBS, signing the Steve Miller Band to Capitol in 1967 with a historic contract that he wrote. They have two daughters. Harvey retired in 2008.

Harvey and Ingrid met in San Francisco in 1966 and in 1976 they got married in Mexico. They moved into this house in 1976 and live there still.

"LA is divine. I have grown to love LA because of the accessibility to so many different cultures. But with gentrification, I have seen so many neighborhoods change, mostly for the worse, and so many gorgeous houses torn down ... definitely not a fan."
—Ingrid

"LA has a diverse city life, very sophisticated, but I hate traffic and homelessness."
—Harvey

KATHRYN SOLÓZANO

Photographed at home with her dog Lola in Marina del Rey on March 19, 2022.

Kathy was born in East LA in 1961. She was the second of four kids for Edward and Erma. Ed was a lawyer and an electrical engineer and Mom taught English as a second language. Kathy spent her young years growing up in the suburbs of Montebello. She was a good kid—shy, funny, Catholic, studious, and artistic in an unsophisticated way. She was the president of her class every year in high school and was student body president in senior year. In her junior year she went to Japan for 30 days, as one of two student ambassadors. Kathy took oil painting classes when she was 12, but doesn't have time to paint anymore. She worked at McDonald's, at a car wash, and at The Gap. She worked at an industrial medical clinic later, while she attended law school, and was an assistant in the legal department at an entertainment agency before she passed the California bar exam. Kathy was Deputy District Attorney for Los Angeles County for over 17 years, prosecuting all kinds of cases, including sex crimes and gang murders. She has been a Superior Court judge for Los Angeles County since 2007. It's her 15th year on the bench and she is up for re-election this year. Kathy is the first and only owner of this loft, and has lived here since 2008.

"In my younger years, whenever I flew into LAX, I felt relieved to see miles and miles of suburbs and freeways and lights and pools and cars. I always uttered to myself: 'I love this town'. The aerial view of the middle-class communities fill me with a feeling of belonging and relief, and I still feel that I belong here because my family is here and we all grew up here. I am privileged to live in this incredibly diverse city. The diversity is what makes LA a great place to call home, hands down. I really loved the eight years I spent in West Hollywood. That was in my thirties and early forties. The neighborhood is largely gay. Although I am not gay, I enjoyed living in this community. I found the residents to be independent, cool, non-judgmental, and tolerant. When I was diagnosed with breast cancer at the age of 40, I felt left alone, but also supported. I lost my hair while going through chemo, and I wore a wig, but it was hot and scratchy and I was miserable, so I would go to the West Hollywood Pavilions Supermarket and walk the aisles: bald, no wig, no bra, with my new asymmetrical chest, and no one seemed to notice. I love anywhere in LA where I can get lost, and you can get lost in LA."
—*Kathy*

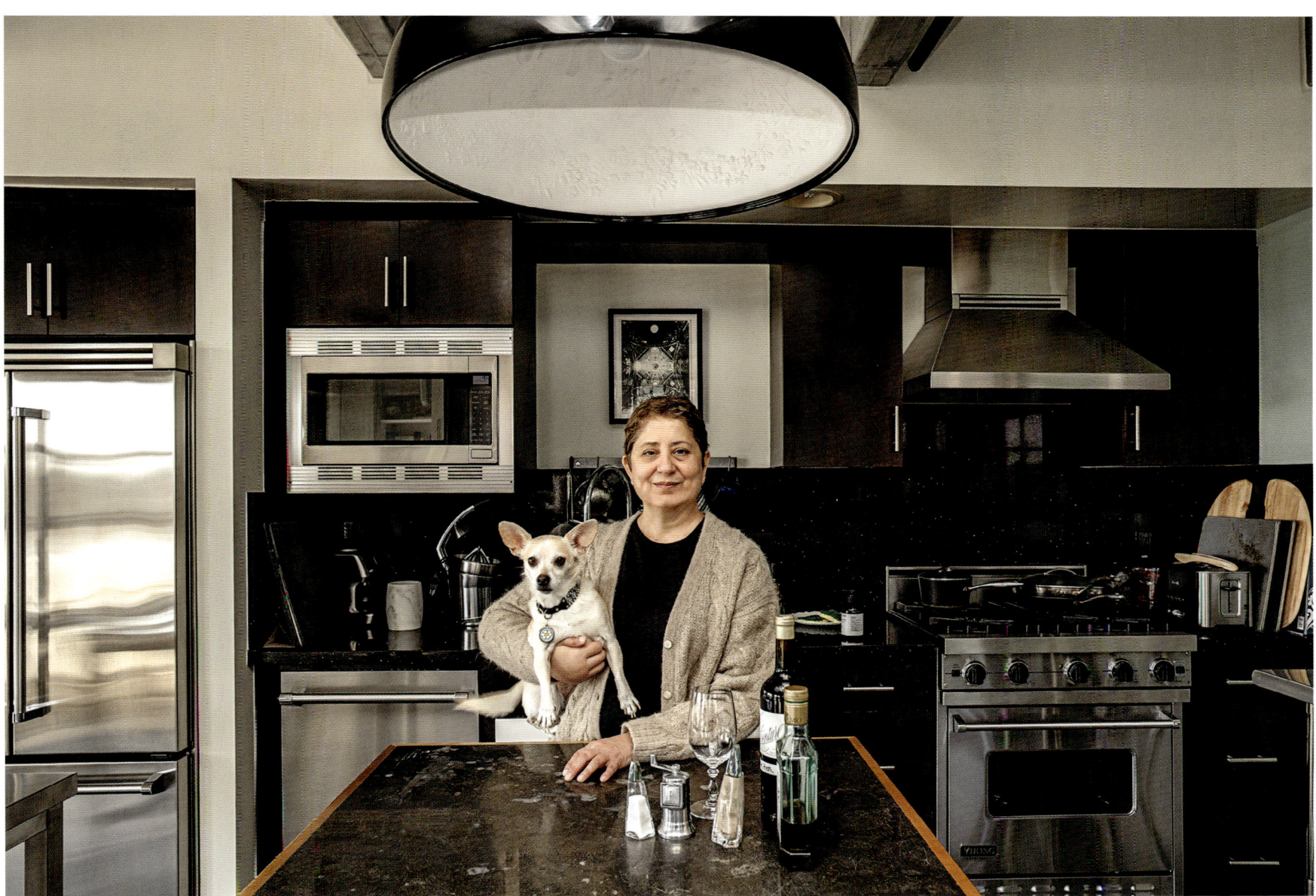

PAMELA DES BARRES

Photographed at home in Reseda on March 30, 2022.

Pamela was born Pamela Ann Miller in Reseda, California in 1948. She was the only surviving baby of five for Margaret Ruth and Oren Coy. Dad liked to be remembered as a gold miner. Pamela spent her young years with her pet dogs and cats in the Valley. She is a Virgo and makes lists from time to time. She always loved the boys and went steady in the third grade. When she was in the 11th grade she met Captain Beefheart, and that changed everything. She read, kept a diary, loved Elvis, Dion, and The Beatles, and she took modern dance to avoid gym classes and showering. Her first job was at a toy factory dipping rubber Batman and Robin boots into little bottles of paint, and she was Moon and Dweezil Zappa's nanny for a few years too. Pamela moved out of the family house when she was 19 and moved into a Hollywood apartment with a woman who was a rock 'n' roll photographer. She took some writing classes at university and when college was done, she stayed in Hollywood. She was a music freak and joined an all-girl group that was produced by Frank Zappa. Pamela acted in B-movies and a soap opera. She met her ex on a film shoot in New York while playing herself. They had a son together before separating in 1987. She started writing her hit book *I'm with the Band* when she was 35, and has published five more books since then. She teaches women's memoir workshops, holds rock tours of Hollywood and Laurel Canyon, and has a podcast. She moved into this house in 2017 and lives there still.

"I loved living on the West Side for 35 of the last 48 years and I miss the fresh, cool air but I've always enjoyed the Valley. The streets are wide, less traffic, easy to get around on the Valley grid, anything you need on any street, all amenities a block away. It is getting hotter every year, however, at least ten degrees higher than when I was a child. I have a great big patio and have music gigs and still dance my ass off."
—Pamela

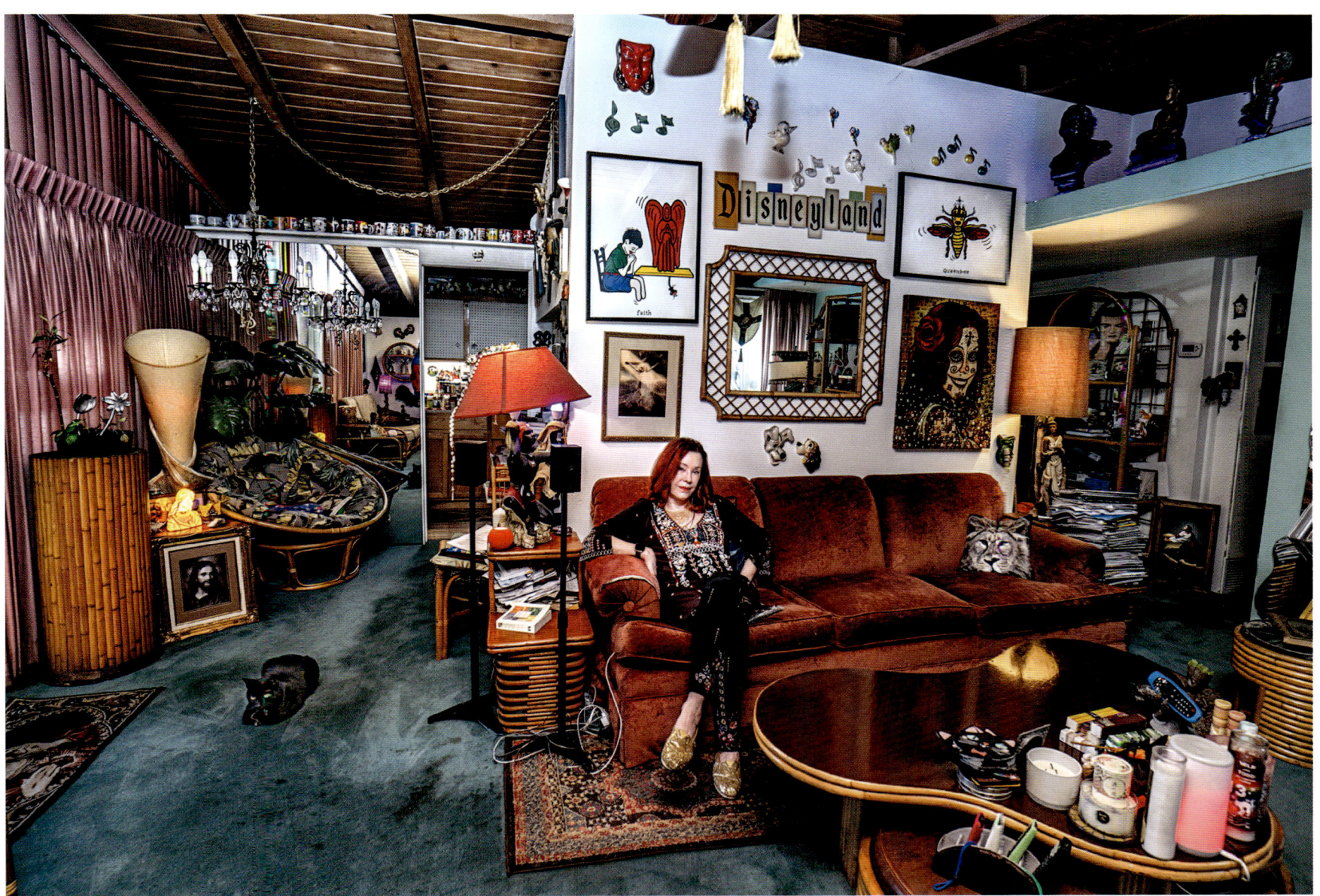

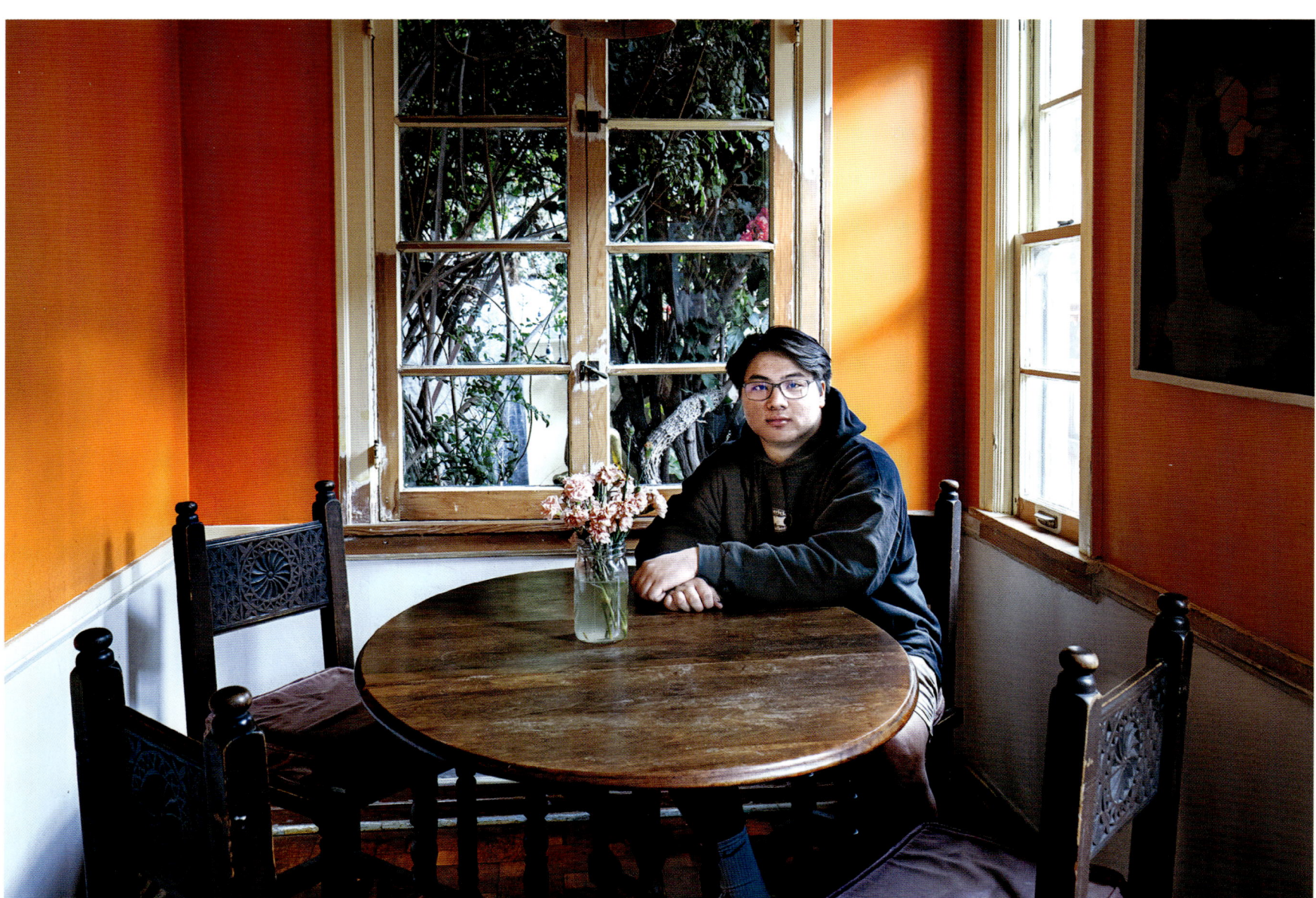

VIN STRATTON

Photographed at his aunt Susan's house in Los Angeles on March 5, 2022.

Vin was born in Ho Chi Minh City, Vietnam in 2002. When he was three months old Bob and Sandra adopted him. He has one older sister. Dad owned an interactive lighting design company and Mom was an art teacher. Vin spent his young years growing up in Brooklyn, New York. When he was ten years old they all moved to Bangkok, Thailand. They stayed there for seven years, then moved back to the United States. They lived in San Diego for a couple of years, then Vin started art college in Santa Clarita, and the rest of them returned to New York. He was a popular kid who loved to dance and he played lots of baseball, soccer, and later, rugby. He wanted to be a professional gamer when he grew up, but that morphed into a love of video production and filmmaking. The family would sometimes spend the summers out east on Block Island where Vin worked at a bike rental and repair store, and where he also drove a truck. Vin lives sometimes at his aunt Susan's in Los Angeles, and also in Santa Clarita where he studies photography at college.

"There is no doubt that the state of California is absolutely beautiful when it comes to natural scenery and weather. However, after living in dense cities for most of my life, coming to California was hard. After living in San Diego for most of the pandemic, I struggled to build a life here, but as things begin to open up, I am exploring the city more and I'm building a relationship with it. I think one of the hardest parts about living in California is how spread out it is. I am still getting used to the constant driving. I love the beach and the constant warm weather, most of the time. I love the carefree lifestyle. I think there are amazing photo opportunities here in California. I hate how expensive everything is."
—Vin

DONALD DIERS

Photographed at home in Los Angeles on May 29, 2021.

Donald was born in Walnut Creek, California in 1958. He was the last of four kids for Charles and Ethel. Mom was a homemaker and a painter, and Dad was a contractor who remodeled homes in the San Ramon Valley. Mom and Dad both hailed from rural Iowa. Donald spent his young years in San Ramon. He wanted to be a filmmaker when he grew up. He excelled at all things creative in school and was not so good at math and science. He was the editor of the yearbook, a photographer, and president of the international club. He was always on the swim team. When Donald was 21 he left home and moved to Los Angeles to go to college. It was 1980 and he was going to study film at UCLA. Don worked doing construction with his father, and later at UCLA he taught film and photography. Right out of college he started in the movie biz as a production assistant. He was a production assistant on *Nightmare on Elm Street* and worked on lots of horror movies after that. Over the years he worked his way up from the production office to being a very successful set decorator. Don is getting ready to open a shop where he will be selling mostly vintage paintings. Don and his husband Taylor foster and rehabilitate baby squirrels. They currently have an 11 week old named Barnabas that they just started releasing into the backyard. He bought this house in 2000. He met Taylor Goodrich in 2009 and five years later they got married in the backyard garden.

"I love Los Angeles. The weather and lights are so beautiful, and I love the open space. My backyard is very sacred to me. I also love living in the city, and these can sometimes be opposed to each other, but Los Angeles lets me have both things. The neighborhood we live in is becoming very gentrified. When I moved here, it was controlled by gangs and largely not desirable. In the past five years it's really shifted and become quite expensive and cosmopolitan. The gentrification of our neighborhood is a natural consequence of living in a very arty area. Artists and filmmakers have lived in this area for a long time, so a Whole Foods, Aesop, and Lassen's are inevitably going to follow. When I first moved here, it was my dream that the neighborhood would change and I've been here long enough to see that happen."
—Don

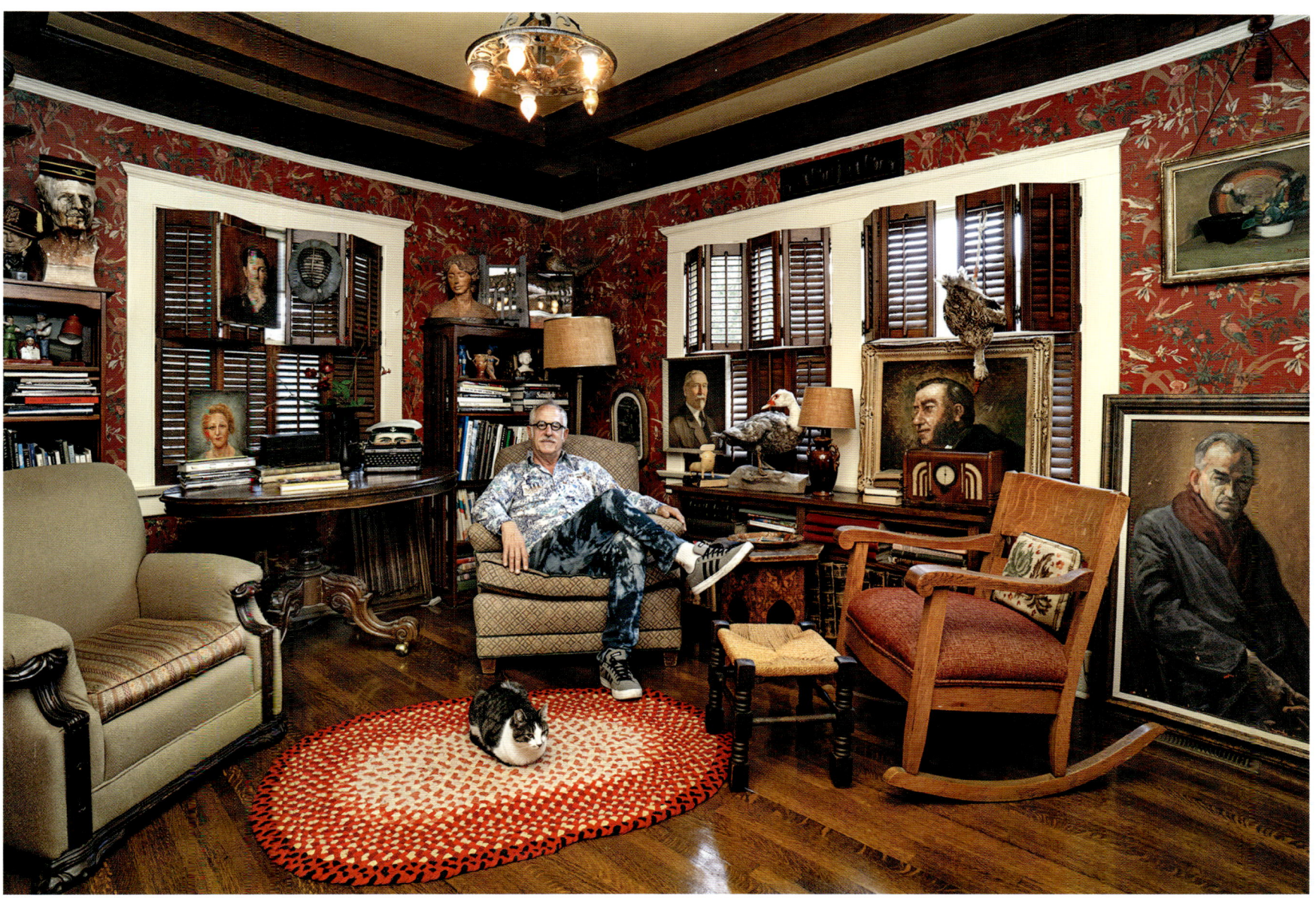

JANE SHIRKES

Photographed at home in Glassell Park on May 15, 2021.

Jane was born in Brooklyn, New York in 1948. She was the oldest of two girls for Rita and Ralph. Mom was a homemaker, taught piano, had a small creative business, and was a champion golfer. Dad sold mutual funds and insurance. Jane spent her first five years in Brooklyn then moved to Westchester. When she was a teenager, she played basketball, tennis, and took modern dance. Jane left home after high school for Carnegie Mellon college in Pittsburgh, to study art and design. Five years later she graduated, and a year after that she got married. They moved to New York City briefly, then to Pittsburgh. Jane got a job as a material designer for the public school system there and not long after that, got a divorce. She played the dulcimer and was in a band for a while before heading west, first to San Francisco, then to Sonoma County where she stayed for ten years. Jane worked in Pittsburgh making creative toilet seat covers, in northern California planting seedlings at a tree nursery, sold her ceramic work, and worked as a window dresser for a shop called Sweet Potato in Santa Rosa. Jane grew three marijuana plants, and sold the pot. With the money, she moved to Los Angeles at 41 years old, hoping to get work in the movie biz. She worked doing this and that, sometimes for free, for about nine months until she got a job as a set decorator. She did that for 29 years, first in music videos, then TV commercials, a few movies, and finally TV sitcoms. Jane is a sculptor and has lived in this house since 1998.

"LA has been good to me in its offerings in the film industry, places to live, and good friends. I found myself an oasis to live so I am far away from the city vibes. LA is toooo youth oriented and filled with selfish people who are egocentric and only concerned with their success. The beach and the mountains are so close, there is a lot of culture here and cultural diversity."
—Jane

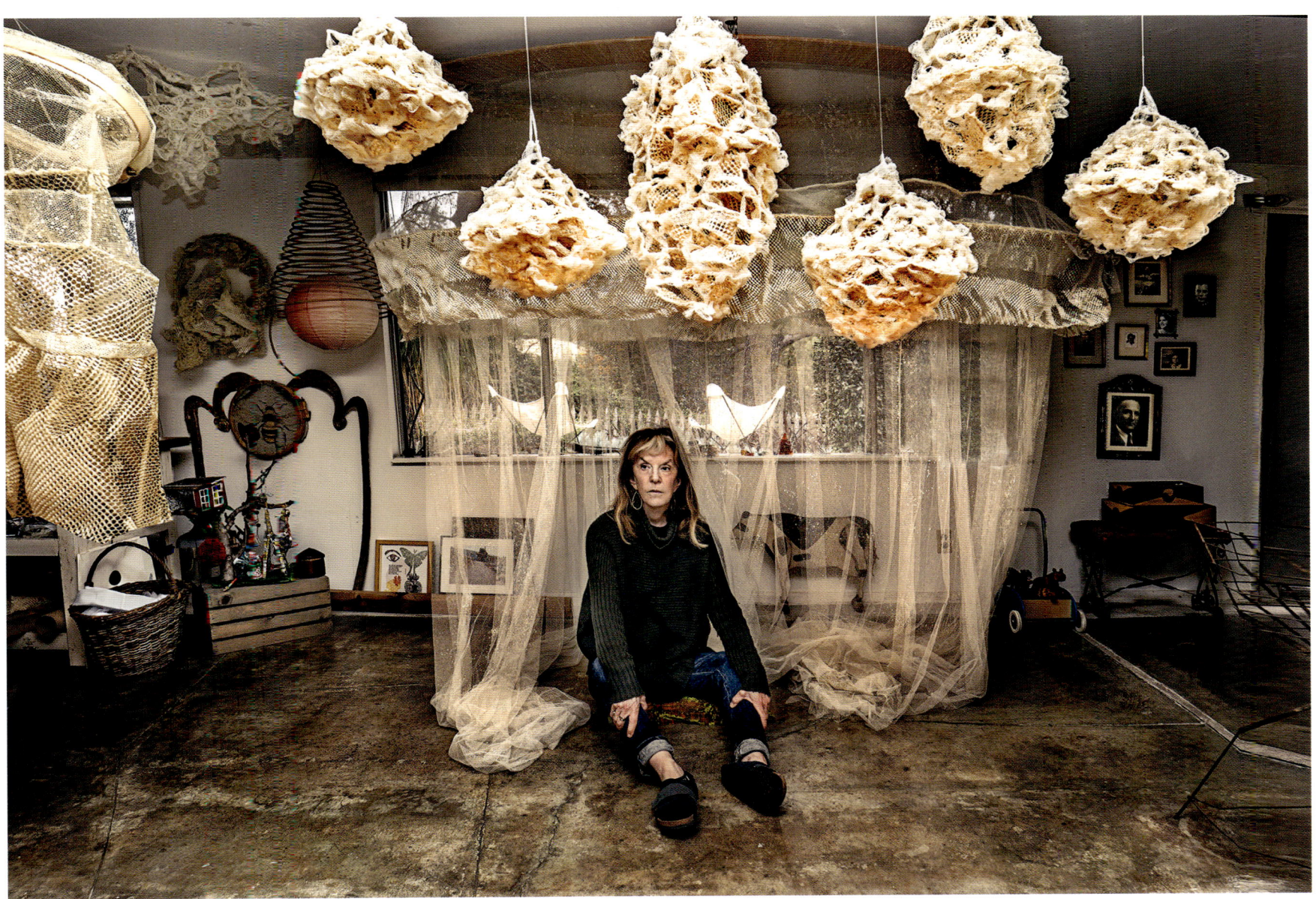

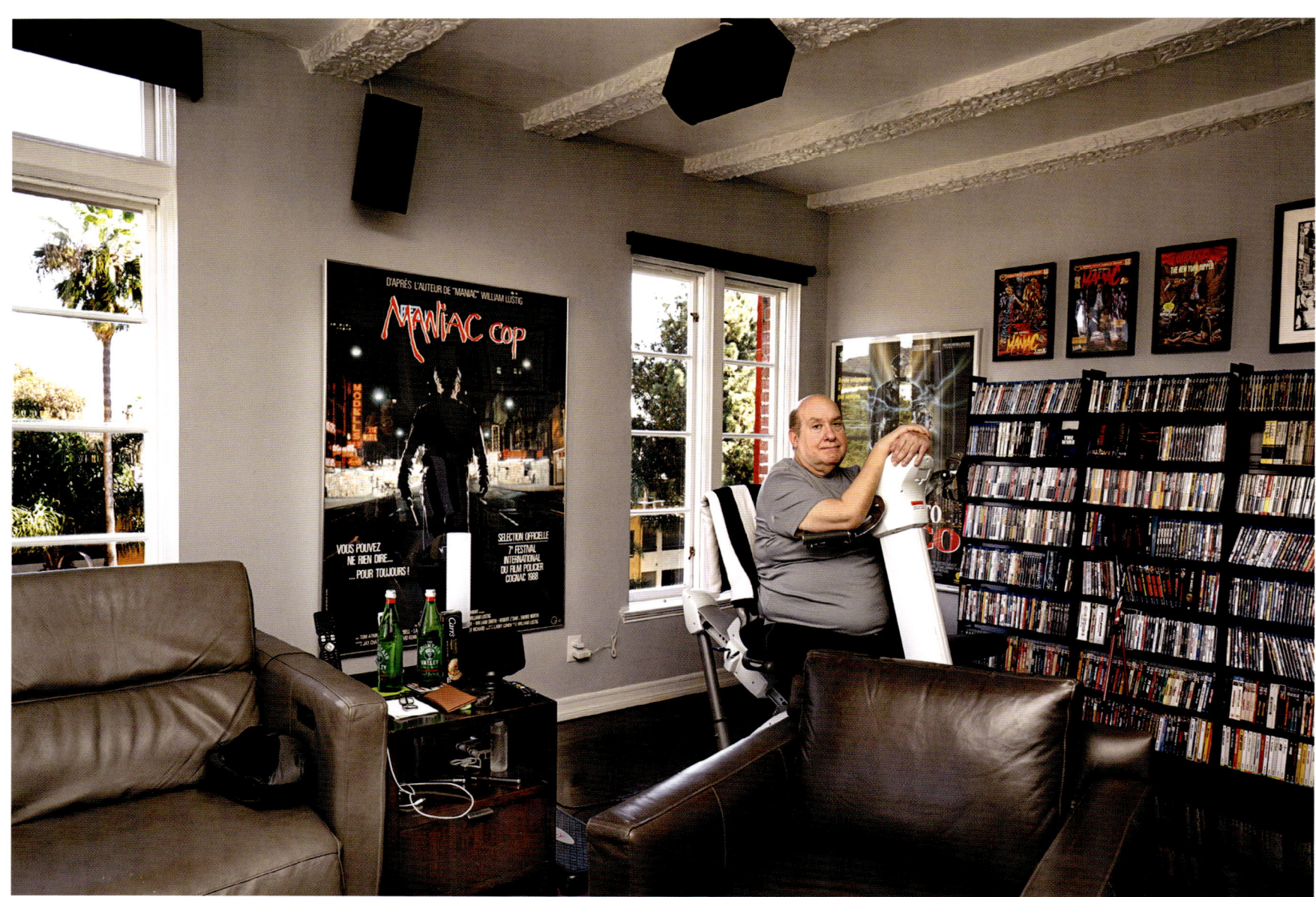

BILL LUSTIG

Photographed at home in Los Angeles on February 18, 2022.

Bill was born in the Bronx, New York in 1955. He was the oldest of two boys for Albert and Maria. Dad worked in direct mail advertising and Mom was a chiropractor. His mom's brother was Jake LaMotta—the former middleweight boxing champion. Bill spent his youth in the Bronx but when he was seven, they all moved to New Jersey. He was a quiet kid who wanted to be a movie director when he grew up. He didn't do that well at school and dropped out at 18. During high school Bill worked as a production assistant and as an assistant film editor on lots of movies, including some porn. He left home when he was 21 and took two semesters of film production at New York University. He worked as a ticket scalper, a theater usher, delivered auto parts, serviced pool tables and pinball machines, and drove a taxi too. Bill stayed in New York until he was 32, and in 1987 he headed west to Los Angeles. He worked as a producer and director mostly in horror movies, and sometimes acted in them. In the 1990s Bill started the home media company Blue Underground. In 1993 Bill moved into this apartment and he lives there still.

"I love the weather here but it's too spread out and I hate driving."
—Bill

BERNIE SHINE

Photographed at home with his dog Maggie in Hancock Park on March 7, 2022.

Bernie was born in 1948 in Spencer, Iowa. He was the youngest of three for Ben and Ernie. Dad was in the scrap metal and new steel business and Mom was a homemaker. Bernie spent his young years growing up in Iowa. He was a popular kid who loved animals, eventually becoming a lifelong vegetarian. He did really well at school in speech class and journalism. He was the editor of the high school newspaper and he was a magician too. He worked in a souvenir store, and in a men's clothing store in an amusement park. Bernie left home when he was 18, bound for college in Arizona. He studied business administration and worked as a magician on the side. In 1970 when Bernie was 22 years old, he moved to Los Angeles to go to law school. He got married and divorced, continued working as a magician, became a lawyer and then went back to magic. Bernie was a favorite performer in the "Close-Up Room" at the famous Magic Castle in Hollywood in the 1970s. Bernie also collects and sells vintage everything, from Bakelite poker dice to 1930s Mickey Mouse and Disney memorabilia. He moved into this house in 1997 and lives there still.

"Great friends here—many in show business. Also the Magic Castle is here, which was very important to me in the 1970s. I really don't have any negatives to say about living here. I subscribe to what the character Elwood P. Dowd said in the film Harvey: *'I always have a wonderful time, wherever I am, whoever I'm with.'"*
—Bernie

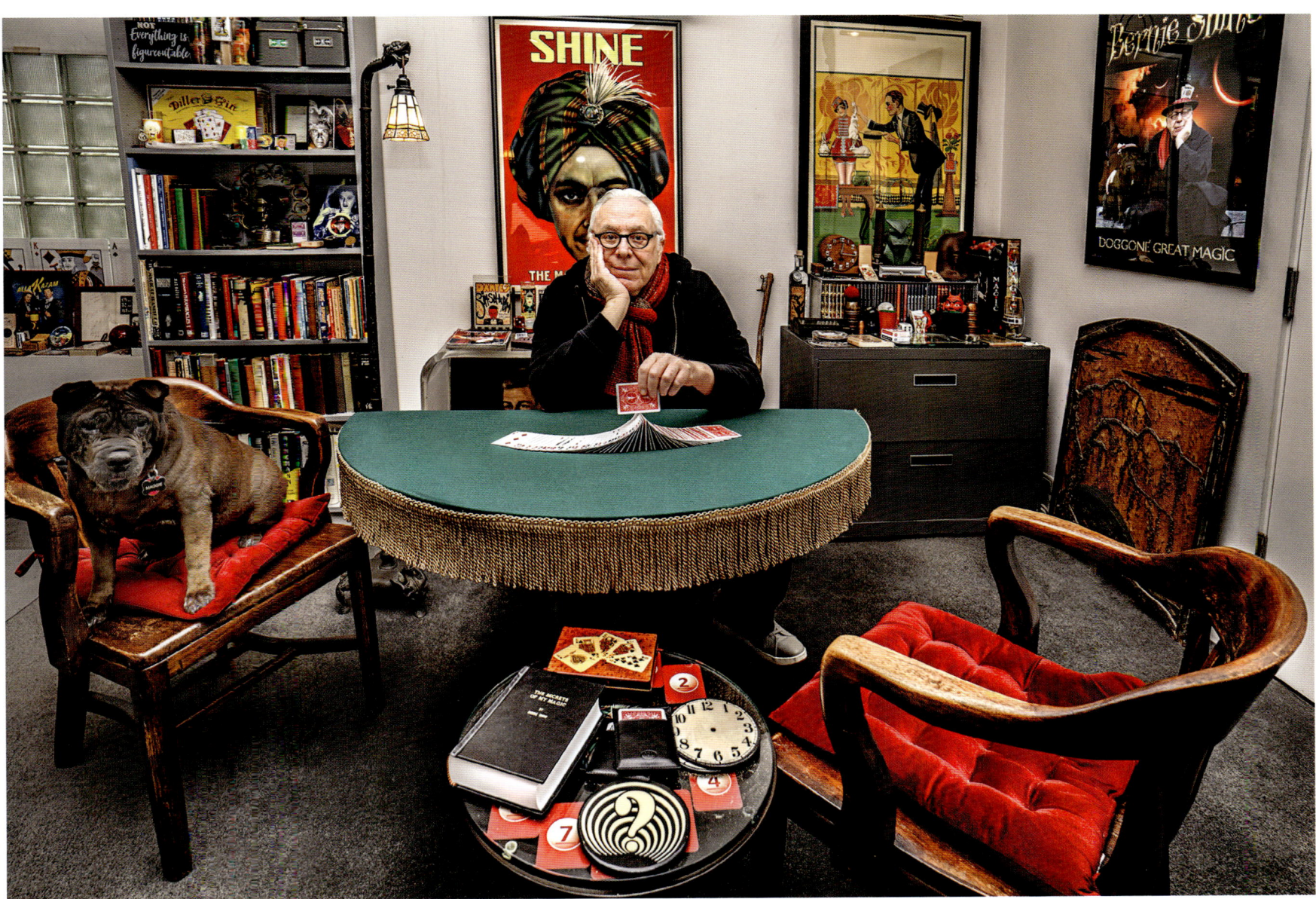

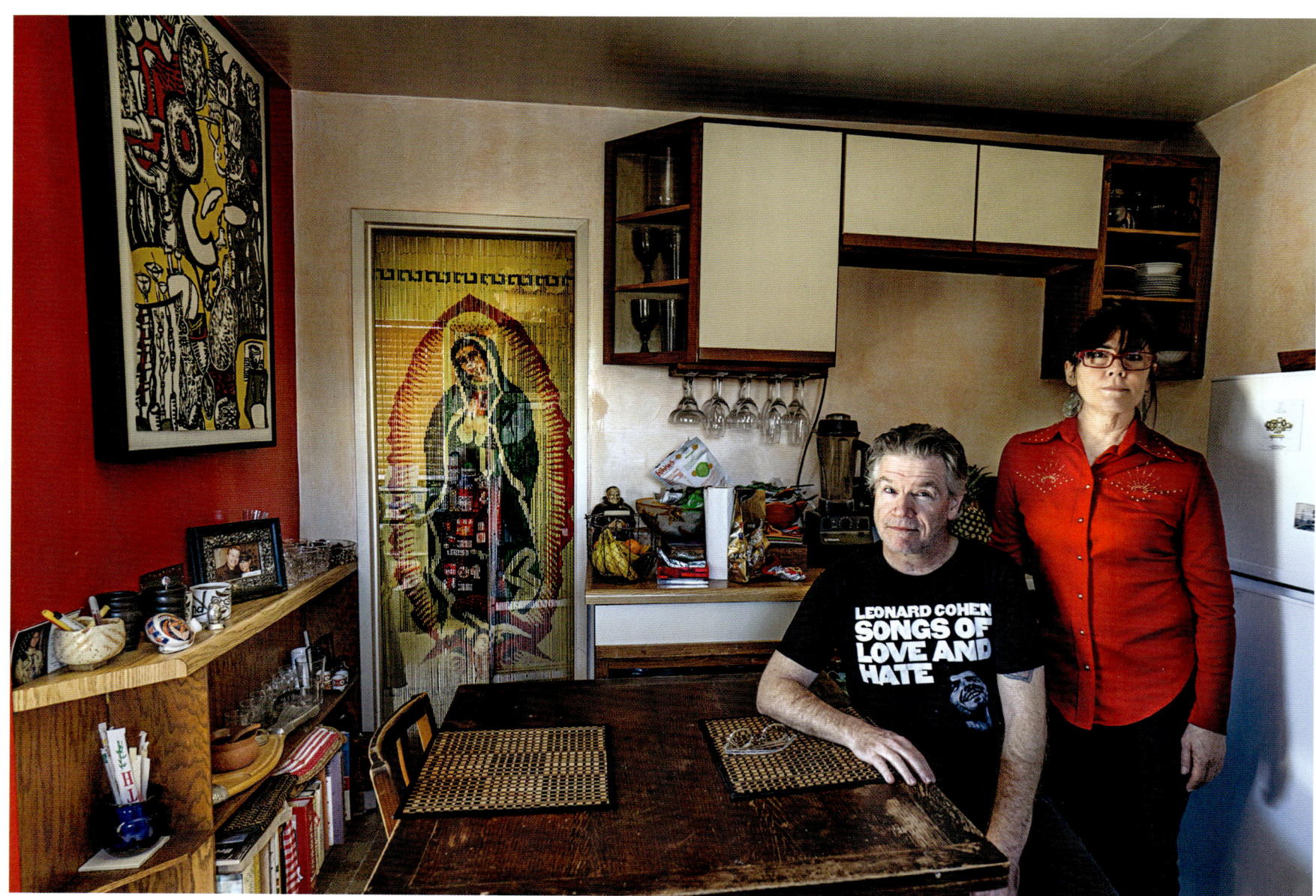

MAT GEASON AND LEIGH SALGADO

Photographed at their home in Huntington Park on February 27, 2022.

Mat was born in 1964 in Fullerton, California. He was the seventh of eight kids for Eugene and Helen. Dad owned his own business and Mom was a homemaker. Both parents came to California during the Depression and met at the Santa Monica Pier. Mat spend his childhood in La Mirada, California. The grown-up Mat was pretty much already in place by the time he was ten. He hated homework and was a resentful kid, and felt alienated most of the time. Mat dabbled in some drama, Dungeons & Dragons, and a nerdy thing called Model United Nations. They would go to conferences with other schools and pretend to be the UN reps for that country. Their assignment was to represent Iran during the 1979 hostage crisis. They got ordered to appear before the security council because he called America "the great satan" as was that country's policy at the time. Despite all this, the highlight was talking to girls. He took a weekend class in magic but was disappointed since it wasn't the spells and voodoo he was hoping for. Mat was expelled from high school and five colleges. When he was 20, his parents moved away to live closer to the family business. They told him and his brother they couldn't come along nor could they stay here, and wished them good luck, so Mat moved to LA. It was 1986. He would still be sitting on the couch with the television remote had they not moved. He worked as a cashier at K-Mart, where he had an affair with a much older woman, and then later worked as a journalist. Mat started an art magazine called *Coagula* in 1992 and really made a name for himself. He got sober in 1993 and replaced liquor with astrology. He is more famous in the art world, but makes more money as an astrologer In 2002 he starting dating Leigh.

Leigh was born in 1954 in San Diego, California. She was the first of four kids for Shirley and Louie. Dad worked for a grocery store chain until he died at the young age of 26 and after that, Mom worked as an office manager. Leigh spent most of her childhood in the San Diego area. She was a shy, quiet kid but she did organize plays in her neighborhood. She was a pretty good student later on except for driving and typing. She was a cheerleader in high school and wanted to be an artist when she got out on her own. It was 1972 and Leigh moved to Los Angeles to attend college. She studied art and art therapy, and later she returned to school to study psychology and more art therapy. She worked as a house cleaner, for a fast food place, for the credit department at Montgomery Ward, as a bank teller, and as a waitress. Leigh worked for programs that helped under-represented kids get into colleges, then as an art therapist and social worker for almost 20 years. Now she is an artist. Leigh got married and divorced twice, then fell in love with Mat.

They moved into this house together in 2007 and in 2013 they got married.

"I took an intermediate Spanish class at Cerritos College and it was the most valuable thing I ever did. I use Spanish every day. My Spanish is not great but I can get my point across. LA is so much easier knowing a little Spanish. Los Angeles is a not a melting pot. It is a segregated buffet. How mixed your plate gets is usually all up to you. "
—Mat

"I love how there are people from many different backgrounds and experiences in Los Angeles. I love that there are lots of art galleries and museums and other venues to hear music or experience the theater. I love that the beach/ocean, desert, and mountains are all accessible as well as city life. I hate that people dump trash around where we currently live and I hate that homelessness is a big problem in Los Angeles."
—Leigh

GWYNNE RIDGWAY AND ROSS VINSTEIN

Photographed with their daughter Pearl and their two dogs Pinky Rose and Nikki, at home in Mount Washington on March 2, 2022.

Gwynne was born in 1969 in Toledo, Ohio. She was the youngest of three kids for Ed and Marlene. Dad was the VP of a jewelry company and Mom was an accessory buyer who looked like Doris Day. They met at work. The family moved around some—New Jersey, Connecticut, St. Louis, and then finally settled in Scottsdale, Arizona. Gwynne was a creative little girl, excelling at all her art and photography classes, and also did some modeling as a young teenager. Modeling put her in a very wild New York City in the early eighties, where she went to all the clubs all the time: Limelight, Area, Palladium, and Studio 54. She attended college first in business classes, but switched to art history, and she still collects art to this day. In the late 1980s, she met and married her first husband, but he was a drug addict and that ended eventually. In 1998 Gwynne moved to Los Angeles. She got a job at Fred Segal department store and worked there for five years. She worked steady in retail, in the fashion end of things, eventually starting her own kids' clothing line.

Ross was born in Indianapolis in 1970. He had a younger sister and a younger half-brother. His dad Arnie was a radiologist and his mom Gail did PR for hospitals. They moved to Los Angeles when Ross was three and when he was seven his mom and dad split up. He spent his childhood years in Los Feliz. Ross wanted to be a truck driver when he grew up. He also wanted to be an actor, a bike racer, and a tattoo artist. He was a very smart kid and teachers always liked him. He was also lazy with bad study habits, so he had to bullshit his way through high school. Ross was a devoted cyclist until he was about 20. It was 1988 and he started getting tattooed the day after he turned 18. From that day forward, he wanted to be a tattoo artist. He attended college at UC Santa Cruz studying labor history. He spent the next four years tattooing full-time at Sunset Strip Tattoo before returning to college for an MBA in 1998. That same year Ross got a job doing post-production accounting on feature films, and that would end up being his second career. He is amazed to this day how well he did at school with so very little effort. Ross works out of Ten Thousand Waves Tattoo Gallery and his main CFO job is at an entertainment marketing agency.

Gwynne and Ross met in August 2007 and in December they married. They had their daughter Pearl in 2009. They lived below the Hollywood sign in Beachwood Canyon before they moved into this house in 2011.

"We are definitely Eastsiders. This area is kind of a bubble, it's super quiet. It's definitely gotten more expensive and is becoming more gentrified every year. I feel like everything keeps moving more east as everything gets more expensive. When I lived with my brother in Silver Lake in '98 he paid $350 in rent. Now you'd have to add another 0 on to that just for rent! It's crazy!! And the main thing I hate about LA ... TRAFFIC!!!!!"
—Gwynne

"While I was not bred, I very much was spread, in LA and I love it to pieces. Having had a pretty broad experience, going to punk shows starting at age 12, writing graffiti for years, and spending an adolescence largely on a bicycle with friends and riding all over the city, I feel super fortunate to really have seen a huge swathe of this huge city. So much more everywhere than most give credit for. I don't really hate any of it, but I do miss a lot of the older landmarks that are slowly being lost to time. Both Gwynne and I always talk about being born too late. While I am thankful I didn't have to live the life of a character in a John Fante novel, that era of LA just seems beyond cool to me. As for gentrification, I am clearly part of the problem, so I hesitate to go too far, but it is a shame to see large populations displaced partly at my expense."
—Ross

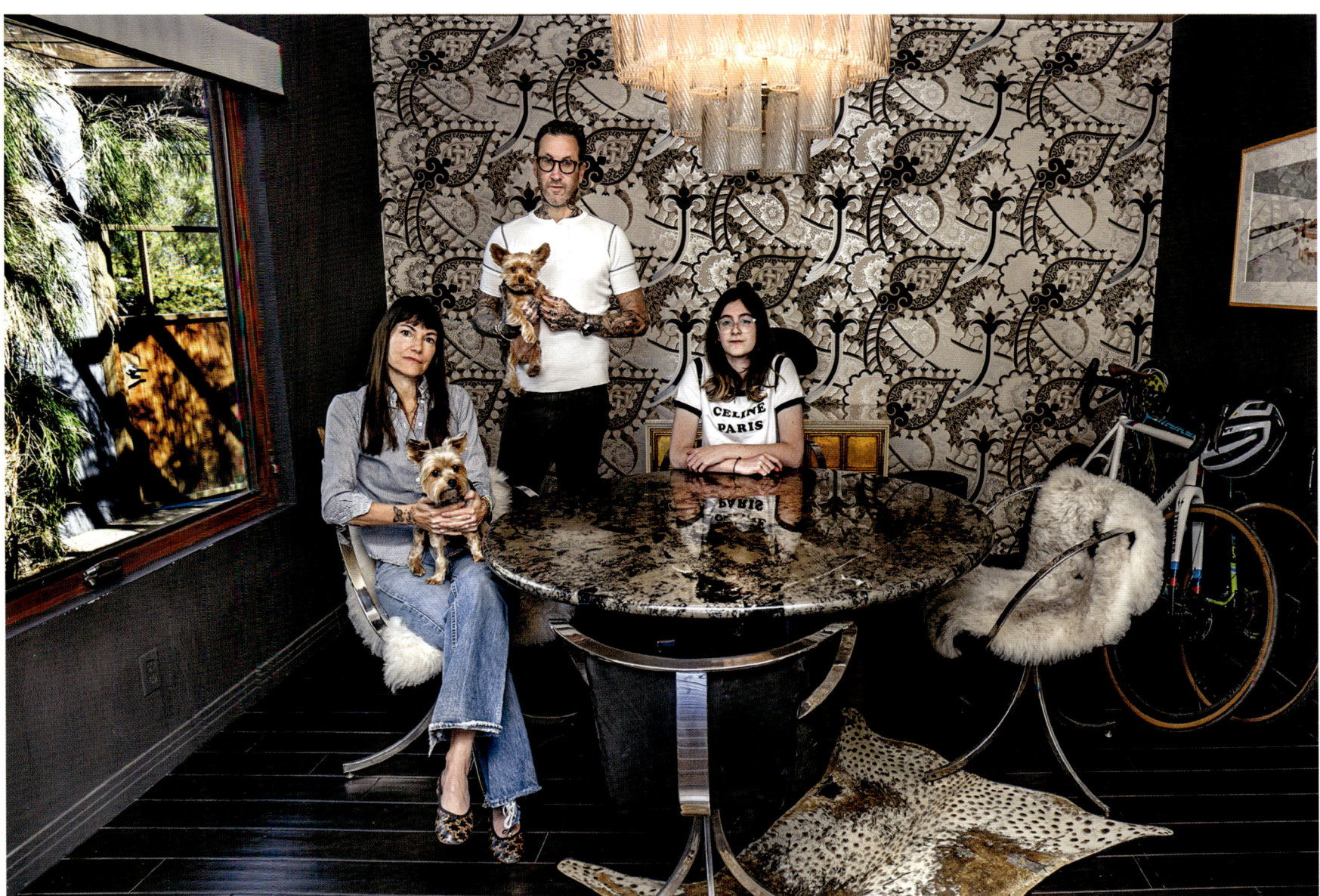

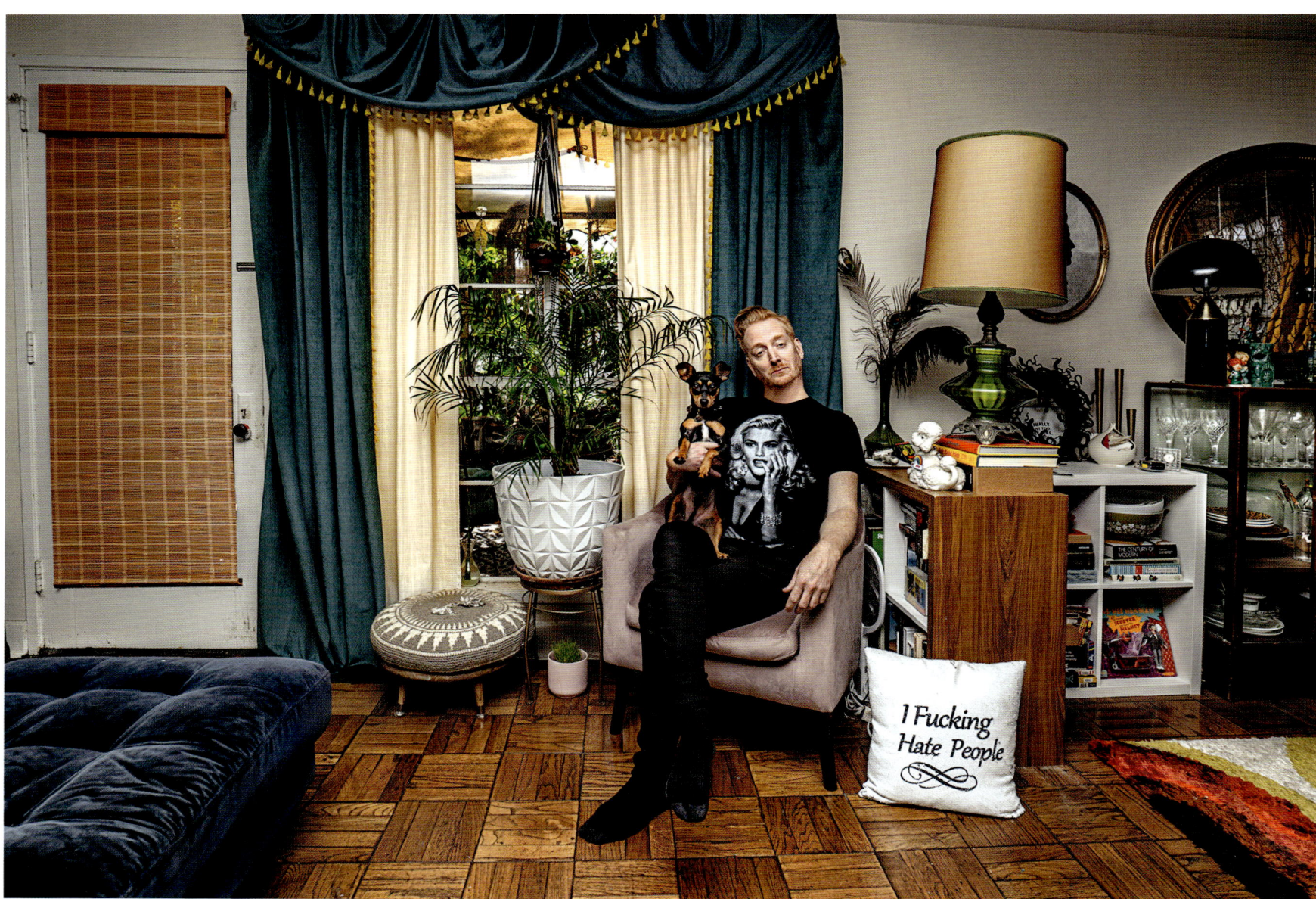

GREG GARY

Photographed at home with his dog Iggy in Fairfax on February 23, 2022.

Greg was born in 1971 on Long Island, New York. He was the youngest of three kids for Joseph and Kathleen. Dad was an aerospace engineer and Mom worked for Canon camera. Greg spent his childhood years growing up in the tiny town of Seaford, Long Island, about 45 minutes from New York City. Like a lot of creative kids, he did very well with English and not so well with math. As a little boy, Greg was more comfortable hanging with adults, and he wanted to be a film director or an actor when he grew up. Always trying to run away from home, he would pack a suitcase daily, and his mom would hold open the door and say: "Nice knowin' ya, kid!" Finally when Greg was 20, he actually did leave home, heading to New York City for school and work. He studied film and creative writing at college. He worked in bookstores, was a production assistant on lots of movies and rap videos, and worked for MTV. His worst job ever was hunched over a table where he soldered computer chips to a computer motherboard. When Greg finished college, he stayed in New York for 29 more years. He started out in film and TV, but eventually he side stepped into the magazine and photography business, becoming an award-winning photo editor. Greg worked in the art department for movies and MTV and then got pulled into the glamorous world of photography in the late nineties—models, traveling, clothes, cocaine, lavish parties—9/11 got rid of all that. In 2013 Greg met his partner Michael Jorris at the East Village dive bar The Boiler Room and they have been together ever since. Five years later when Greg was 47 he was offered a job at *Entertainment Weekly* magazine in LA. The two of them said yes and headed west. Greg works as a creative director for PETA now, doing their celebrity campaigns. Greg and Michael moved into this townhouse in 2018 and live there still.

"It ain't NY! New York has a vibrancy and energy no other city really has. LA isn't really a city to me as much as a long, stretched-out bunch of neighborhoods. But I'm grateful to have spent the pandemic here rather than in my little veal fattening pen in NY. I would have lost my mind there. I love my garden and the mellow weather, love driving but hate parking! It's harder to make real friends here because everyone's a bit phony, always on the make. Even the supermarket checkout person wants something from you. Luckily I already had a bunch of friends out here when I arrived, mostly ex-New Yorkers."
—Greg

ANNIE SPERLING

Photographed at home in Echo Park on March 25, 2022.

Annie was born in 1975 in Norfolk, Virginia. She was third in the lineup of one brother and two stepbrothers for Kit and Harris. Her parents divorced when she was 11. Her mom married Steve and brought two stepbrothers into her life. Dad was an executive at an aerospace and defense technology company, Mom wrote mystery books, and Steve was a college professor. They moved around a lot when Annie was little because Dad was in the Navy. She wanted to be an artist when she grew up and always had pets: kittens, cats, dogs, hamsters, and bunnies. She did really good at school, almost always straight A's. She discovered punk rock music and that changed her life. When she was 18 she left home and moved to San Francisco's Haight Ashbury. She went to college there and studied fine art for a year, and then for three more years down in Los Angeles. She worked odd jobs on Sunset Strip selling cards and flowers, and as a waitress too, but she got fired three times from that. She got married in 1995 and they divorced six years later. Annie directs music videos, paints murals, designs installations for an eco-ocean group, is a production designer in the entertainment business, and is a set designer. She moved into this house in 2006 and lives there still.

"Echo Park and Silver Lake were communities of gangsters, artists, immigrants, and a large, leather homosexual, pan-, transexual community for many years. A place rich with succulents, palms, little gardens for every renter and homeowner, with mixed cool architecture and views of the Hollywood sign and downtown Los Angeles—a hub. Although there is still a large population of these people, the neighborhood has relentlessly gentrified. The result has been a misshaping of the beauty of this place. There are a multitude of homeless with seemingly no way out from the city's programs; garbage in the LA river piled high on the trees and yet white and rare blue herons populate the river too. LA is infused with this dichotomy. Super-interesting artistic people making dreamy cool projects amongst the ruins of infrastructure, all under a continuous perfect sunny day."
—Annie

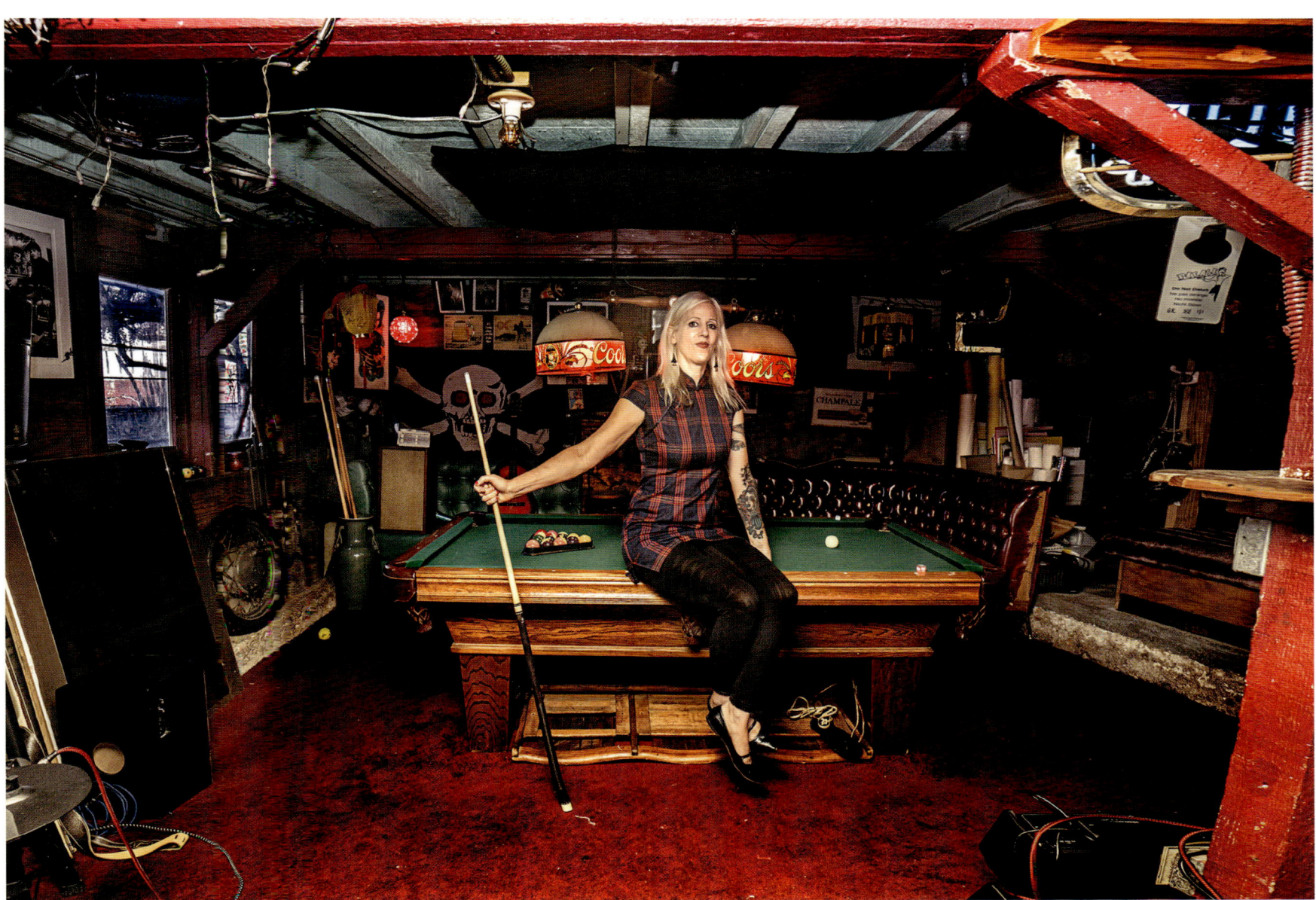

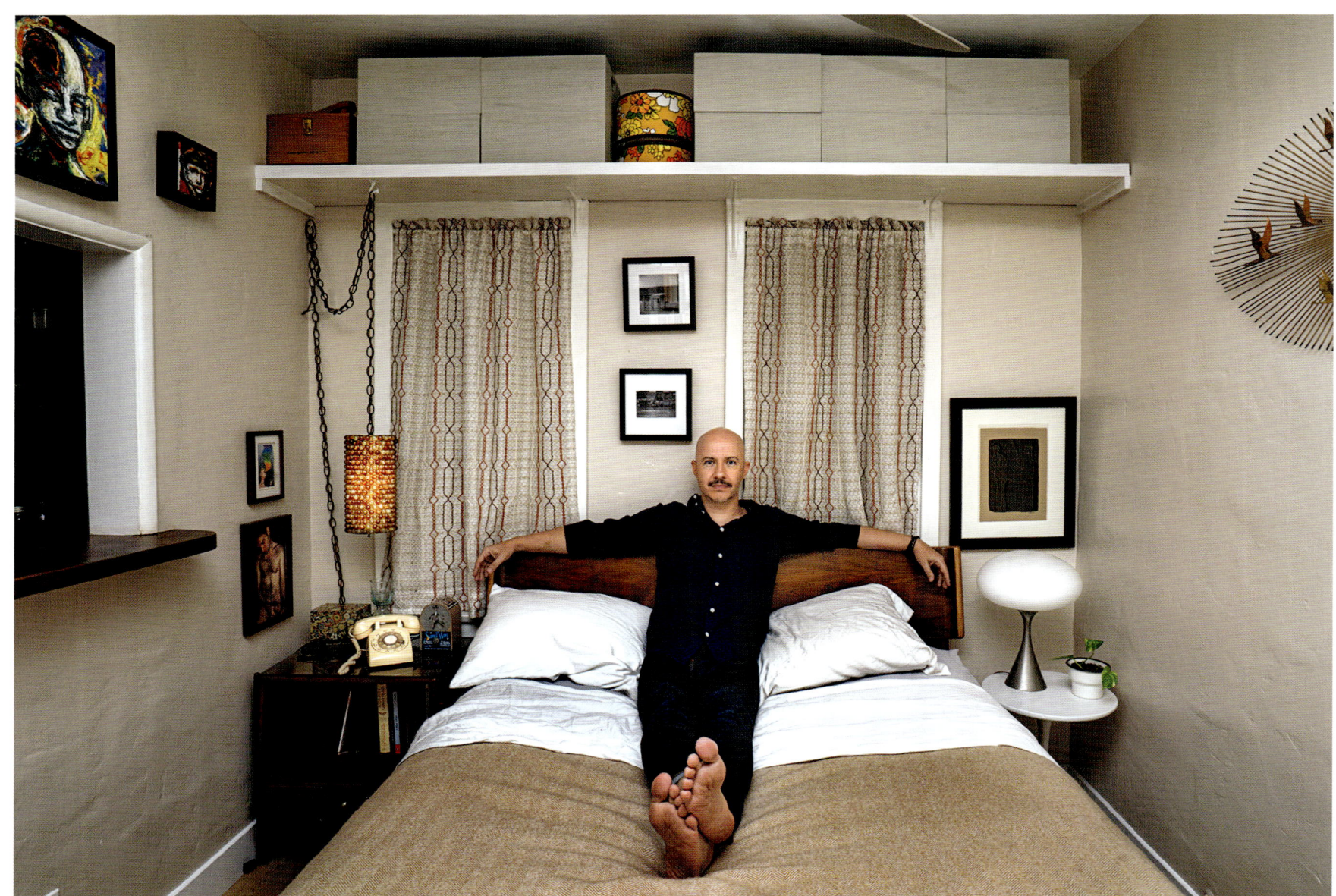

STEVEN REIGNS

Photographed at home in West Hollywood on February 17, 2022.

Steven was born in St. Louis, Missouri in 1975. He was the youngest of two for Barb and Chuck. Dad was an engineer and Mom was a homemaker who decorated cakes. Steven suffered through his youth being abused by his parents and molested by a neighbor. Those younger years were followed by high school torment because he was gay. When he was little he wanted to be a truck driver, or a schoolteacher or maybe a sculptor. He left home when he was 18, Florida bound. He went to college there and took creative writing. He lived in an apartment that Jack Kerouac once lived in. Later he got a master's degree in clinical psychology back in California. He worked at a cotillion teaching young people how to button their sports coats and sit properly, at an art store, at The Gap, as a window washer, a public school teacher, a doorman at a club, fetish clothing salesperson, bartender, underwear model, magazine columnist, cashier at a porn shop, and wrote blog entries for a funeral home's website. It was 2005, and he was almost 30 years old. After ten years of living in Florida, he moved back west to Los Angeles. Steven's parents divorced around this time. He worked in LA as an HIV test coordinator, and as an HIV test provider at bath houses. After thousands of hours in therapy, and reading countless self-help books, Steven's life continues to get better and better. He writes poetry, teaches autobiographical poetry writing workshops to LGBTQ seniors, and is a part-time psychotherapist. He has a new book out called *A Quilt for David*, and he was appointed the first Poet Laureate of West Hollywood. Steven moved into this tree-house apartment in 2005 and lives there still.

"LA has evolved and changed so much since I moved here in 2005. Devaluing or stereotyping LA for its superficialness is tired and untrue. It's a city loaded with creative people supportive of arts, equality, and diversity. There are stunningly beautiful people here but that makes beauty the equalizer, so people need to bring more to the table than just their looks. Other aspects and talent gets cultivated. I absolutely love LA and refer to it as home. I correct people when they ask if I'm 'going home for the holidays?' and tell them that this is my home. It might be easier to appreciate the city since I'm not involved with the industry. I am thankful for rent control and how it's created an opportunity for me and being like me to really thrive in this city. I'm glad I've been able to stay in this part of the city. West Hollywood feels like its own little pocket of progressiveness and gayness. I was elected the first Poet Laureate of the city, so obviously I think they have good taste in poetry too."
—Steven

PHIL AND LISA NOYES

Photographed at home in Mid City on February 26, 2022.

Phil was born in San Francisco in 1965. He was the youngest of three boys for James and Isabella. Dad was a Middle East expert who worked for the Pentagon and the CIA, and Mom was a real estate agent. Phil lived in Sri Lanka until he was three, then in Virginia and San Francisco. He was an outgoing little boy who spent his young years socializing with high-ranking Pentagon officials at his parents' dinner parties. He had tons of friends and a dog named Digger. Digger died when Phil was 19. Phil wanted to be a firefighter, actor, photographer, or a veterinarian when he grew up. He did super good in school with history and super bad with math. His great love has always been art and theater. Phil went to boarding school when he was 14. After high school he moved back to San Francisco and lived in Haight Ashbury. He went to college and studied theater and photography, but working at a really cool nightclub was just too distracting and college ended after one year. Phil worked as a street sweeper, box loader, forklift driver, lumberjack, house painter, caterer, doorman, bartender, waiter, mover, at a candy store, and as a kayaking instructor. In 1990, when he was 25, he moved to LA. There he worked as a production assistant, photographer's assistant, and as a bartender. He worked at PBS where he produced a popular TV series about California history. Now he is a producer and a director at a small production company in Santa Monica. Phil loves vintage travel trailers and owns four of them. He has written two books and produced a documentary about their history in the US.

Lisa was born in Hollywood, California in 1966. She was the only child for Cammy and Cliff. Mom and Dad both worked in the film and TV business, Mom a hairdresser and Dad worked in wardrobe. When Lisa was five, her parents divorced. She spent her first five years in North Hollywood and then after the divorce, she moved around a lot with her mom. She spent two years in Australia but mostly she was in West Hollywood. Lisa was an outgoing kid who grew up fast. She wanted to be a bail bondsman when she grew up so she could have a beeper and a cool car, then she wanted to be an actress. She did pretty well at school if she liked the project. Her mom was young and they spent a lot of days on Hollywood Boulevard skipping school together where they would go to the movies and eat chocolate sundaes. She acted, modeled, loved to roller skate, worked in retail, and was an assistant teacher for preschool later on. She did some college on and off for two years so she could teach. When Lisa was 25, she left home and moved in with Phil. Now she works for a non-profit that provides aid and relief from conflict, disaster, and disease. She married her soul mate; he won her heart with a motorcycle ride. They got married in San Francisco and have been together ever since.

One night when Phil was bartending, the most beautiful woman he had ever seen walked into the bar. Her name was Lisa and in 1994 he married her. They have a son and a daughter. In 1998 they bought this house and they all live there still.

"The thing I love most about Los Angeles is the diversity. Every corner is filled with immigrant families. When I first moved here, I thought mini malls were a disaster until I realized that they were the spaces that were available to people just starting out. Almost all our favorite restaurants are tucked into mini malls, and we have grown to know and love many of the families who own them. This really is the City of Angels and I like to think she opens her wings to anybody who is willing to come here and work hard."
—Phil

"LA is part of my soul, born and raised only here I can only feel an immense love and loyalty to this city that has raised me and a hate sometimes for keeping me from leaving here. This city is everything you want in a day, which I think is its beauty. You can go to the beach and go to the snow and ski and take a hike in the desert in the same day. You can also find your place and people and community everywhere and not feel like an outsider."
—Lisa

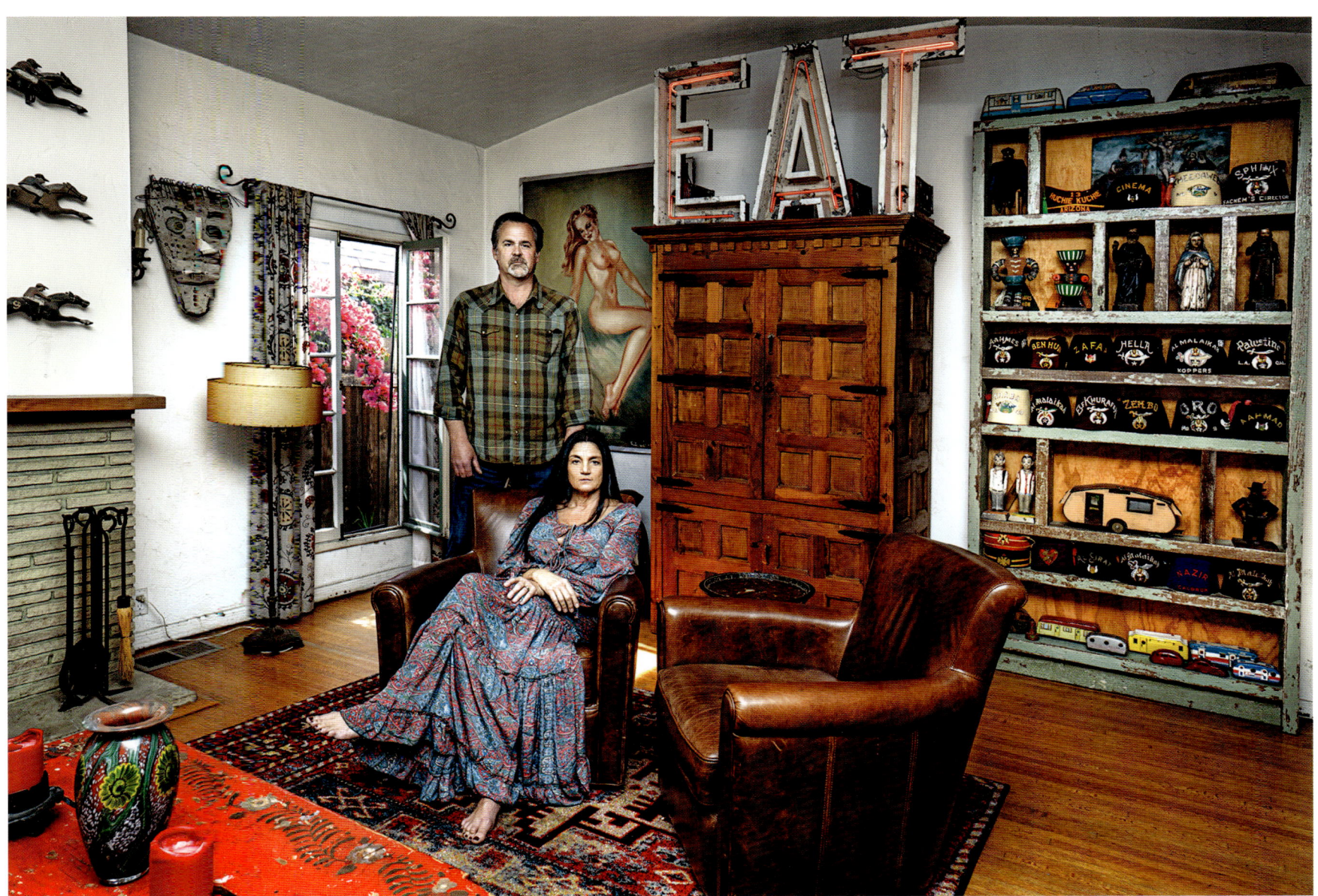

JOHNNY CUBERT WHITE

Photographed at home in Downtown LA on March 5, 2022.

Johnny was born in 1966 in Hammond, Indiana. He was the first born for Georgia and J.C. and he had one sister named Jackie. Mom was a teenage runaway, housewife, bathing-suit runway model, real estate agent, farm wife, and a jewelry counter manager at JCPenney. Dad was a teenage runaway too, a petty criminal, steel mill worker, waiter, wife beater, topless bar owner, disco manager, heroin dealer, and an inmate who eventually retired on disability. Johnny wanted to take dance lessons when he was ten, but his dad put him on the football team instead. When Johnny was 12 years old, his mother filed for divorce, and they went into hiding. "Dead women don't get divorced," is what his dad said. Johnny spent his youth growing up in sunny Tarpon Springs, Florida, known as the sponge capital of the world. He wanted to be a writer, lawyer, actor, politician, filmmaker, and a gynecologist when he grew up. In fourth grade he organized "raising money for charity" and went door to door for that. When he was 12 he raised the second-most money in the state of Florida, coming second only to an adult aged 35. He was a junior rotarian in high school and college. Johnny's first job was at a Greek restaurant. The owner always flirted with his mom, so one day she asked him to hire Johnny. He told her to bring him back when he was old enough to work. On the day he turned 16 his mom dropped him off at the restaurant. Johnny left for college when he was 17: Atlanta first, then the School of the Art Institute of Chicago. He worked at a movie theater in high school and college. Johnny stayed living in Chicago for eight years after earning his MFA. He worked part-time at a media arts center doing their press and marketing and waited tables while working on film gigs. It was 1999 and Johnny was 33. He already had four feature films being shown at film festivals. He left Chicago and headed for Los Angeles. When Johnny arrived, he lived in Hollywood and did game shows for money. He was living in a 4,000 sq ft warehouse loft and got a job with a premier manufacturer of fetish latex and leather clothing. He did a 22-year stint teaching 16mm filmmaking to kids, received a National Endowment of the Arts Grant, was an early NFT artist, and exhibited at the 2017 Venice Biennale. Johnny is an artist, filmmaker, photographer, and all-round creative force. He moved into this loft in 2004 and lives there still.

"I love LA. I love industrial loft living. I was lucky, I am the last man standing—18 years and counting. My landlord doesn't sell or develop so I lucked out. Gentrification happens and those who bitch the most are usually the ones who are a major cause of it. When I leave this loft I will most likely move to Europe. My friends range from porn stars to nuns and priests. I am a fortunate individual able to live a creative life and thrive."
—Johnny

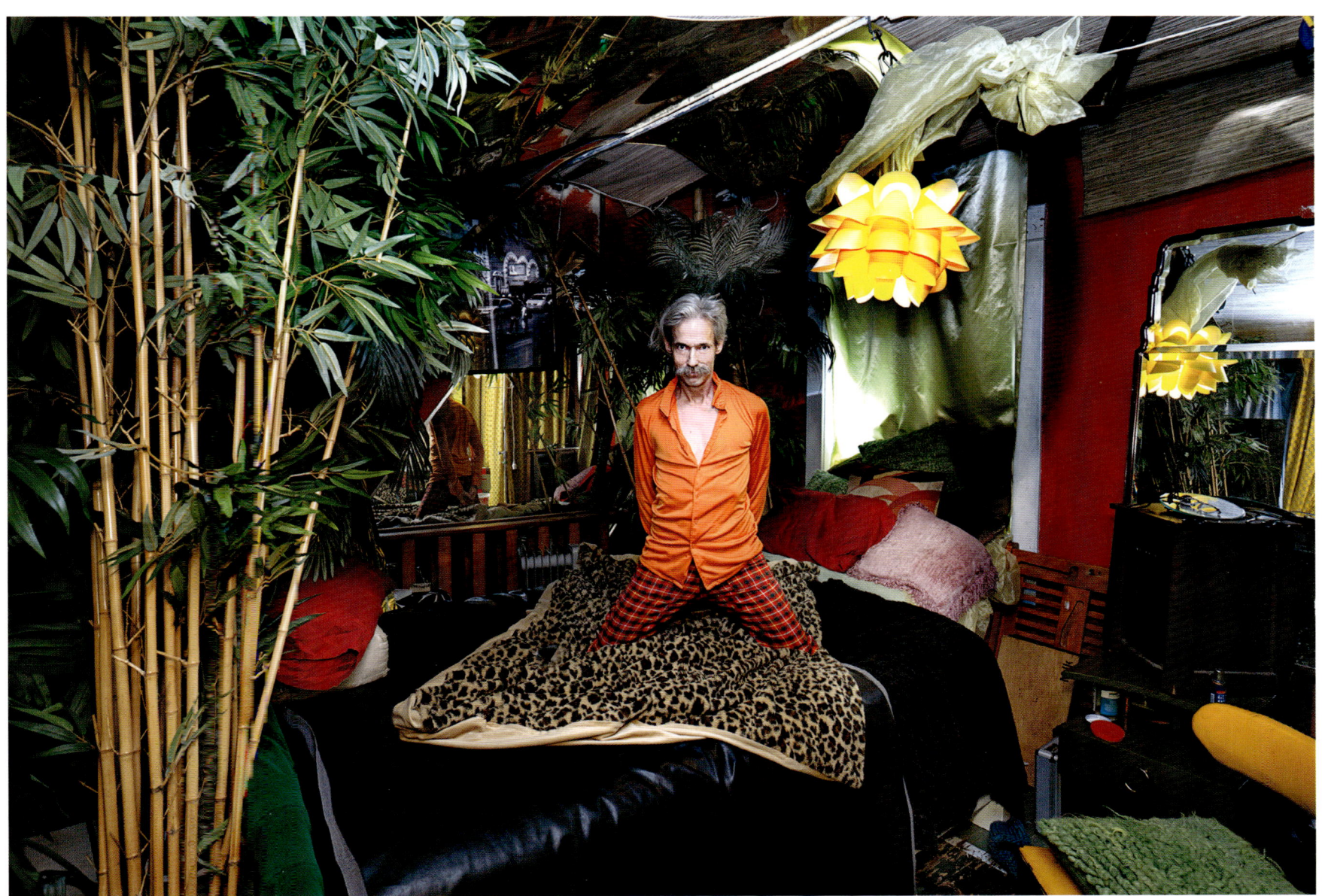

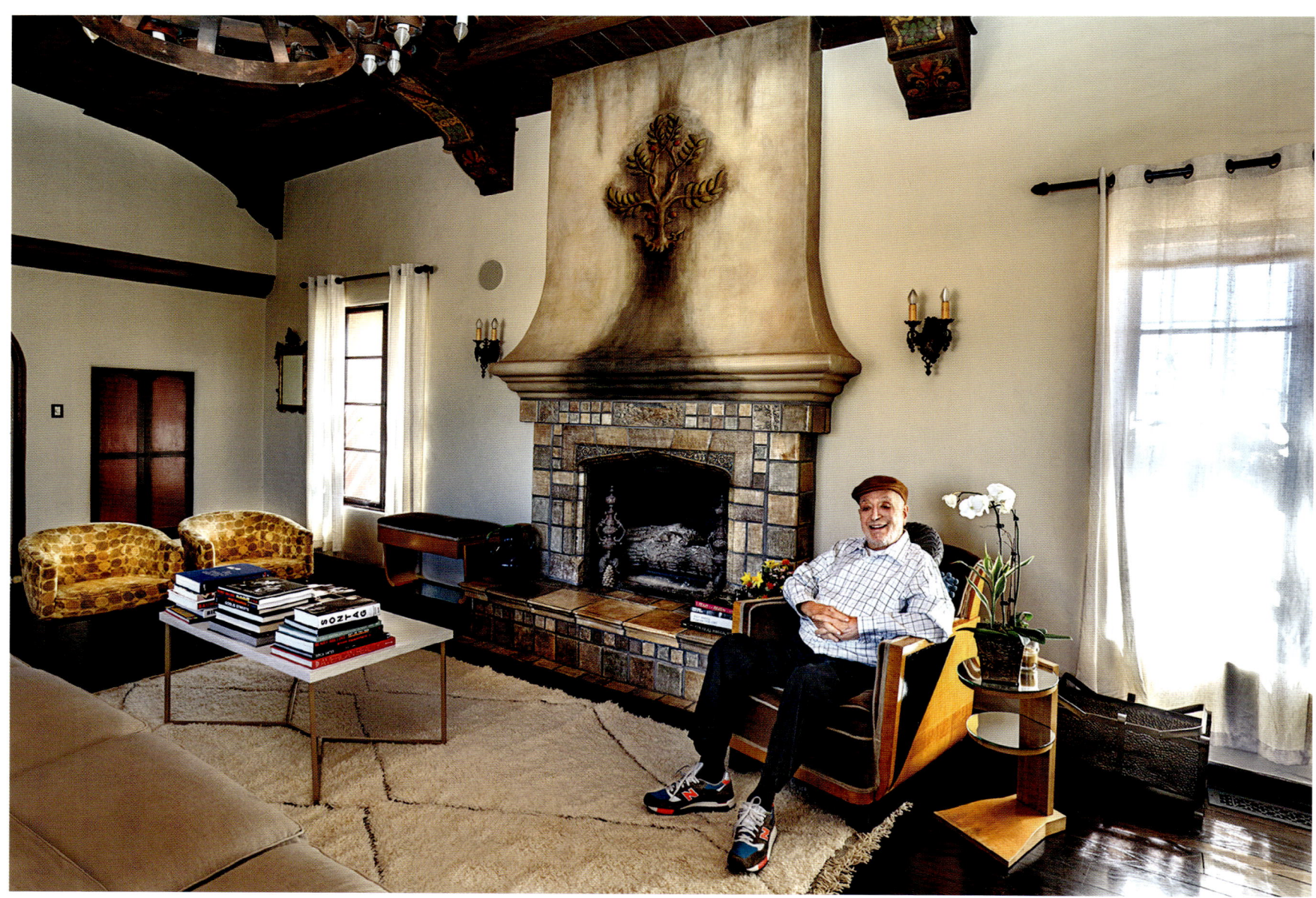

SEYMOUR STEIN

Photographed at home in Los Angeles on March 14, 2022.

Seymour was born Seymour Steinbigle in 1942 in Brooklyn, New York. He was the youngest of two for Dora and David. He spent his young years in Brooklyn. Seymour was born with a heart defect. Because of that he was exempt from sports, and was also a bit spoiled by his mother. He took on a clerk position for music industry magazine *Billboard* in 1958 and in 1961 he began a two-year work run for King Records in Cincinnati, Ohio. Seymour was recruited there by Syd Nathan, who somehow convinced his dad, an ultra-conservative Orthodox Jew, to allow him a trip to Ohio to be a summer intern. In 1971 Seymour married Linda Adler, and they had two daughters, Samantha and Mandy, before divorcing later in the seventies. In 1966 Stein and record producer Richard Gottehrer founded Sire Productions, which led to the formation of the legendary Sire Records. Sire signed the Ramones and Talking Heads, The Pretenders, Madonna, Depeche Mode, The Smiths, Ice-T, The Undertones, Echo & the Bunnymen, and so many more. Seymour was the President of Sire Records and also Vice-President of Warner Bros. Records until he announced his retirement on July 18, 2018. He was inducted into the Rock & Roll Hall of Fame on March 14, 2005 and on June 9, 2016 Stein was honored with the Richmond Hitmaker Award at the Songwriters Hall of Fame. Seymour believes in music's ability to change the world. He feels that music is a way for people to cope with the misery of day-to-day life.

"I really have to thank my older sister Ann for my early introduction to music. We were not rich, and when I was a little kid, we slept in a two-bedroom apartment. Ann had a radio and we would listen to the songs together and she got me to love the music too."
—Seymour

CYNTHIA BACH AND JIM MATTHEWS

Photographed at their home in Los Angeles on March 11, 2022.

Cynthia Bach was born in Tachikawa, Japan in 1955. She was the second of two kids for Dave and Lucie. Dad was in the US Air Force and Mom was a homemaker. Cynthia spent her young years in Germany. She wanted to design jewelry when she grew up. She did well in school at art and philosophy but not so good with math and science. She took ballet, dance, and she skied too. When she was 18 she left home and went to college: first in Germany and then she moved to Texas where she went to school again for six more years. She studied art, jewelry history, and philosophy. Cynthia worked as a cocktail waitress and as a bartender until 1978. She met Jim and apprenticed as a jeweler in his trade shop.

In 1983 Jim and Cynthia got married. Six years later they moved to Los Angeles to run design and fabrication for Van Cleef and Arpels jewelry company, then launched their own jewelry collection. They design and make jewelry for movie stars and celebrities, and Jim works on his brightly colored wood assemblage art sculptures, inspired by his time in Mexico. They moved into this house in 1999 and live there still.

Jim Matthews was born in 1941 in Brownwood, Texas. He was the only child for Eric and Lilly. Dad worked for the highway department and Mom was a housewife. Jim spent his childhood years in Abilene, Texas. He wanted to be a psychiatrist when he grew up. When he was young, his parents noticed he was always dancing to music on the radio, so they bought him a violin and private lessons. Later it became clear—Jim just wanted to dance. He was a self-described troublemaker, attending a conservative Baptist university in Abilene on a music scholarship. He rebelled against the religious part of it all, but loved being part of the World Famous Cowboy Marching Band. Jim worked as a gunsmith apprentice until he was 17, and then somewhere around 1965, he left home and headed for Las Vegas. Jim joined the Army reserve and was stationed in Fort Polk, Lousiana. He never did get drafted, so he headed back to Las Vegas. He worked for two years in California at a factory, then moved back to Texas to be closer to his aging father. He worked at Timex, moving up quickly to become an engineer, inventing the machines that assembled the watches. When Jim was 30 the Timex factory closed its doors and that job loss marked the beginning of his jewelry life. A big jewelry chain store needed a freelance person to size their rings and a friend got him the job. He quickly taught himself and five years later Jim was doing custom jewelry as well as repairs and sizing. About a year later he opened Goldesign, his own jewelry store.

"I love LA. It's sunny, bright, happy, and anything is possible. I love the art, Hollywood, movie stars, the food, the beaches, the culture, the desert, the mountains, and the ocean. The world is your oyster here. That said, I hate the traffic, the crowds, the pollution, the lack of rain and seasons, the extreme homelessness, and the poverty here."
—Cynthia

"I'm happy living in Los Angeles largely because I'm just naturally happy, but being 30 minutes from the mountains, 30 minutes from the beach, 30 minutes from the desert, 30 minutes from the forest, and 30 minutes from LAX are but a few of the reasons to live here. Access to world-class dining, entertainment, shopping, healthcare, museums, antiquing, and fashion are additional plusses. Besides, I couldn't leave Los Angeles even if I wanted to for fear of the door hitting me in the ass on my way out."
—Jim

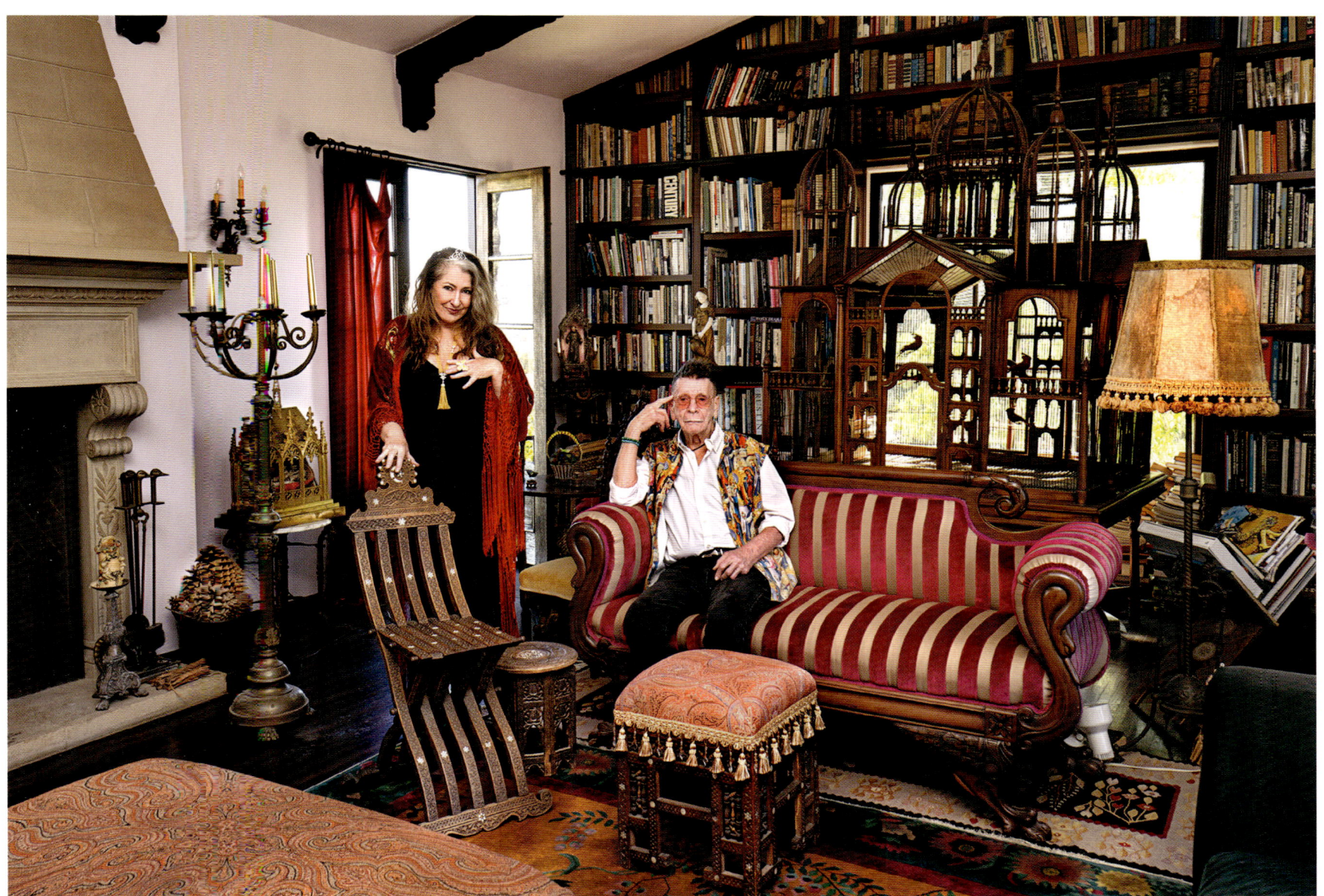

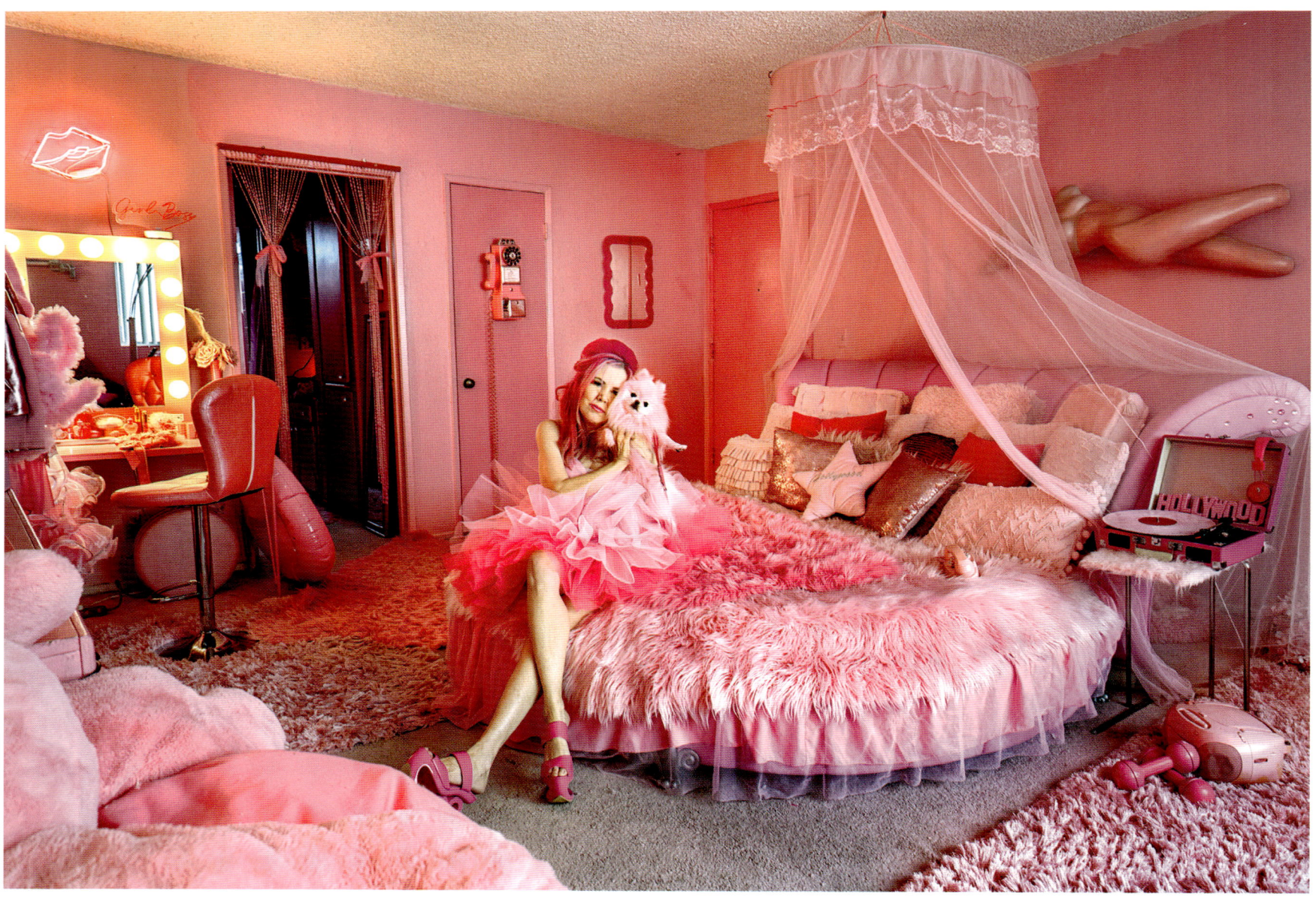

KITTEN KAY SERA

Photographed at home in West Hollywood with her dog Pinkaboo on March 4, 2022.

Kitten was born in Houston, Texas in 1963. She was the youngest of five for Carole and Jack. Dad was a house appraiser and Mom managed the girls' singing group. Kitten spent her young years in Houston. She wanted to be a singer or a TV star when she grew up. She didn't do that well at sports, but she was super good at choir. She sang in a girl group with her four sisters from the time she was six until she was in her late twenties. They sang at rodeos, BBQ joints, resorts, furniture stores, and malls; they even sang with Johnny Cash. Kitten learned how to promote and be her own manager from her mom. Dressed in all her pink clothes, she worked at record stores during the day, where she could play her music that she was recording at night. In 1998 she followed a friend to California. Nothing much was happening in Houston and she needed to be where the action was. One day Kitten was walking down the street in her pink clothes with her pink dog and a big fancy car pulled over. She gave the man her business card and three days later she was on the set of a famous movie. She officially became the pinkest person in the world, even gracing the cover of *Vogue* magazine's PINK issue. She dyes Pinkaboo's fur with beet juice, never using anything toxic. She loves her dog. She has been photographed with the likes of Meryl Streep and Dolly Parton, and did a fashion shoot with Paris Hilton. On New Year's Day in 2022, Kitten married the color pink at a ceremony in Las Vegas. She moved into this apartment in 1999 and lives there still with Pinkaboo.

"California is where it's at. I love the weather. I always see posts from my friends on Facebook saying how they hate the cold winters and snow where they are and I think, 'you are no tree ... MOVE!' I need the swimming pools and movie stars ha hah—I have a pink convertible and adore the way I ride with the top down, music blaring, and the pink fuzzy dice swaying. It was a dream to have a pink convertible. I visualized me doing this and when it happened I smiled and knew what I am capable of. If anyone is saying you can't do something or no to your dreams, remember: If you don't ask, the answer is always no. I also love my city West Hollywood. It's a very cool place to be and I am tickled pink to be in a place where they accept me as I am. I can be outrageous with my pink fashion and no one bats an eye. I don't come any other way. I am a monochromatic. I also have a big gay following and support the LGBTQ community and here ... we are family!"
—Kitten

STEPHEN HENRY

Photographed at home in Silver Lake on May 23, 2021.

Stephen was born in San Diego in 1961. He was the youngest of five kids for Annie and Willie. Mom was a dietary supervisor at a hospital and Dad wasn't around. Mom raised all the kids by herself. Stephen spent his childhood growing up in Perris, California. Because he was dyslexic he didn't do all that well in school. Back in those days, they didn't know what that was. When he was still 17 he left home to live with a friend and her family. Stephen moved around a lot in those early years, unsettled and neither here nor there. As a teenager, Stephen loved to dance and, together with his friends, would sneak into a West Hollywood gay bar before he was 18. He went to fashion school for a short stint, taught dance classes, worked as a stylist, worked at Trader Joe's, and bought and sold some real estate. In 1989 Stephen moved to Los Angeles. He got sober on July 21, 1990 and finally his life started to come together. In 1996 he bought his house in Silver Lake, which was very different back in those days—it had a large Hispanic community and lots of gay men. He loved it and fit right in. In 2001 he sublet his house and moved to San Francisco, but he came back to Los Angeles in 2017 and lives here still.

"I get mail from real estate agents asking if I would like to know the value of my house, because they have a buyer … would I please give them a call. I'm not in need of either. There was a time in Silver Lake when they put up signs saying 'No Cruising.' It's a sign of the times they have all come down."
—Stephen

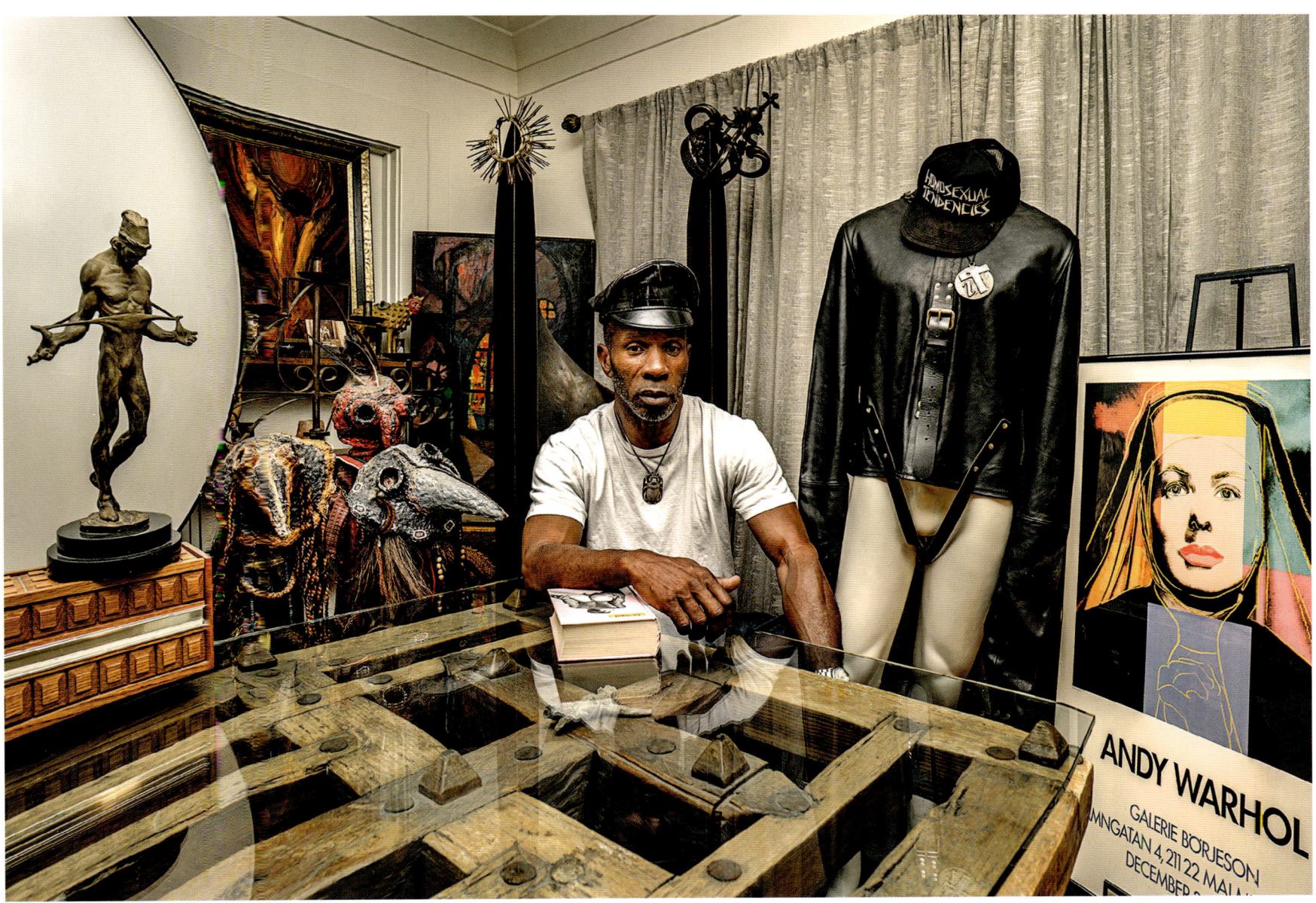

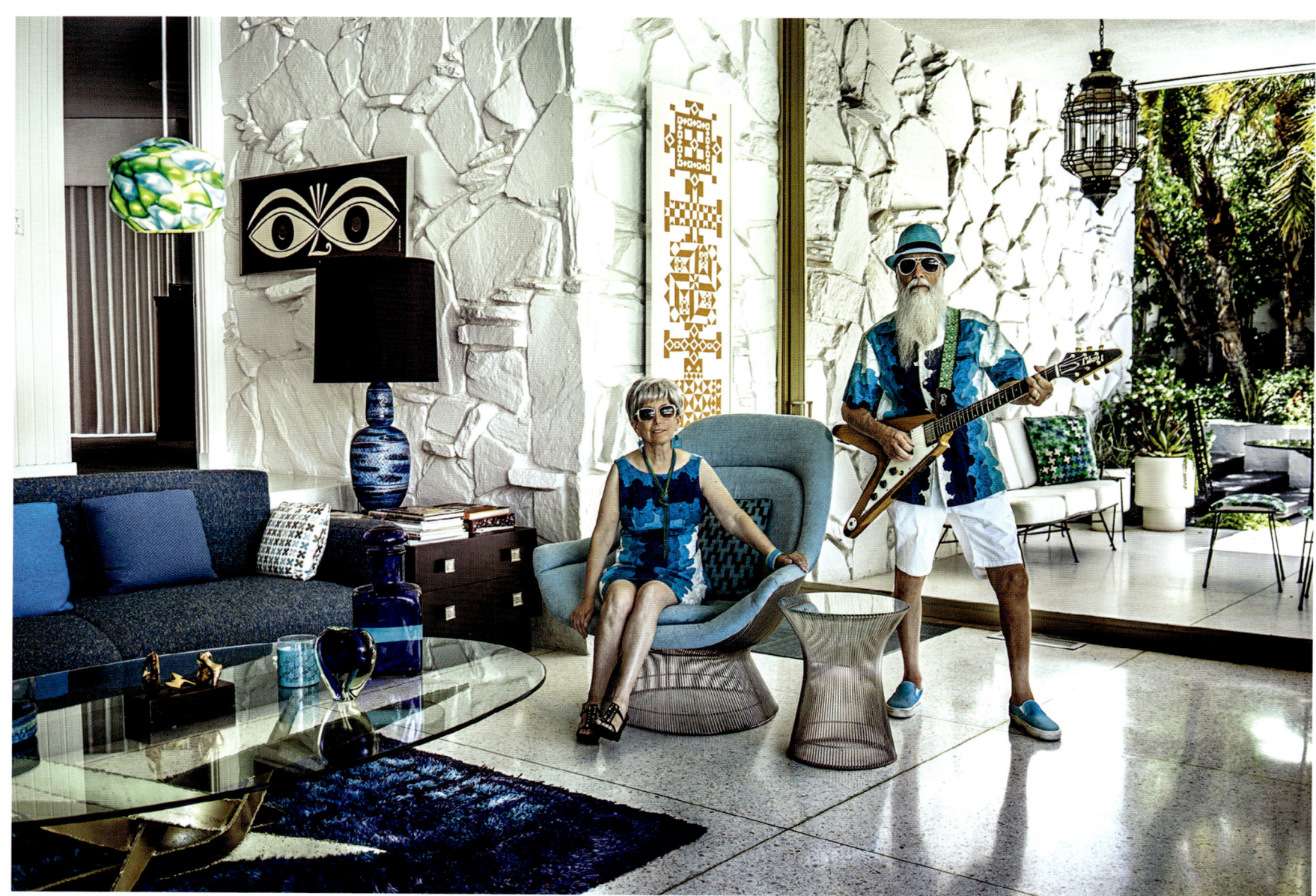

JOAN AND GARY GAND

Photographed at their home in Palm Springs on April 30, 2021.

Joan was born in upscale Chicago in 1953, a short walk from the beach of Lake Michigan. She was the youngest of two kids for Harriet and Harold. Mom was a homemaker who had studied at the Institute of Design and Dad was a tax attorney. They were both music lovers. Mom sang in the choir and Dad was a big jazz fan. Her brother Cliff manages the Red Hot Chili Peppers, The Black Keys, Muse, and Metallica. When Joan was five, she told her parents she wanted to play the piano, so they bought one for her and got her signed up for lessons. Her ability to play by ear and learn songs quickly allowed her to join a blues band when she was 15 years old. Her parents lent her the money to buy a portable Farfisa organ and she paid them back with her part-time high school jobs. Joan was an industrious young girl and kept busy with music and art. She taught guitar and piano, accompanied the local dance studio, and sold leather belts, purses, and guitar straps that she made.

Gary was born in St. Louis, Missouri in 1953. He was the oldest of two kids for Robert and Myrna. When he was two and a half they moved to Deerfield, Illinois. Mom and Dad met at university. He was Catholic and she was Jewish. They met in the middle and became Unitarian. In 1963 Dad quit his day job and started a folk music school in the basement and formed the Gand Family Singers. Gary was ten and his sister Gale was seven. While his friends were playing little league baseball, he was riding all over the USA and Canada in the family station wagon going to folk festivals, TV and radio stations, JFK rallies, and world fairs. They shared the stage with Peter, Paul and Mary, Muddy Waters, and Buddy Guy, to name a few. They traveled to Appalachia to visit with Doc Watson and met Pete Seeger and Arlo Guthrie and dozens of other artists. Later Gary would work with these same people as their concert sound engineer. In 1964 Gary took up the electric guitar. He met Eric Clapton and Frank Zappa when he was 14. He only lasted two years at high school because he was playing every night and making more money than his teachers were making. Gary was also making multimedia slides for bands, hiring a driver because he was too young to drive himself to gigs.

Gary and Joan met when they were both 17 and have been together ever since. In 1970 they opened a rock music equipment store selling vintage guitars. By 1977 Gary was traveling as a sound engineer with all the stars of the day: Talking Heads, Emmylou Harris, Stevie Ray Vaughan, U2, The Temptations, Tom Jones, and many more. In 1986 they bought a mid-century house in Illinois and became friends with Julius Schulman. He convinced them to buy a house in Palm Springs. They made a book together and produced a documentary on Trini Lopez. They moved into this house in 2013.

"Palm Springs is a magic place where the best creative minds land after escaping the maze of life elsewhere."
—Joan

"We never had any kids, too busy. I always say, 'We have employees, they do all the same stuff as kids: lose the car keys, need to borrow money, end up in jail, ask for advice, which they ignore. The difference is you can't fire your kids.'"
—Gary

ACKNOWLEDGMENTS

Thank you

Christopher Bryson

Claire Jeffreys

Frances Pilot

Janet Halpin

Linda Heidinger

Michael DeJong

Michael Ernest Sweet

Phil and Thea Scotti

Sean Corcoran

Tom Storey

for your enthusiasm and patience, and for supporting me
in every way imaginable.

Thank you

Stuart Horodner for his ongoing understanding of my journey through the universe,
his friendship and his sense of humor.

Thank you

Vin Stratton, my assistant and driver, for joining the adventure.

Special thanks to

Adam Normandin, Arturo Mirafuentes, Bob Stratton, Claude Hall, Donna Lee, Ed Valfre, Gillian McCain,
Greg Gary, Jane Shirkes, John Lansing, Jonathan Paley, Johnny Cubert White, Kimberly Biehl, Kristian Hoffman,
Steve Warden, Susan Stratton-Pruitt, and Thuc Doan Nguyen-Brophy for introducing me to so many of the
remarkable people who grace these pages.

Thank you

to everyone at Ammonite who made this project better—
Jonathan Bailey, Robin Shields, and Virginia Brehaut.

Thank you

to every single Californian who welcomed me into their home
and shared their story with the world.

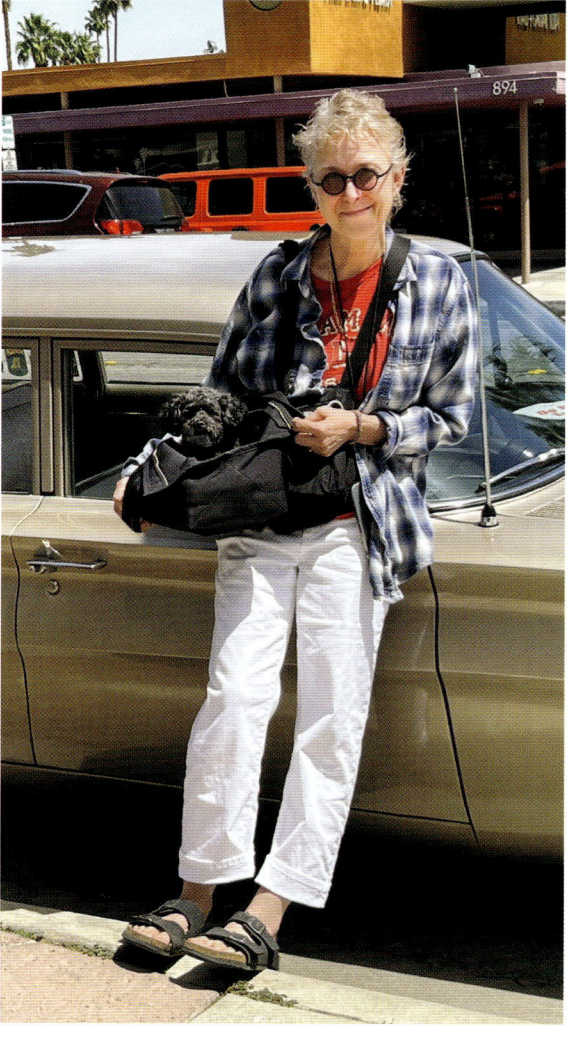

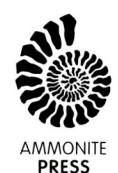

AMMONITE
PRESS

www.ammonitepress.com

BIOGRAPHIES

Sally Davies is a photographer whose works are in the Museum of the City of New York and the 9/11 Memorial Museum. She is the author of the acclaimed McDonald's Happy Meal Project (1.5 million online hits) and her archive is part of the Downtown Collection of Fales Library at NYU. She took Allen Ginsberg's old apartment when she moved from Canada to New York in 1983, and she still lives in the East VIllage with her dog Bun. Her book *New Yorkers* (Ammonite Press) captures intimate portraits of people in their apartments and studios along with their unique stories.

Stuart Horodner is director of the University of Kentucky Art Museum. He has also been artistic director at the Atlanta Contemporary Art Center; visual arts curator at the Portland Institute for Contemporary Art; director of the Bucknell University Art Gallery; and was co-owner of the Horodner Romley Gallery in New York City. His writing has appeared in many periodicals including *Art Issues; Art Lies; Art on Paper; Bomb; Dazed & Confused; Sculpture;* and *Surface*. His book, *The Art Life: On Creativity and Career*, was published in 2012 and explores the philosophical and practical issues that affect art-making and the marketplace.